PENNSYLVANIA LIVES

(*Volumes previously published*)

JOHN WHITE GEARY
Soldier-Statesman
1819–1873
By
Harry Marlin Tinkcom

JOHN and WILLIAM BARTRAM
Botanists and Explorers
1699–1777   1739–1823
By
Ernest Earnest

JOHN ALFRED BRASHEAR
Scientist and Humanitarian
1840–1920
By
Harriet A. Gaul and Ruby Eiseman

JAMES BURD
Frontier Defender
1726–1793
By
Lily Lee Nixon

JOHANN CONRAD BEISSEL

Mystic and Martinet

1690–1768

By

WALTER C. KLEIN

UNIVERSITY OF PENNSYLVANIA PRESS

PHILADELPHIA

1942

FOREWORD

FEW subjects worthy of inclusion in "Pennsylvania Lives" present such difficulties as does Conrad Beissel. He was not a man of action in public affairs; nor was he, in the purely religious sphere, the founder of any important institution or movement. Yet despite a lack of the trappings of greatness, there is something fascinating about the American career of this German peasant. One feels this vaguely, as he stands today before the old buildings in Ephrata and wonders what manner of man or what strange dream was at work here two centuries ago. What could be more incongruous, at first glance, than monastic institutions on a Protestant frontier? Where else, in all the English colonies, can one find their counterpart? Was the Ephrata community a sort of "missing link" between the monastic groups of the past and the utopian experiments that lay ahead? Was the founder really an idealist, or simply another earthy figure in the long list of religious humbugs? Such questions seem to echo through the long empty rooms of the old Cloisters. Clearly, the answers are not to be found in the ordinary course of human events, but rather in the elusive wanderings of the human mind. Beissel himself would doubtless have held that his physical meanderings in the Rhineland and finally to America were but incidental to his pilgrim's progress in the spiritual realm.

Such history is more difficult to trace, and requires more insight in its preparation, than does the story of more mundane developments. Dr. Klein, in the pages that follow, displays the rare discernment that is needed to reveal the significance of this apparently insignificant figure. To begin with, he provides a careful account of the mystic who was the founder and long the leader of the Ephrata community. One follows, critically but not without sympathy, the origins and growth of his strange personality and influence. Viewed simply as a psychological study, this is in itself a compelling portrayal.

Even more enlightening than the biographical analysis, however, is the historical background against which Beissel's career is presented. The ebb and flow of German religious forms in the seventeenth century, the conflicts between what one might term conservative and radical Protestantism in that period, and the projection of that conflict into the free air of Pennsylvania, are all described with incisive clarity. Dr. Klein's familiarity with the general history of Christian thought enables him to bring into sharp focus the usually blurred outline of such divergent sects as the Anabaptists, the Inspirationists, the Dunkers, and the others which influenced Beissel in the course of his spiritual adventures. As a result, one has here a case history of a particular pietistic sect which provides, more lucidly than many volumes, an interpretation of the radical, "separatist" phase of post-Reformation Protestantism. It is the more enlightening for the fact that in dealing with the German story, it suggests parallels with the English Baptists, Quakers, and other sects with which American readers are likely to be more familiar.

The account of Beissel's life in Pennsylvania provides an interesting narrative, in which events, difficulties, scandals and near-scandals in the Cloisters, are skillfully interwoven with an interpretation of the thought and practice which lay behind them. The Ephrata experiment is seen as one of the first attempts in a long line of idealistic communities in America, and the problems of the community as well as of its leader receive due consideration. In the Priar Onesimus, there emerges a figure even more bizarre in some respects than the *Vorsteher* himself. Occasional contacts with English-speaking groups suggests the possibility that the Germans exerted some influence on their English compatriots. But the decline of Beissel's prestige, and of the Cloisters after his death, is shown to have been inherent in his own limitations.

Dr. Klein is thoroughly familiar with the sources, as well as with later writings on his theme. He does not glorify Beissel or the leader's associates. In a bibliographical note, he admits frankly that he has spent many hours "in the society of some of the weakest minds of the eighteenth century, not to mention the defectives of subsequent generations." Indeed, throughout the work, the author expresses incisive comments on men and their principles that lend zest to the entire narrative. While such comments are often critical, and even caustic, most readers will find them eminently fair. In any case, they are usually so given as to be clearly the author's own—to be judged accordingly—and are not insidiously confused with the story itself. It is not too much to say that Dr. Klein has illuminated a whole phase of early American religion that had hitherto, for most of us, remained relatively unappreciated and obscure.

RICHARD H. SHRYOCK

University of Pennsylvania
November 1941

CONTENTS

I

THE ORPHAN OF THE PALATINATE

HUMAN existence would lose many of its complications if a drastic judgment could be pronounced upon worn-out ideologies and their concrete results. Society groans under the weight of outmoded institutions, and the rubbish of the past hampers movement in the present. The emancipated and exasperated modern, impeded by this wreckage in his attempts to grapple with the disquieting enigmas of his own day, is disposed to give it short shrift. Yet many discarded social and intellectual patterns were extraordinarily sound in their generations, deriving much of this soundness from their bondage to the supernatural or their alliance with other concepts now largely abandoned, and, even though their vestiges are irrelevant and incomprehensible in the modern scheme of things, they merit, by reason of their earlier sufficiency, a friendly and unprejudiced study.

This principle must govern an inquiry into the life and exploits of Johann Conrad Beissel, who may well, at the outset, impress the average reader of these pages as a mere crackpot with a title to nothing but the oblivion from which the present biographer proposes to deliver him. In reality, Beissel was the principal author of a highly significant social experiment, and this, of itself, should endear him to the philosophers of our own time. His paramount virtue was his unremitting fidelity, in the none-too-sympathetic surroundings of a new and materialistic society, to the ideal of the Christian life that had engaged his devotion before he left his native country. His greatest achievement was the foundation and maintenance of a community in which that ideal was the most potent force. For the student of thought, Beissel is interesting because, though destitute of formal schooling, he assimilated, and imparted fresh life to, many venerable ideas. The church historian discovers a great deal to marvel at, and not a little to applaud, in his erection and moderately successful operation of a monastic institution without the sustaining tradition in which Catholic asceticism is rooted. Paradoxically, there is much in this undertaking that, when justly evaluated, commends itself to the secular historian, for, with no deliberate effort towards that end on Beissel's part, the regimentation prevailing in his compact and self-contained settlement rendered possible the execution of corporate enterprises for which the isolated pioneer had neither the leisure nor the resources. The cohesion that existed in the Kloster at Ephrata originated in the common respect for Beissel. He was incompetent as an executive, tactless, vacillating, and devoid of aptitude for the small intrigues by which influence is won and consolidated; but, even when he was obliged to yield the practical control of the settlement to others, he retained the spiritual power that animated and inspired his supporters and his opponents alike. His preëminence as a ghostly father was the foundation of the solid continuity that made his curious anachronism a civilizing agency.

However, the divination of such a career at the beginning of Beissel's life would have required exceptional foresight. The unembellished facts of his first twenty-five years, the formative period that preceded and included his conversion, are soon told. He was the son of an improvident baker of Eberbach, in the Palatinate, and at the moment of his birth in 1690 his father, after dissipating his means with drunken irresponsibility, had lately been summoned to account for his demerits in another world. The widow and Beissel's brothers shared the task of rearing the child, and, at his mother's death, which occurred when he was seven years old, he was committed, presumably, to the care of one or more of the other sons. He passed through a precarious and unregulated childhood and, when he attained a suitable age, was bound out to a baker. During his apprenticeship he showed a pronounced enthusiasm for such carnal diversions as fiddling and dancing, and people were rather surprised when, after he had left Eberbach to seek his fortune, they were informed that he had entered the ranks of the Pietists. Without the assistance of a tutor he made remarkable advances in arithmetic, but these absorbing studies gave him no interior repose, and, again without guidance, he experienced a crisis that terminated in his conversion.

It is impossible, in the absence of the requisite materials, to recapture in their living reality the mind and sentiments of the small community in which Beissel reached maturity, and therefore an attempt to interpret his origins is hazardous. Nevertheless, the biographer may well pause, as perhaps Beissel did before setting out as a journeyman in search of practice, to ponder the effect of these years of insularity upon a robust intelligence and an introspective temperament. They had determined the direction of his interests. Religion was his refuge and his opportunity. Circumstances had schooled him in the virtue of detachment at the start. He had begun with the disadvantage of a fatherless and poverty-stricken home. His mother, to whom the perplexities of widowhood were still new at the time of his birth, had resigned herself to, but could scarcely have welcomed, the untimely addition to her beggared brood. At her death he was left without a home of his own. During the remainder of his childhood, he probably discovered that his existence was a distinct inconvenience to his nearest relatives. His unimpressive stature and his stolid elders' indifference to the first manifestations of his vigorous mind accentuated a native inclination towards self-scrutiny. In his studies and recreations he found, no doubt, a fleeting escape from himself, but the instability of his childhood had fostered in him an abnormally sharp sense of the ephemerality and unpredictability of life. This provided an admirable groundwork for subsequent renunciation. Beissel had made, at a tender age, the discovery that he did not belong to this world. Ignorant of the consolations of domestic life, he held them in low esteem. For such a person, when later mischances had confirmed these nascent antipathies, the austerities of the cloister were not forbidding.

The *Ephrata Chronicle* (*Chronicon Ephratense*), the only source of knowledge concerning Beissel's early years, is to all intents and purposes an authorized biography, and therefore not seldom uncritical and misleading. When it was published, eighteen years after Beissel's death, he was a person of hallowed memory, and the idealization that blurs the outlines of every religious leader's personality in retrospect had obliterated from the authors' minds such recollections as did not agree with the community's legendary portrait of the founder. To say this is not to charge the blameless writers with intentional falsification; they could not have performed their task in any other manner, since, for them, Beissel was clothed in uncommon holiness. Moreover, Beissel must have been their authority for the beginning of their account, and it would be singular if his memory had not felt the transfiguring touch of time. It was one of the fundamental beliefs of those who eschewed the ministrations of state-controlled churches that the Holy Spirit operated independently of the wooden preachments so prosily delivered by the uninspired clergy of such bodies to long-suffering congregations. Beissel's conversion under the prompting of an inward monitor, with no intermediary between God and himself, patently conformed to this ideal pattern. The realities of the case, if they were known, would no doubt show that some more tangible force was brought to bear upon his development. His mother, who is described as a "godly person," can scarcely have neglected to ground the boy in the rudiments of ethics and religion as she understood them. Her influence may have been deeper than the paucity of information indicates. Dr. Fahnestock, without offering proof, says that Beissel was "educated in the Calvinistic faith." If this is true, it is not likely that he escaped baptism as an infant, and his early training may account for a lingering attachment to the Reformed Church, which ended only with his bitter experiences in Heidelberg. Before his departure from Eberbach, he had incurred the displeasure of the local pastors, probably because he attended illicit conventicles. Yet he frequented Calvinistic and perhaps other churches during his subsequent association with the Pietists, apparently with an open mind. During the period of his residence in Eberbach one contact with a congenial spirit is recorded. All in all, the data do not justify a conclusive judgment, but a careful reader of his biography may venture to suspect that Beissel was not entirely self-instructed in spiritual matters.

An alert intuition may have taught him, even before his mother's death, that he was the heir and victim of a tempestuous age. Social conditions were unfavorable to normal and placid living. Since early in the seventeenth century the buoyant Palatines had been compelled again and again to repair the ruin that ensued upon the blighting passage of armies across the land. For the ordinary man there was not much to choose between the excesses of the hostile forces and the depredations of the hirelings who fought on his own side. The frigid winter of 1708–9 brought insupportable hardship to an already spent peasantry. For many America held out the only prospect of release from a life of laborious futility. Seductive descriptions of its resources and advantages were circulated among the discouraged people, and glib representatives of proprietors and land companies traveled about to gather colonists for their employers' holdings. So profound was the effect of this adroit salesmanship that Pennsylvania was inundated with German settlers.

If Beissel had possessed less native fortitude his morals might have yielded to the solvent action of want and discontent. As it was, he felt the sharp pinch of penury before he decided to follow the drift towards the new continent, and the instability of his environment in youth and early manhood probably determined his sentiments more potently than he was aware. He made his gesture of defiance towards the forces that had vanquished him by remaining a revolutionary to the end of his days, but, with interests and emotions that had been conditioned to run their course in the cramped channels of piety, he could assert his independence solely by establishing a religion of his own.

The turbulence of the times had not an exclusively economic

origin. Religion played a prominent rôle. The heritage of the Reformation had proved calamitous to prince and subject. During the first thirty years of Beissel's life the Palatinate was in the grip of a bitter, unedifying competition for influence and favor in which all three of the recognized cults, Catholic, Lutheran, and Reformed, participated. For the separatists, whose faith was outlawed, there could be no lasting security; yet to many of the underprivileged the abnegations that separatism entailed were a pledge of future abundance, perhaps even in this world, or, failing that, an assurance of compensation in another life for their manifold frustrations. The movement drew to itself malcontents and individualists of every stripe. The antecedents of this confusion must now be traced.

The Reformation, following hard upon an epoch of renewed interest in antiquity, dissolved the integrated culture and devotion of the Middle Ages. Luther's followers preserved much of the old religion, while the Swiss, or Reformed, made a more fundamental break with the past. These two groups failed to discover a common ground, except in their vigorous repudiation of the Anabaptists, who soon appeared as the advocates of a third kind of reformation, and the Catholics, who, when the breach was beyond mending, mobilized their forces for a tardy defense and counter-attack. When the impulses that motivated these four currents of Christian belief and practice had lost much of their original force, Pietism, with multitudinous divisions, ramifications, and variations, flourished as a discordant protest against the dreary flatness to which the Lutherans and the Reformed had succumbed. An amplification of these summary statements will help to elucidate Beissel's spiritual origins.

While the principles of the Lutheran school were disseminated with startling rapidity in certain parts of Germany, they found no enthusiastic sponsor in the Palatinate during the first forty years. The complacent apathy of the venerable University of Heidelberg, founded by Ruprecht I in 1386, and the politic indecision of the Electors retarded the progress of the

Reformation, even though no obstacle was placed in the way of its infiltration.

The new movement made an impotent beginning under Frederic II (1544–56) and speedily suffered a temporary check. Otto Heinrich (1556–59), a convinced champion of reform, remodeled the church in the Palatinate after the Lutheran pattern. Anabaptists lived unmolested in the Palatinate while he was head of the state. The next Elector, Frederic III (1559–76), adopted the views of the Swiss Reformers. The appurtenances of worship that the Lutherans had left untouched were removed as relics of idolatry. In 1563 the Elector issued a new service book and published the Heidelberg Catechism, which was the work of Ursinus and Olevianus, both steadfastly opposed to Lutheranism, which they regarded as only imperfectly purged of medieval errors. Frederic showed the lenient aspect of his character to the Anabaptists, whom he invited in large numbers to a discussion of disputed matters in 1571. Frederic's son, Ludwig VI (1576–83), promptly demolished the structure his father had laboriously reared. The Palatinate returned to Lutheranism.

These unhappy changes, pivoting upon the will of each Elector in turn, had first unsettled and were at length demoralizing the Palatinate. Many, finding no alternative, were obliged to quit the land. Those who remained lived in apprehension of further upheavals.

Ludwig's successor was his nine-year-old son. The late Elector's will entrusted the direction of affairs to Casimir (1583–92), with whom three Lutheran princes were associated. Before long Casimir abandoned his thankless attempt to compose the differences of the two parties and devoted himself to the rehabilitation of Calvinism.

The Lutherans suffered a fatal disappointment when the new Elector, Frederic IV (1592–1610), resolutely defeated their intrigues and began a reign during which the Palatinate attained to a hazardous preëminence among the Calvinistic states of

Germany. In the Palatinate Calvinism made good its losses, and before many years had passed it penetrated Anhalt and Brandenburg. Frederic dedicated his exceptional gifts to the unification of Protestantism in Germany. Efforts to find a common doctrinal ground expired for the most part in impassioned fusillades of insults, but the Protestant forces expressed their solidarity, such as it was, in the Union of 1608, which in an agitated career of thirteen years brought ruin to the Palatinate. Cordial relations were established with the Netherlands, and Frederic V's marriage with Elizabeth Stuart fortified the cause. A few tranquil years, distinguished by luxury and the cultivation of French manners, preceded the cataclysm of the Thirty Years' War.

At the centenary of the Reformation occurred the event that released the accumulated rancor of several generations and ushered in a chaotic and far-flung conflict, which, as it passed through one phase after another, hopelessly blurred all issues and loyalties. Its only palpable result was the acknowledgment that the religious disunion of Europe was permanent.

Pitted against the Union, which by no means commanded the solid allegiance of Protestant Germany, was the Catholic League, directed by Maximilian of Bavaria. The Emperor Matthias counted for little in the tumultuous affairs of the period. Ferdinand of Styria, the Emperor's cousin, was chosen King of Bohemia at the Diet of 1617, but the election was not acceptable to the Bohemian Protestants, and two years later this faction raised Frederic V (1614–32), the Elector Palatine, to the throne. Frederic received the dubious honor with misgivings. The reverses of the next four years almost extinguished the Palatinate. Frederic became an importunate fugitive, and his cruel adversaries oppressed the country.

The tribulations of the people now and later were grievous and their impoverishment defied computation, but even more lamentable was the overthrow of church and school. The work of the University came abruptly to a standstill. A spiritual army of Roman Catholic ecclesiastics addressed itself promptly to the task of cleansing the two Palatinates of Protestantism. Instructions were given for the methodical and heartless restoration of Roman Catholicism. The Palatinate Library was transported to Rome. The vindictive pleasure with which the Lutherans at first contemplated the oppression of the Calvinists quickly vanished as they themselves began to feel the heavy hand of the Counter-Reformation. Multitudes, unable to accept the calamity, left the country. Many lingered in the expectation of retaining both their faith and their possessions, but their alien taskmasters had chosen an inflexible policy, which they enforced with undeviating consistency, and those who withstood it were banished. Bewildered and resentful, a large part of the population reluctantly submitted. Within seven years the intruders could congratulate themselves on the disappearance of the last vestige of Calvinism, for they were unaware that a fresh revolution was imminent. At the first intimation of deliverance, the traditional preference for Calvinism asserted itself.

During the years of servitude in the Palatinate, Frederic was preoccupied with plans for retrieving his title and lands. Optimistic to the end, he exhausted every possibility of assistance, but such advocates as he found were faint-hearted and disinclined to put themselves in jeopardy for his sake. When Christian IV of Denmark joined the Protestant forces, the north became the battleground, and a train of Catholic victories, forcing Christian out of the struggle, culminated in the Edict of Restitution (1629), which decreed the cancellation of all Protestant rights to ecclesiastical possessions confiscated since 1552 and prohibited the toleration of Calvinists and Zwinglians. Not long after this, the machinations of the League accomplished the downfall of Wallenstein.

Wallenstein was soon recalled. A much more redoubtable Scandinavian had appeared in Gustavus Adolphus. His meteoric successes ended in his death at Lützen in 1632, though not until he had nullified the advantages lately gained by the Catholics. His entry into the Palatinate brought release from an execrable bondage. Frederic rushed to the conqueror, in the vain hope of early reinstatement. Gustavus was sympathetic, but would not pledge himself, and the forlorn Elector died before he could reclaim his inheritance.

Frederic bequeathed his rights and injuries to his son, Karl Ludwig (1632–80), but for the present the conduct of affairs was entrusted to Ludwig Philip, Frederic's brother. The regent entered upon the labor of reconstruction, in which the cheerful disposition of the people and the uncommon fertility of the land would have seconded him, had he found it possible to make satisfactory terms with all the powers that had interests in the Palatinate. A settlement with the Chancellor of Sweden protected the Lutherans against discrimination and granted them the church properties and revenues in districts where they outnumbered the Calvinists, among whom there was now a quick renewal of life. The ecclesiastical situation was replete with possibilities of friction and disorder, but the lull was too brief for their exploitation. Once again the currents of war changed direction. The Swedish forces lost the Battle of Nördlingen (1634). Across the Palatinate streamed the shards of the beaten army, reduced by defeat to bandits, and the Swedish guardians retired in terror. The enemy's troops appeared and invested Heidelberg. It was relieved by the French, who remained long enough to irritate the inhabitants, but not long enough to insure their safety. The imperialists pressed their advantage, and in the Peace of Prague (1635) the Calvinists were given no legal standing, and the Palatinate was abandoned to partition. Bernhard of Saxe-Weimar and the French fell back as the Catholic host advanced, the government fled, and the deadly foes of Calvinism occupied the country once more. Again war traversed the land, and the people, loathing by this time the social dislocation and material hardship that trailed the unmanageable armies of the two sides equally, were neither elated at the arrival of the French nor downcast at their departure. The mass expulsion of pastors and their households, the command to frequent Catholic services under threat of fine and imprisonment, and other measures for the reconversion of the emaciated land can scarcely have inspired zeal or provoked resentment in the fashion of like tyrannical decrees a few years before. The initial purposes of the war had been lost in a labyrinth of futile operations and desultory discussions; the prodigal sacrifice of men and supplies had exhausted the combatants; still the Calvinists could not content themselves with such a treaty as the Peace of Prague. The Elector had recourse to every expedient that courage, ingenuity, and desperation could suggest. In the end the indefatigable patience of the Electoral family, supported by diplomacy, accomplished its purpose. In the Peace of Westphalia (1648) an eighth electorate was founded and given to Karl, and he received the Lower Palatinate, somewhat shorn. The beginning of the year 1624 was selected as the norm in matters of religion. The state of things prevailing at that time was to continue without modification. Confessional changes in ecclesiastical foundations were rendered impossible. Certain concrete rights were bestowed upon those who could not conform to their ruler's religion. The effect of these provisions in the Palatinate was to lift Lutherans and Roman Catholics to the position of tolerated and recognized minorities.

Karl Ludwig, at one time inclined to frivolity, had matured and was ready to grapple with the stupendous difficulties that blocked the way to restoration. He was not a bigot, and his generous policy accelerated the repopulation of the country. In ten years the improvement was startling. In his relations with Lutherans and Catholics Karl was considerate of their rights. He tried to add Spinoza to the faculty of Heidelberg, and this invitation, which Spinoza did not accept, indicates as clearly as any other single act he performed that the strait opinions of his ancestors were not his own. Sabbatarians and Anabaptists shared in the benefits of this liberality. It was the Elector's ardent wish to bring all confessions into harmony under one ecclesiastical roof, but his efforts in this direction miscarried.

The hereditary Calvinism of the Simmern line assumed its

most repulsive form in the next Elector, Karl (1680–85), under whom, although French Calvinists were given strong incentives to make their homes in the land, Lutherans found their liberties curtailed. Karl's dearest wish in matters of religion was to reproduce the ecclesiastical glories of the days of Frederic III, but he lacked the zeal of his honored predecessor, and the times did not favor his plans. He failed in his most pressing duty, that of providing himself with a son, and the title fell into the hands of the older branch of the Zweibrücken line, then represented by Philip Wilhelm, Count Palatine of Neuburg.

In the negotiations that led to his assumption of the electorate, Philip (1685–90) had bound himself to the terms of the Peace of Westphalia and undertaken to safeguard Protestantism against the perils that now menaced it, for he was a Catholic, and there was no assurance, apart from such a promise, that he would resist the temptation to favor his own confession. He was conscientious in the execution of this pact. Nevertheless there was a gnawing dread of the oppression that would begin as soon as his tactful influence was removed. This apprehension was confirmed when Johann Wilhelm (1690–1716) became Elector.

Louis XIV had long contemplated the Palatinate with greedy eyes, and when the last elector of the Simmern family died without male issue he found an excuse for aggression in the Duke of Orleans' marriage with Elizabeth Charlotte, Karl Ludwig's daughter. The lady herself had no interest in the aggrandizement of her adopted country, but this did not deter Louis, who, gaining little by the use of diplomatic stratagems, at last had recourse to violence. French troops crossed the frontiers of the Palatinate and subjected the populace to the force of a carefully devised savagery. Women were assaulted, large sums of money were extorted, monstrous outrages were inflicted upon the very old and the very young. These brutalities began two years before Beissel's birth, and Louis did not formally relinquish his groundless pretensions until the Peace of Ryswyk in 1697, and then not entirely, for the settlement of the quarrel was entrusted to Clement XI, who ruled that the Elector should pay the Duchess a sum of money in consideration of her rights. Infant though he was, Beissel can hardly have been immune to the contagious anxiety of such an era.

At the start Johann Wilhelm defended Protestant rights and even tried to stimulate immigration by offering prospective settlers complete religious freedom. The Catholics, however, made astute use of the presence of French forces and the disorganization of the Reformed system. The Lutherans, alert to secure their independence, did not make common cause with the Reformed, and some of them in 1699 set up a consistory, which maintained a dubious power by truckling to the state. Protestant churches fell into Catholic hands. Catholic missionaries filled the land. At the very end of the peace conference that brought the war with France to an end, a clause legalizing all the questionable gains of the Catholics was forced through. Thus the stage was set for a period of religious strife to which the past hardly offered a parallel. The clause was used as a pretext for depriving Calvinists of the use of churches in places where Catholics formed only a minority. In 1698 all Reformed churches were turned over to the other two confessions as well, for the simultaneous use of all three. Catholics, nevertheless, were not obliged to share their churches with Protestants, who were required to display at least a perfunctory respect for the public aspects of Catholicism. The temporal affairs of the Reformed Church now fell at least partly under Catholic control, and the Reformed no longer enjoyed the full use of church revenues.

The diplomatic intervention of the Protestant Estates brought a measure of relief to the Protestants in 1705. A declaration incorporating the concessions forced upon the Elector by Prussia gave the Palatines leave to change their religion and to contract mixed marriages, and decreed that Protestants were no longer to be dragooned into attending Catholic services. The experiment of housing more than one confession in a single building was generally recognized as unwise, and dropped. The

Catholics nevertheless had secured an impregnable position, and Calvinism, though its sufferings might be partially alleviated by legislation, could not dislodge its rival and recover its old authority. Jesuits were appointed to the faculty of Heidelberg, the ancient citadel of Calvinism. Karl Philip (1716–42) went so far as to forbid the use of the Heidelberg Catechism. This command was issued in 1719, a year before Beissel left his native soil. Steadfast resistance prevented its execution, but we may accept it as a symbol of the end of an age. Roman Catholicism, Lutheranism, and Calvinism, each capable of educating and enriching as well as sanctifying, had reached a stalemate. None of them had much charm for people like Beissel.

Elaborate comment on the protracted wranglings thus baldly recounted would be superfluous. The final effect of this spectacle of uncharity upon Beissel was to confirm his early distaste for steeple house Christianity. His own words show how he despised the subsidized churches of his native land:

Everything has been brought to such a pass with so-called external divine worship that not alone do people generally not need to be converted, but the preachers themselves are, for the most part, unconverted, natural, and carnal men, who live in pride and love of the world, and do the will of the flesh and of the reason in evil works; who have not the eternal, living, and self-sustaining Word of God, which regenerates there, dwelling in them nor, much less, remaining; but they prate and teach out of natural learning in erudite discourses of human wisdom and deal with spiritual affairs carnally, which should be dealt with spiritually; who interpret Holy Writ, which no natural man understands, with their wholly earthy and blind reason; who cause the people to sin through their preaching that neither they themselves nor any other human being, fundamentally, can be improved.

The Reformed belief in faith is as impotent to redeem mankind as the Catholic reliance upon works. "Since all parties lead equally evil and godless lives, I should like to ask by what one is to know the pure teaching people claim to have. For certainly, if a doctrine produces no piety, it is false and evil, whatever it may seem to be." The impious dogmatism of those who spoke for Catholicism, Lutheranism, and Calvinism in the acute crisis of his youth had made an indelible impression upon him, and the disillusionment he suffered then conditioned his own subsequent conduct in the no-less-bitter squabbles that took place in Pennsylvania.

Beissel's biographers attribute to the Pietistic movement the impulse that gave rise to the Dunker sect, of which Beissel's community was an offshoot. The formal act with which the separate existence of the Dunkers began was the rebaptism of Alexander Mack and a small group of his adherents (1708). Their renunciation of a sacrament in which all the state churches believed implied an approach in doctrine and sentiment to Anabaptism, the next type of Christianity to be discussed in this hasty review.

Beissel may have had some intercourse with Anabaptists in his early years. The humane treatment these dissenters received from some of the Electors Palatine has already been mentioned. Of those who had settled in the Palatinate during the sixteenth century few remained at the conclusion of the Thirty Years' War. Faced with a decimated population and depleted resources, Karl Ludwig adopted the policy of importing companies of Anabaptists and naturalizing them so far as their essentially illegal position permitted. In 1658 the Huterites, a Hungarian group of Anabaptists, were made citizens of Mannheim and granted exemption from military service and duty as policemen and magistrates. In 1664 liberty of worship, but not the privilege of building meetinghouses, was bestowed upon the other Anabaptists. Under the pressure of persecution in Zürich and Berne large numbers of these Apostolic Christians emigrated to the Palatinate in 1671 and 1709. Apart from the friendly disposition of the government, they had no protection against the violation of their rights.

The designation "Anabaptist" is comprehensive, and a regrettable carelessness in its application has embraced in a motley fellowship a vast assortment of saints and scoundrels. It is difficult to conceive of the emergence of Anabaptism early in the period of the Reformation as an entirely new phenomenon. Side by side with the intricate dogmatic development of Christianity and, much of the time eclipsed and repressed by it, there ran, from remote times, a current of evangelical religion, severe and often ascetic, grounding its doctrine, devotion, and discipline upon the Bible, and striving to maintain and enforce the ideal of Apostolic plainness. It is improbable that there was an unbroken tradition; independent and spontaneous insight, casual borrowings, and indirect influences furnish a sufficient explanation of the meager data. It is not always possible to trace every step in the derivation of a group representing these views, and such sects often exhibit an admixture of bizarre doctrines that can be assigned to non-Christian sources. Neo-Platonism exerted an abiding and continuous influence upon many groups within and without the Church, and frequently their doctrines were tinctured with dualism. Nevertheless there is an arresting similarity between the principles of many of these older parties and those of the Anabaptists. In all likelihood the spiritual ancestry of the latter is to be found in one or more kindred movements of medieval times, even though there is no conclusive proof of a direct historical link. These protests against the prevailing order of things were never completely liquidated even under the most unrelenting persecution, and they took a new lease on life soon after the Reformation began.

In their statements of doctrine Lutherans and Reformed alike dissociated themselves from the Anabaptists. The Second Helvetic Confession (1566) declares flatly, "Therefore we are not Anabaptists, nor do we share with them any of their doctrines." Similar language is used in the Augsburg Confession (1530) and the Belgic Confession (1561). The Formula of Concord (1576), while it justly makes the prefatory remark that the Anabaptists flourish in a host of sects, some of which surpass others in the number of their aberrations, considers their teaching, as a whole, a menace to organized Christian life. It presents a lucid and systematic digest of Anabaptist errors. The

Anabaptists deny Christ's incarnation and His divinity. They rely unduly upon the power of good works, and their asceticism, like that of religious orders, is a human fabrication. According to their principles, baptism is only for adults. God's wrath is not directed towards children, since they are "just and innocent," and for them baptism is not indispensable to salvation. The holiness of Christian parents sanctifies their children. The Church is an association of perfected persons; sin has no place in it. The saints must have no commerce with the unholy: one may not hear sermons in churches that have been contaminated in the past by the recitation of the mass, and contact with Protestant ministers is to be avoided. The duties of a magistrate's office, private property, the manufacture of arms, innkeeping, and trade are incompatible with the practice of Christianity. One may not invoke the power of judges, nor may one take an oath. Married people of divergent religious views may dissolve their unions and take more congenial partners.

If the chief schools of Protestant thought shunned the Anabaptists as pestilent and subversive of order and decency, the Münster orgy, to cite a single perversion of the Anabaptist spirit, could be utilized as an excuse for such a sentiment. At Münster (1534–35) a pack of licentious fanatics, headed by the astute John of Leyden, perpetrated a variety of atrocities and abominations that brought grave discredit upon the Anabaptist movement. Menno Simons (1492–1559), after whom the Mennonites are named, disavowed these excesses. The Anabaptism of Northern Germany and the Netherlands is deeply indebted to his writings and missionary labors.

Anabaptism, whatever affinities it may or may not have with earlier trends that bear some likeness to it, was an acute manifestation of a fundamental dissatisfaction, which could not content itself with the established churches that Luther and other reformers had substituted for the iron hand of the Papacy. There were doctrinal differences between Protestantism and Catholicism, to be sure, but the old principle of one religion for all remained. The secular princes simply wrested from the

Pope the authority to determine the religion of their subjects. The most obvious mark of allegiance to an established church was infant baptism. The Anabaptists rejected this badge of submission, and a great deal besides. Strictly speaking, they did not advocate a second baptism, since they held that the baptism of an unconsenting child had no validity. Adult baptism was the logical consequence of their contention that faith must precede the seal of incorporation into the company of believers. Christianity must be voluntarily chosen, and a free choice could be exercised only by one who had reached the age of discretion.

The definitive formulation of their beliefs was alien to the temper of the Anabaptists. Their writings abound in vindications and expositions of their principles and doctrines, but it would be an error to regard such creeds as binding upon the entire body. It will suffice to indicate the most common and characteristic of their teachings.

(1) Perhaps their most nearly universal principle was their acceptance of the Scriptures as the only standard and arbiter in matters of faith and conduct. Their apparent deviations from orthodoxy in their beliefs about the Trinity and the Person of Christ are normally to be explained by reference to this fundamental. The theology of the Roman Catholic Church and the Reformers did not confine itself within these bounds. It added to, and therefore misinterpreted, what the Bible taught.

(2) The Church was a fellowship of believers. Faith and repentance were the first tokens of eligibility to this society of elect souls. Baptism was the sign of reception into the fellowship. It was the recognition, not the cause, of the change brought about by the Spirit. In like manner, the Scriptural ordinances of the Lord's Supper and foot-washing were pledges of union and love rather than channels of grace.

(3) The partnership of church and state was therefore abhorrent to the Anabaptists. The two must not be equated, as they were when people brought their children to the font and shared in prescribed observances simply and solely because

as citizens they owned the authority of a certain government, and that government had imposed upon all those who fell within its jurisdiction the form of Christianity it preferred. This repudiation was extended to all the functions of the secular power: judgment, the execution of sentences, and war.

(4) The principle upon which established churches are based is reduced to absurdity when vital differences of opinion and moral offenses are tolerated for the sake of a fictitious uniformity. Within the sphere of the Christian fellowship, which a man entered without compulsion, the Anabaptists employed the disciplinary measure of excommunication, in order to maintain the integrity of the fellowship. A single unrebuked backslider could pollute the saints, and his imperfections, which impaired the holiness of the community, had to be disavowed.

(5) Finally, in their pursuit of evangelical simplicity, the Anabaptists demonstrated their genuine unworldliness. This trait is distinctive of the Mennonites in the United States to the present day. It did not escape inimical observers, who found in it a detestable imitation of medieval monkery. In so far as the same motives actuated the two, the resemblance is more than superficial. Yet religious orders often employed their resources in endeavors that Anabaptists could not have countenanced. If the simple life of the Anabaptists was fashioned after the likeness of anything in the Middle Ages, the pattern was furnished by such informal monastic groups as the Beguines, the Beghards, the Brethren of the Common Life, and possibly the Third Order of St. Francis, or by sects outside the frame of Catholicism, the Cathari, the Waldenses, the Bohemian Brethren, and the like.

The cardinal teachings of Anabaptism are less a condemnation of dogmatic theology itself than a rejection of the view of Christianity upon which the tortuous refinements of dogmatic theology are founded. If the foregoing résumé may justly be regarded as setting forth the basis of Anabaptism, the rest of the opinions ascribed to the sect may be considered subordinate, and indifferent from the point of view of Anabaptism in its totality. Its emphasis upon the "inner word" is consonant with its conception of the operation of divine influence upon the soul. Its most reasonable apologists accepted original sin and the necessity of good works. Scripture could be quoted in defense of the common ownership of property, but many Anabaptists admitted the lawfulness of private property. Some believed in universalism, but others denied it with conviction.

If Beissel had no commerce with these people before he quitted his birthplace, he fell under their influence when he joined the company of the Pietists, among whom Anabaptist ideas circulated, and his removal to Pennsylvania brought him into close touch with Mennonites and Quakers. Quakerism, along with its aloofness from what is ordinarily called "the world," surpassed the less extreme form of Anabaptism in its repudiation of outward ordinances and its cultivation of the interior light, which for John Denk (1495–1527), an early Anabaptist, had been the mainspring of religion. Other ramifications of the movement may be seen in the Baptists and the Independents.

These sectarians did not shrink from the most excruciating tortures in loyalty to their tenets, and their steadfastness, commonly regarded as obstinacy, sometimes moved their enemies to chivalrous praise. They perished cheerfully for an apocalyptic dream; little did they understand that their heroism was to produce, not the millennium of their infatuated visions, but a new nation erected in no slight measure upon principles borrowed from them.

II

DEFEAT AND FAREWELL

BEISSEL, setting out, after a stuffy and thwarted youth, in quest
of experience, had a certain capital of skill and charm, and
sanguine expectations, if not precisely brilliant prospects. Life
in Eberbach had been galling to an exceptional lad who lacked
connections to facilitate his entry into a career commensurate
with his talents. The narrow rural society in which he passed
his early days had not provided fertilizing contact with cultivated minds, and, in consequence, he knew neither his poten-
tialities nor his limitations. He was unduly stubborn and self-
reliant, but his most crippling fault was his perfectionism,
which rendered him incapable of innocent and necessary compromise. He was to find that he could never acknowledge a
leader, never identify himself submissively with any cause, because there was always something that became a stumbling-
block to his conscience. It would not be difficult to cite other
examples of such pig-headedness among the separatists, many
of whom were honored as sticklers for pure religion when in
truth they were merely self-willed.

Yet at the start a reckless elation and an eager inquisitiveness
must have overshadowed even the morbid inhibitions of Beissel's increasing piety. He was alive to the opportunities that
awaited the itinerant journeyman as he tramped from city to
city. The freedom of bachelorhood and the impressionability
of a rustic lad at liberty to pursue his fortune in a world bris-
tling with unproved possibilities gave him a sharp appetite for
the interesting things that were to come his way. As he wandered, he would acquire a liberal education, and it was exactly
the sort of training that a self-tutored youth could most easily
assimilate.

He roamed, under the Spirit's control, as far as Strassburg,
where the Spirit halted him. Prince Eugene of Savoy was engaged in his second war against the Ottoman Empire, and, if

some lucky circumstance had not intervened, Beissel would
have joined a contingent of four hundred journeymen bakers in
a junket to Hungary, where all of them perished. It would be
interesting to know how he felt when the shocking news of
the disaster reached him, for devout people often take an illog-
ical joy in their preservation from death and injury. Next he
lingered awhile nearer home in Mannheim, where a certain
Kantebecker gave him work and became so fond of him that
Frau Kantebecker was moved to sharp words. Beissel was always prepared with a barbed retort. The inflammability of his
temper is a point in his favor. In a fit of annoyance he told
the shrew that she was a Jezebel, and Kantebecker had to dispense with his services. Wedlock had very likely, by this time,
inspired in him an incipient disinclination, and this encounter
fortified it. At length he settled down in Heidelberg, where he
was to have his first and last taste of human happiness.

Beissel now came under the tutelage of the Pietists, and
formed friendships strong enough to last through many years
of separation. He soon outdistanced his first guides and was
hurled into the disorder of a less timorous kind of Pietism, but
he never suffered himself to forget his obligations to the Heidelberg circle. For him it was only a halfway house, and the ran-
kling memories of the perfidy its members had shown when
he most needed their support must often have troubled him,
later, in his prayers. Yet the tenderness he felt towards them
was stronger than his resentment. Through their fellowship
he had passed from conventional religion to complete separatism, and he was grateful, even though, in a sense, they had
betrayed him.

Since Pietistic ideals, in one form or another, governed the
rest of Beissel's life, it is necessary, at the risk of putting too
great a strain upon the reader's patience, to explain the nature
of Pietism. Interpreted broadly, the name covers not only the
work of Spener (1635–1705) and those of about the same period who shared his views, along with the movements that arose
out of their efforts to raise individual Christians to a higher

level of personal devotion, but also the careers of earlier teachers of the type of Jean de Labadie (1610–74), who, as the
founder of a congregation in which he hoped to reproduce
the fervor of the first church in Jerusalem, was the precursor
of many later enthusiasts. The one element common to the
various forms of Pietism is an intense yearning for personal
sanctity. Certain constitutional defects in Protestantism and the
gradual exhaustion of the reforming impulse had shown clearly
that a renewed cultivation of this aspect of religion was imperative. Both Lutherans and Reformed had fallen into a condition
of torpid sterility, and this unhappy state may be attributed,
not only to the spiritual insolvency that is the ultimate lot of
most religious institutions, but also to the limited foundation
upon which the two churches attempted to base the Christian
life. The perfect Protestant is orthodox, and meticulous in the
discharge of his religious duties; but he does not renounce the
world, because he believes that sanctification is to be attained
by the godly pursuit of ordinary ends in ordinary ways. His
civic obligations and the frequently onerous claims of family
and business give him ample opportunity for the mortification
of his self-will and the development of Christian virtue. These
things, unfortunately, do not meet the requirements of all,
and in neglecting to provide for the exercise of extraordinary
vocations Protestantism had done those who lived under its rule
a grave disservice and had shown less wisdom than the unre-
formed Church, which, though sullied by concubinage and
simony, had contrived to maintain a rich latitude of practice
and to enlist every honorable calling, from that of the Car-
thusian recluse in his cell to that of the workman at his bench,
in a broad fidelity to the common cause, to which men might
make, as their consciences dictated, any contribution from the
complete self-dedication of the religious to the average person's
mere minimum of conformity. Moreover, Protestantism, in
sweeping away many of the customs, pious and profane, that
ordinary people had been accustomed to observe, had rendered
it difficult for Christians of the rank and file to express their

piety. To pompous dogmatists, well paid to execute the will of the state in ecclesiastical matters, these blemishes were not evident, but not all the Protestant clergy were blind to them. Lodensteyn (1620–77), though unimpeachably sincere in his acceptance of Calvinistic doctrine, was aware of the usefulness of many things the Reformers had discarded in their hasty zeal, and lamented their failure to purge and utilize the heritage that fell to them. Censure, when it emanated from such persons, was friendly and constructive, and if Pietism could have directed its energies entirely towards the vitalization of a moribund system, its history would be more creditable, though less entertaining, than it actually is.

In the hands of discreet pastors the movement became a rejuvenating force and enriched the spirituality of their charges, but the event proved that the desires it awakened and the energies it released could not always be regulated. Its passion for the holiness of the individual too often led to a loss of confidence in organized religion. Many pastors and many laymen declined to believe that the churches had wholly forfeited their power to sanctify, but even among such persons the clash of loyalties must sometimes have been acute. They had set up "small churches within the Church," and by means of extra-liturgical services had implanted in themselves and others a lively desire for holiness. They found it revolting in the extreme to see the Lord's Supper profaned by complacent Christians who, at best, showed a glaring want of zeal and piety. Baptism had frequently to be administered to children whose parents had no intention of bringing them up to be devoted servants of God. Could one meekly tolerate such desecration? In exploring their consciences for an answer to this question, sincere inquirers reached different conclusions. Some remained in the churches or were driven back to them. These are the Church Pietists. They may now be dismissed, since Beissel did not belong to them. His leanings were towards the other group, the separatists, who, in despair of a regeneration of traditional Christianity, slipped away from its control and either lived in self-sufficient isolation or formed sects, for the most part rather tenuously organized.

The Anabaptists had been the separatists of the sixteenth century, and between the remaining Anabaptist groups and the new separatists there was a real, if not always cordial, sympathy. The name "Quaker" was bandied about freely and sometimes applied to people of Pietistic proclivities who had never been in the presence of a Quaker. The old movement and the new resembled each other in the weight they both gave to the holiness of the individual, in their unwillingness to compromise with organized religion, in their refusal to submit to the authority of the state in matters of conscience, in the ease with which they assimilated fantastic doctrines, in their rejection of ecclesiastical theology, and in the readiness with which they encouraged the growth of sects. Though less closely identified with a specific social class than Anabaptism, Pietistic separatism, in a society in which the interests of the state were interwoven by law and habit with those of the church, had political and social implications that could not be overlooked. Its hospitality to chiliastic, theosophic, Anabaptist, and quietistic views rendered it suspect. Like Anabaptism under John of Leyden it sank to execrable lewdness in the brazen lawlessness and blasphemy of Eva von Buttlar, who was accused of having maintained liaisons with upwards of sixty persons. At the opposite pole was Gichtel's almost psychopathic distaste for marriage, and the pains he took to keep his followers in the virgin state gave great offense. In forsaking his church the separatist exposed himself to the penalties of the law, which could not tolerate him; but a few petty nobles, moved by their personal inclinations and sympathies, welcomed an amazing variety of fanatics and provided for them. During the first half of the eighteenth century Wittgenstein teemed with separatists. The life they led will be described presently.

A passing reference to the Philadelphians will serve both to conclude this outline of Pietism and to introduce the reader to a constellation of mystical notions that lodged in Beissel's mind and formed the groundwork of his theology. These ideas were set forth in the writings of Jacob Böhme, which enjoyed great vogue among such persons as Gichtel, Arnold, Jane Leade, Pordage, Bromley, Petersen, and Johanna von Merlau, Petersen's wife. The Philadelphians conceived the plan of founding a new non-partisan church, in which brotherly love was to meet all difficulties. Its members were to live as a separate group, withdrawn from the Babel of the churches. Maintaining a pure, Apostolic type of divine service, they would constitute a visible witness to the reality of the invisible church of true believers, members of which were to be found in all churches and even outside Christianity. Beginning as an effort to abolish sectarianism, it merely intensified the confusion that already existed. It was this strain in Pietism more than any other that influenced Beissel.

In Heidelberg Beissel encountered Pietism in a mild and un-heroic form. He gained the friendship and interest of Haller, an educated Pietist who exchanged letters with Gichtel. Assured of Beissel's good faith and discretion, Haller sponsored him and secured his admission to the local Pietistic society. The members of this circle, one of whom was a Frau Professor Pastoir, gathered in retired places with great circumspection. Their convictions kept them from church services, but in a city as large as Heidelberg the habitual absence of a few persons probably passed unobserved, and the practice of Pietism, though excitingly furtive, was not unduly dangerous. Haller, nevertheless, was mindful of the punishment that would ensue upon detection.

Pietism, whatever else it accomplished or failed to accomplish, leveled social distinctions and other disparities. Because he was one of the awakened, Beissel had the privilege of rubbing shoulders with a few persons of provincial eminence. Pastoir, whose wife was a Pietist, had occupied a chair at the university since 1706, and the discourses of his colleagues, Kirchmayer and Mieg, who had joined the faculty at the same time, made a deep impression upon Beissel. In Eberbach there had been no such charming society. It went to one's head.

Beissel's success brought about his downfall. He applied himself assiduously to his trade under a master baker named Prior, and before long Prior's bread enjoyed such a reputation that he had virtually a monopoly, and his rivals were in desperate straits. Beissel was elected treasurer of the bakers' guild, partly, we may suppose, for his honesty, and partly in recognition of his skill. His meticulous performance of the duties of this office was the proximate occasion of his ruin. The bakers gave way at their carousals to unbridled merriment, and Beissel was shocked at the spectacle of ribald hilarity, paid for with money that should have been devoted to less questionable uses. As a responsible officer of the fraternity he could not acquiesce in such conduct. His puritanical admonitions were received with vigorous resentment. His accomplishments and rectitude had alienated a number of his fellow craftsmen, who resolved to disgrace him and procure his expulsion from the city. They invented a charge against him; but, finding the accusation too hazy to serve their purposes, they denounced him as a Pietist. An influential Jewess intervened in his behalf; Mieg recommended nominal membership in the church as a painless solution of his problem; Prior tried to purchase his release; and other dodges may have been urged upon him by people who liked him or felt sorry for him. Beissel was adamant, difficult as it was to relinquish a solid position and an alluring future. Haller did not approve of Beissel's impetuosity and could only hope that he would not imperil the safety of his Pietistic friends. The authorities inquired into Beissel's association with these people, but the prisoner shielded his friends with an evasive answer. In the end, the court reluctantly imposed the sentence of banishment upon him. He made a hurried visit to Eberbach, probably surrendering his small share of the paternal estate to his relatives at this time, and escaped with the police at his heels.

What had this sojourn in Heidelberg done for him? It had given him a glimpse of an attractive life, in which prosperity and piety could have been combined without detriment to either, but this prospect had been snatched away and he had been dismissed into ignominious exile. Haller, with a penetration that surpassed his loyalty, had become convinced that Beissel's spiritual demands could not be met in Pietism. It is possible that the urgency of a clamorous need would have incited him to further wanderings, even if he had suffered no misfortune in the chief city of the Palatinate. At any rate, his months of labor and self-improvement had not been lost. He had listened with profit to the eloquence and learning of Kirchmayer and Mieg, perfected himself in his calling, established fast friendships, and entered profoundly into a type of religious experience that would retain its hold upon him to the end of his life. To be sure, such comforting thoughts did not present themselves at the time. In spite of all these gains, he felt a desolate disgust as he turned his back upon a land bitter with the wormwood of confessional conflict. Time did not efface his recollection of that forced departure. The following rabid denunciation expresses the misery he felt at the moment as well as the conclusions he reached in subsequent reflection:

O land, land! what will happen to you? O Palatinate, Palatinate! what are the burdens that rest upon your conscience? How many days of God's gracious visitation have you let slip by! Upon how many of God's witnesses to truth have you heaped outrage and torture and made them sigh against you in their wretchedness! Oh, what will happen to you in the day when God afflicts you? Then will your wickedness and wantonness, which you have committed against God's elect, be brought to light. For you have not thought upon the time wherein you were afflicted, and have fattened yourself for the slaughter in the day of Almighty God's fierce wrath, and the blood of the poor and wretched lies heavy upon you; wherefore a merciless judgment will come upon you, because you have shown God's elect no mercy, but have persecuted them and banished them from you; wherefore your sins have become so numerous that they are, so to speak, concealed by their very multitude, so that you can no longer see them, until the day that the Lord has appointed, inasmuch as then every covering will be taken away. Oh, how exposed will you stand there then, when the garment of shame and sin will render you naked, and you will be manifest before God and His elect and the angels! Then you will begin to cry and say, "O mountains! fall upon me, and hills! cover me before the presence of Him who sits upon the throne, for the time of His judgment is come, and who can endure it?"

Severe as the pain of this persecution must have been, Beissel was not a solitary sufferer. The dignity of pronounced spiritual uniqueness was not to be his. Even in the untiring pursuit of his own bent he merely followed the trend of the times. In the next phase of his life he became conversant with a more consistent, radical, and courageous school of Pietists. Compared with their tribulations, his own had little glamor.

Beissel now had no choice but to hasten to some place where he would be safe from the law. Such havens were to be found in Wittgenstein, Berleburg, and Büdingen. In 1698 Heinrich Albrecht of Wittgenstein, upon taking his father's place as ruling count, had granted liberty of conscience and safety to refugees from other states. Hedwig Sophie of Berleburg, who governed as regent for her son Casimir, practised a similar liberality and insured her protégés against a reversal of policy by supervising Casimir's education with minute watchfulness. So complete and unbroken was the protection the separatists enjoyed in Berleburg that they had leisure to print their own version of the Bible. Under Count Ernst Casimir, who must also be listed among these warm-hearted and open-handed rulers, Marienborn in Isenburg-Büdingen sheltered many separatists. Scores of Pietists were beholden to these tolerant aristocrats for protection and sustenance, and Beissel naturally gravitated towards such an asylum.

The next period of his life is one of profound dejection. His austerities had impaired his health, and he was so cowed by adversity that a temptation to renounce Pietism assailed him. Ill and unsettled, he strayed into a district inhabited by In-

spirationists—his biographers are not very precise concerning
the place—and was taken in by one Schatz, a baker, who was
at that time an Inspirationist but later, like many of his fellows,
yielded to the blandishments of Count Zinzendorf and joined
the Moravians. Schatz extended his hospitality to many Pietists,
and Beissel acquired further knowledge of the nuances of this
type of religion during his sojourn in the compassionate baker's
house. Doctor Carl, a well-known Inspirationist, restored him
to health. His interest renewed, he studied eagerly the enthusiasts of those parts. No doubt the life of the hermits, of
whom there were many, was first brought to his notice during
these months of tentative inquiry. This ancient form of self-
consecration was sedulously cultivated, and not a few of those
who elected it, finding that custom has apportioned certain
accomplishments and duties to each of the sexes, making them
indispensable to each other, comforted their celibacy by con-
tracting alliances of dubious propriety. Such unions, into which
the principals entered for reasons of convenience, were often
too sore a trial for the flesh, and spiritual marriage, under the
pressure of emotion, became carnal indeed. A knowledge of the
pitfalls that surrounded those who ventured upon this manner
of life may well have been a safeguard to Beissel when his fame
as a spiritual guide attracted women to him in Pennsylvania.
He was not spared the attentions of the prurient, but there is
no reason to suppose that his conduct gave any real warrant
for the unsavory reports his enemies circulated. There will be
occasion to consider these matters at greater length later; for
the present it is important to observe that celibacy, the solitary
life, and the partnership of the two sexes on a purely spiritual
plane were familiar to him before he emigrated to Pennsylvania.

He had leisure, at this time, to contemplate the practices and
ascertain the merits of two sects. Alexander Mack, with whom
Beissel was to cross swords some years later, led the Dunkers
of Schwarzenau, in Wittgenstein. This small coterie of saints
was now about ten years old. Its founder was deeply indebted
to Ernst Christoph Hochmann von Hochenau, an eminent and

godly separatist, who, after his conversion in Halle under Francke, had led a roving life, striving to convert Jews as well as Christians, and gaining a wide acquaintance among people who were interested in matters of the soul. In 1702 Hochmann was required by the Count of Lippe-Detmold to prepare a statement of his beliefs. He repudiated the baptism of infants, advocated the exclusion of the unconverted from the Lord's Supper, and held that perfection was possible in this life. According to his conception of it, the ministry was charismatic; it was Christ, and not men, who gave ministers their authority. He regarded the civil power as valid in the realm of nature, but declined to obey such of its commands as violated his conscience. He looked forward to universal redemption, but admitted that serious obstacles stood in the way of its execution. This creed, it is worth observing, was published at Germantown by Christopher Sauer, and at Ephrata. The Count, not completely satisfied with it, demanded an abstract of Hochmann's views on marriage. Hochmann replied by describing five kinds of wedlock. The first is merely a respectable form of prostitution. The second, though less carnal, is, like the first, purely natural. The third is the physical union of two Christians, and sexual congress is permitted only for the purpose of reproduction. The fourth is a wholly spiritual union, designed to further the salvation of the two parties. The last degree is virginity in the proper sense. In due time, these views are reflected in Beissel's own teaching.

Mack attended Hochmann on his journeys and was his faithful follower until they disagreed on the question of rebaptism, Mack adopting the uncompromising opinion of the English Baptists that the immersion of adults in running water was indispensable, since the baptism of infants was totally unavailing. Mack, a Palatine of Schriesheim, had been reared a Calvinist and had paid for his separatism with the loss of considerable substance. He and his master illustrate the two divergent tendencies of separatism. Hochmann represents those who viewed its work as the multiplication of individual converts and depre-

cated the attempt to set up barriers in the form of exclusive
creeds and principles. Mack and his partisans valued their own
method of baptism, with its doctrinal implications, to such a
degree that they felt obliged to part company with those who
were less firmly convinced of its necessity. Obviously the position of the unattached separatist was untenable. Unless he succeeded in uniting his disciples and friends in a common life, the
propagation of his ideas, except within narrow limits, was impossible. A common life demands a creed. The work of men
like Hochmann, whatever its effect while their conviction and
zeal exerted an immediate influence upon their followers, was
barren because it remained nebulous and was never reduced to
the concrete form of a social pattern. Beissel, like Hochmann,
was unwilling to formulate his tenets and never assumed a genuinely unequivocal and determined position, regarding even the
Scriptures as an inadequate statement of eternal truth. Since
Hochmann's death did not occur until after Beissel's departure,
it is conceivable that the two met.

Beissel was not drawn to the Dunkers. The Inspirationists
were more to his liking, but, although he shared in their exercises, he never joined them. The sect was only a few years old.
The movement that led to its formation began early in the
eighteenth century in southern France, where people claiming
to possess the gift of prophecy had appeared among the dissenters of the Cevennes Mountains. They led a revolt against
their Catholic oppressors and, when the insurrection had spent
its force, traveled through England and Scotland, and finally
reached Germany. During the years 1713–16 they made a deep
impression upon some of the German Pietists. A band of Inspirationists journeyed to Pennsylvania in 1726. Among them
was Johann Adam Gruber, the author of a long and incoherent
plea to the isolated German settlers who had been "awakened"
in the old country. He implored them to assemble in small
groups and renew their fervor. The pamphlet was published,
without the author's consent, in 1742, when Zinzendorf's attempt to merge all denominations in one Christian body was in

full swing. Zinzendorf had made a similar attempt at amalgama-
tion a few years before, when he established amicable relations
with Rock, the leader of the Inspirationists, and detached a
number of his followers from him, to Rock's enduring indignation. Unquestionably, Gruber's recollection of Zinzendorf's
former slyness motivated his refusal to join the wily count in
the new enterprise.

The Inspirationists soon discovered that Beissel was resisting
their advances. He was not tractable by temperament, and his
disenchantment at Heidelberg had left him sour and cautious.
His want of docility irritated the prophets, and the tension
reached a climax when two young women were visibly upset in
Beissel's presence. The leader of the meeting attributed this agi-
tation—no doubt correctly—to Beissel's personal charm and
dismissed him promptly. Although he submitted with humility
to a reprimand, he soon dissolved his connection with the sect,
suspecting that he was about to be demoted to the children's
class. In spite of this second disillusionment, he cherished no ill
will and cordially acknowledged the reality of the awakening
he had found among the Inspirationists. His pulpit manner at a
later stage in his career suggests that their influence did not
cease when he severed his relations with them. Caught in the
swell of the Spirit, he preached disjointedly and with little attention to grammar. In writing, he "suspended his considering
Faculty, and putting his Spirit on the Pen, followed its Dictates
strictly." It is evident that he cultivated prophetic ecstasy, and
it may be that he began to develop his capacities in this direction during his brief intercourse with the Inspirationists. Perhaps the spectacle of their unbridled abandonment to the surge
of emotion taught him to be moderate in the use of such gifts
as he himself possessed.

By the time of his arrival at Schatz's establishment, Beissel
had become so enamoured of poverty that he signified his desire to work without remuneration. Schatz, a man of broad
experience, preferred a more businesslike arrangement. After
a time Beissel gave up baking and became a wool spinner,

sharing quarters with George Stiefel, whom he had known at home in Eberbach. Junkerroth, an eccentric nobleman, befriended him, and, in all likelihood, he eked out the pittance he contrived to earn at his new trade with occasional gifts from this odd Pietist. At last he made up his mind to devote the residue of his days to a hermit's life in America. His friends begged him to stay where he was, but he was adamant, and in 1720 he set sail with Stiefel, Stuntz, Simon Koenig, Henry von Bebern, and others. He was so impecunious that Stuntz paid his passage.

The discomforts and perils of a sea voyage to the new world in those days have been exaggerated, but they were unquestionably severe. Either Beissel was inured to such tribulations and did not mind them or the passage was unusually smooth, for his biographers give no details of the journey. The ship docked at Boston in the fall of the year, and Beissel made his way to Germantown.

At the age of thirty, a man cannot leave the world of his youth behind and begin his life anew. Beissel was neither a pioneer nor a missionary. He had not come to America to fill his purse, for he had long viewed money and other possessions with serene indifference. His father, a spendthrift, had exhibited his contempt for money by getting rid of it as rapidly as possible. In Beissel the family trait assumed the form of voluntary poverty. He was so deeply preoccupied with his own spiritual concerns and so uncertain of his doctrine that he was not impelled to seek converts. His efforts in this direction had been confined to his family, and within this limited circle they had been startlingly successful. We are examined more searchingly by our own flesh and blood than by those who know us less intimately. Since it sustained this most rigorous of tests, Beissel's piety must have been genuine. If he could win those who were least inclined to discount his faults, he might expect to make swift strides among people who were predisposed to accept his teaching. Yet, with these advantages and gifts, he had a negativistic shyness that neutralized them. Superbly equipped, in some respects, to propagate a faith to which he

clung with the deepest sincerity, he exercised his talents with
unaffected reluctance. He never really surmounted the barriers that divided the Germans from the other linguistic and
national groups of Pennsylvania. He remained a German among
Germans and failed completely to respond to the impulse
towards unification and growth that stirred his adopted country. In later years Beissel's followers, with his approbation, reviled the Moravians as exponents of a shallow Christianity. It
did not occur to him that his own religion was defective, since
it could claim nothing comparable with the efficiency and fruit-
fulness of the Moravian missions to the Indians. For Beissel the
savages, like the magnificent natural beauties of the new world,
were merely a part of the passing scene, which he saw dimly as
through a mist and from a great height. To him such things
did not matter. In short, his emigration to Pennsylvania made
only one difference in his life: it gave him liberty to follow
his soul's promptings. He wanted to be alone. Surely in the
backwoods there would be a secluded spot where he could live
in contemplation, unruffled by the interminable dissension of
Wittgenstein and Berleburg. He did not know that the new
life was to be merely a continuation of the old.

III

A RECLUSE IN CONESTOGA

THE most exacting German separatist could find little to carp at in the legal foundation upon which life in Pennsylvania rested. When he crossed the ocean, Beissel relinquished a precarious toleration, which depended upon the indulgence of the reigning count and might readily be converted into oppression at the caprice of his successor, and gained in its stead the assured protection of a government that subscribed almost without reserve to the principle of freedom in religious matters. The charter of 1701, which remained in force until the American Revolution, states this principle explicitly in the following words:

I do hereby grant and declare that no person or persons inhabiting in this province or territories who shall confess or acknowledge one Almighty God, the creator, upholder and ruler of the world, and profess him or themselves obliged to live quietly under the civil government, shall be in any case molested or prejudiced in his or their person or estate . . . nor be compelled to frequent or maintain any religious worship, place or ministry, contrary to his or their mind, or to do or suffer any other act or thing contrary to their religious persuasion. And that all persons who also profess to believe in Jesus Christ, the Saviour of the world, shall be capable (notwithstanding their other persuasions and practices in point of conscience and religion) to serve this government in any capacity, both legislatively and executively, he or they solemnly promising, when lawfully required, allegiance to the king as Sovereign, and fidelity to the Proprietor and Governor, etc.

There is little ambiguity in this declaration. It clearly envisages the toleration of all religious views, except atheism, so long as they do not imperil order, and extends to the harassed sects of Europe the pledge of emancipation from exasperating disabilities. Even the single qualification for office—in addition to theism, which is required of all—is loosely defined, perhaps intentionally so. A liberal construction of the terms of the charter might have admitted Unitarians to public office, since a confession of belief in Christ's divinity is not expressly prescribed. In this broad constitution the visions of many a persecuted dissenter were fulfilled. Indeed it was too broad to be palatable to the English crown. Penn's designs were pruned by an order, issued in 1702, compelling colonial officials to meet the requirements of the Toleration Act of 1689, by which they were forced to repudiate transubstantiation and the veneration of the Virgin and the Saints. Three years later the Assembly gave its assent and support to this ruling. Thus abridged, the liberty accorded to the settlers in Pennsylvania was still wide, and all but Jews, Unitarians, and Roman Catholics, even when the law was strictly interpreted, were eligible to public office.

William Penn did not arrive at such a measure of magnanimity by chance. Converted to Quakerism in 1667, he had sought to further the interests of his sect by waiting upon a number of influential persons on the continent and had, in the course of his peregrinations, acquired considerable knowledge of the separatists and sectarians of Germany and the Netherlands. William Ames, an indefatigable Quaker missionary, had gained a following in Krefeld a decade before Penn's conversion and had formed a congregation of Quakers at Krisheim in the Palatinate. Penn stopped at Heidelberg in order to intercede with the Elector for the latter group. He called upon the Labadists and heard accounts of their spiritual experiences. This intercourse with people whose opinions were closely related to his own opened his eyes to the servitude in which they lived and helped to develop in him a humanity that was almost without parallel in his day.

In 1681 Pennsylvania was granted to Penn in settlement of a debt. In the late summer of the next year Philadelphia was founded, and in 1683 Germantown was settled by Dutch Quakers. There was little difference between the Mennonites and the Quakers, and many of the former had adopted Quakerism. At first the community was predominantly Quaker in religion

and Dutch in nationality. It is highly probable that Francis
Daniel Pastorius, the chief citizen of early Germantown and
the only member of the Frankfort Company to set foot upon
the soil of Pennsylvania, was a Quaker. In 1686 the first Quaker
meetinghouse was erected, and the Quakers retained their ascendancy over other sects, despite some friction with the Mennonites, at least until 1707, when the first Mennonite immigrants
from the Palatinate arrived. The torrential influx of Germans,
beginning in 1709, altered the character of the settlement. Soon
the German Baptists constituted an important element in the
population. The first wave came in 1719, under Peter Becker,
and ten years later Alexander Mack disembarked with a second
group.

The traits that were common to all these sects helped to
accentuate their disharmonies. Seelig, one of the hermits of a
community soon to be mentioned more particularly, wrote,
"The religions here are in constant opposition . . ." The dis-
cord that characterized their relations was too plain to escape
notice. Not only did sect clash with sect, but there was also
acute internal dissension. In 1691 and for a time thereafter,
Quakerism in Pennsylvania was shaken to its roots by the
Keithian schism. George Keith, an energetic, disputatious person with a flair for vituperation, ended his stormy career as a
parson in the Church of England, but not until he had "made
a great bustle" in Pennsylvania, as Sewel, the Quaker historian,
informs us. Keith, while still a Quaker, was suspected of be-
lieving in the transmigration of souls. He berated two fellow
Quakers for holding "that the light within was sufficient to salvation," from which it might be inferred that Christ's redemption was superfluous. He also asserted that Stockdell had
charged him with teaching that there were two Christs. The
precise issue is of little moment, but the deplorable result of
the quarrel was felt sorely by the Quakers. "And seeing several
Mennonites of the county of Meurs, lived also in Pennsylvania,
it was not much to be wondered, that they who count it un-
lawful for a Christian to bear the sword of magistracy, did

stick to" Keith, "and to get adherents seemed the main thing he aimed at; for he himself was not trained up under such a notion, but in the doctrine of the kirk of Scotland." Beissel learned the doctrine of the seventh day sabbath, if we may trust Morgan Edwards, from Keith's adherents. Speaking of the Ephrata community, the writer says, "They keep the seventh day of the week for sabbath, to which their founder had been proselyted by the remains of the keithian baptists, particularly Rev. Thomas Rutter, who in this affair was the disciple of Abel Noble."

The principles so stoutly cherished by the Quakers impeded the execution of a program of defense for a colony exposed to the raids of the Indians and the French, and both the Proprietor and the Crown made concessions in an effort to reconcile their divergent interests. The two most formidable hindrances to the ordinary operations of government were the Quakers' objection to oaths and their refusal to participate in war. They also advocated a mitigation of the rigors of English criminal law and would, if left to their own devices, have imposed the death penalty only upon those guilty of murder or treason. The government, in deference to the conscientious scruples of the Quakers and others, accepted an affirmation as the equivalent of an oath. The Quakers were as accommodating as their convictions permitted, placing no obstacles in the way of persons whose consciences allowed them to bear arms, and agreeing to a more extensive use of capital punishment than they had contemplated at the beginning. Quaker rule terminated in 1756.

The freedom suddenly bestowed upon people accustomed to persecution and frustration was not merely a sedative for their frayed nerves. In many instances, it stimulated and intoxicated them. Land had to be settled, cleared, and cultivated, and the immigrant's back-breaking combat with the inexorable forces of the natural world claimed so much of his time and energy that religion was thrust into a subordinate place. Except in the few towns of the colony, the settlers lived far apart, and regular attendance at religious meetings entailed great fatigue and the neglect of pressing business at home. Some of those who had been most zealous in the old country showed little resistance when confronted with the attractions of the new. There was a revulsion of feeling: nauseated with the acerbities of sectarian strife, which raged unrestrained in Pennsylvania, men began to glimpse the possibilities of a world built upon material foundations and actuated by secular motives. The theology with which the Anabaptist and Pietistic groups were saturated was one of abstraction and withdrawal from the natural interests of life. It stifled the genius of a man like Conrad Weiser, who, to a greater degree than any other German colonist, epitomizes the conflict between allegiance to the religion imported from Europe and a desire to share in the formation of a culture that would express the mind of a nation rapidly becoming conscious of its separate existence and its dazzling future. This was the environment in which Beissel did his appointed work. If we limit our view to the period of his life, we cannot deny that the times, on the whole, favored the execution of the project that matured in his mind as ways were opened to him, but in the long run the drift of national sentiment and ambition was not in his direction. His course ended logically in the calm of decay, and, not many years after his death, Peter Miller, his successor, pathetically confessed that the surviving brothers and sisters at Ephrata could not hope to "propagate the Monastic Life upon the Posterity," because "the Genius of the Americans" preferred action to contemplation.

Beissel was wisely reticent about his plans. A period of orientation was necessary before he could begin to carry them out. He had several reasons for spending a year in Germantown. He had probably heard from some Pietist, or read somewhere in a communication from Pennsylvania, of the monastic community founded on the Ridge, a short distance from Germantown, by Johann Kelpius, in 1694. It had forty members at the start, and later accessions gave some hope of permanence, but the enterprise dissolved after the untimely death of Kelpius. When Beissel arrived, it had dwindled almost to the vanishing point. Beissel's disappointment must have been keen, for it is not unlikely that he had intended to begin his solitary life in fellowship with the hermits of "The Woman in the Wilderness," as this company styled itself. He may have regarded himself as in some sense a member of this community, for he sent an "offering" to it from Conestoga after his departure from Germantown, and he appears to have made this gift, which perhaps he looked upon as tribute, from a strong sense of duty.

The influence of Jacob Böhme's theology permeated several Pietistic groups and had a powerful effect upon numerous individuals. Beissel's debt to this curious system of thought is incalculable; he appropriated both its substance and its language, and it is, beyond dispute, the ultimate source of the intellectual groundwork upon which he raised the structure of the monastic life. His biographers, realizing—perhaps without full consciousness—that an acknowledgment of his obligation would detract from his prestige, have dealt very unsatisfactorily with the matter. Beissel could not have hobnobbed with Pietists very long without becoming acquainted with Böhme's writings or, at least, with his teachings as they appeared in the works of his interpreters. Beissel's familiarity with Böhmism presupposes an intense study of its doctrines in written form, and, although it is quite possible that he had an opportunity to immerse himself in them before he left Europe, it may reasonably be conjectured that he gained his first intimate knowledge of them from his association with the survivors of Kelpius' abortive venture. The first head of the group, before Kelpius and his companions journeyed to America, was John Jacob Zimmermann, an ardent Böhmist. Kelpius himself had known some of Böhme's disciples in England. "The Woman in the Wilderness" was a theosophical fraternity as well as a religious community. The erudition of its members was one of the marvels of the colony, and Beissel, during his sojourn in Germantown, can scarcely have lacked either tutors in the mysteries of Böhme's theology or books to aid his studies. With such means at his command, he probably made remarkable strides in this branch of learning while he found his bearings in the new world.

Beissel's second reason for choosing Germantown as his first place of residence in Pennsylvania was the presence there of a number of German Baptists who had lately made the voyage to America under the guidance of Peter Becker. Beissel had not been friendly with this sect in Germany, but he had broken with his earlier friends, the Inspirationists, who, moreover, had as yet no representative in America, and the prospect of living among people who were not wholly strangers to him probably helped to determine his choice. No doubt he had several acquaintances in Germantown before his arrival, but, even if he had not, he knew that he would find fellow countrymen there. Among those who came to America with him was Henry von Bebern (van Bebber), whose father and brothers had lived in Germantown.

A less important, but not entirely negligible, factor in the situation was Beissel's empty purse. He was a pauper. Happily, the expenses of the trip to America had been met by a generous friend, and Beissel was not pressed for immediate payment of the loan, but it soon became clear that he would fare ill as a baker, and he found himself under the necessity of learning a new craft. Peter Becker was a weaver; he was willing to accept Beissel as an apprentice; and the two came to an agreement, with or without articles of indenture. Beissel's relations with the Baptists grew more cordial. They found that he had a receptive ear for complaints and confidences, and soon he knew as much as they did of the uncharitable quarrels that had divided them before they reached their new home. He urged them to try, quietly and circumspectly, to restore their shattered unity, and his biographers credit him with helping to bring about the revival that took place a few years later.

At the conclusion of his brief term of apprenticeship, Beissel retired, with Stuntz, to Conestoga, then an outlying district of the colony, sparsely settled and therefore well suited to his purpose. It was customary for a master to outfit his servant when the latter's period of service expired, and frequently the equipment to be furnished was mentioned in the contract. There was nothing niggardly about Peter Becker, and he probably did not dismiss Beissel without a parting gift of tools and supplies. The two young men found a convenient site at Mill Creek and built a cabin, where, for a season, they led an untroubled existence, with boundless leisure for contemplation. Their solitude was broken by Isaac von Bebern, a Dutchman related to the von Beberns of Bohemia Manor in Maryland. In his company Beissel made an excursion to Maryland. The authors of the *Chronicon* wrote warily at this point in their narrative. Bohemia Manor was the seat of a branch of the Labadist sect. Beissel's biographers are reluctant to suggest that he learned anything from these people, and studiously avoid saying in so many words that he made their acquaintance, but the *Chronicon's* summary description of the iniquitous prosperity of the Labadists may be construed as an indirect admission that Beissel knew them and disapproved of them. Certain of the writings of the Labadist leaders de Labadie and Yvon, no doubt scrupulously and legibly copied in the manner of the time, were to be found among the settlers at Bohemia Manor. These manuscripts must have aroused Beissel's interest, if he had an opportunity to consult them. Perhaps portions of them were translated for him. He could hardly have read them in the original, for, since he never mastered English, it is not likely that he had a command of French, and his Latin, if he had any at this time, must have been limited to a few common words and phrases. In any case, the writings of the Labadist fathers contained little, if anything, that could not have reached him through other channels. The community, however, was a living example of degeneration, and he cannot have failed to be impressed by its decay.

If Beissel is typical of separatism at its most thriving period, the career of Jean de Labadie will serve to illustrate its beginnings. To a remarkable degree, the same characteristics appear in the two men. Both believed themselves, and were believed by their followers, to be in direct rapport with supernatural reality, so that the importance of the various human influences brought to bear upon them is obscured; both evinced an obstinate loyalty to the interior light and to a sense of destiny, with the result that they never genuinely belonged to any religious group not of their own creation; both were such unyielding perfectionists that they finally established congregations of their own, concluding that it was impossible to purge existing religious bodies of their impurities; and both relied inordinately upon their personal influence, to the detriment of their work, on the whole. It is not certain that Beissel knew the older separatist well enough to be aware of the traits they had in common, but, if he did, a salutary moral was to be drawn from the decline into which de Labadie's sect had fallen.

Outwardly de Labadie was first a Catholic, then a Calvinist, and at long last, a Labadist. Within, he was Labadist from the start. He entered a Jesuit school as a child and did not sever his connection with the Society of Jesus until he was almost thirty. His honorable dismissal was the culmination of at least ten years of growing antipathy to the combative theology of the Jesuits and resistance to their attempt to impose upon him a stereotyped spirituality. His own position was exceedingly simple: truth was to be found in the Scriptures, not in the jejune expositions of professional theologians; the earliest Christian community had taught and practised this truth with immaculate perfection and purity; and it was de Labadie's appointed task to restore the Christian religion to its primitive holiness and vigor. As a secular priest, he preached in Bordeaux, Paris, and Amiens, founding, in the last place, a brotherhood for those who had felt the touch of the Spirit and were therefore qualified to belong to the select company of sincere and fervent Christians. The Jesuits pursued de Labadie with vindictive accusations and finally hounded him out of the Church.

The transition from Roman Catholicism to Calvinism was

not difficult for him. He had by no means discarded his headstrong belief in the commission entrusted to him and had no intention of assuming the rôle of pupil at the ripe age of forty. He soon became a Reformed pastor in Montauban. He rose to high position with a celerity that must have exposed him to the envy of many who were Calvinists born and bred. After a pastorate in Orange, he received a call to London and was on his way to England when the congregation in Geneva detained him and insisted upon his accepting their urgent invitation to remain and become their pastor. Higher than this it was not possible to ascend, and de Labadie seemed to have attained the pinnacle of an illustrious career, only to find that Geneva was not a suitable scene for his projected reformation. Apparently the majority of his congregation believed that one reformation was sufficient. Since there were obstacles in his way at Geneva, an invitation to Middelburg in the Netherlands was welcome. Middelburg ranked far below Geneva in dignity and renown, but it opened a vista of reforming activity in which de Labadie would have the support of several very earnest saints. His plans were thwarted. Not deeming it proper to dissemble, he preached indiscreetly on the journey to Middelburg. Presently he was embroiled with the ecclesiastical authorities. His millenarianism, as well as his opinionated and disingenuous conduct, made his orthodoxy dubious. His maneuvers, cleverly calculated to embarrass his opponents, were infuriating in a newcomer, who arrogated to himself the part of judge in the dispute and responded to the courteous patience of the Synod by calling its soundness into question. In view of de Labadie's intransigent stand, there was only one way to conclude this protracted altercation. He was deprived of his office and at last enjoyed complete liberty to follow his vocation.

One-third of the congregation at Middelburg sided with him. After the rupture he moved to a nearby town, and, when it became desirable to quit this place, Anna Maria von Schürmann, his most noted convert, joined him in the establishment of a curious ménage in Amsterdam. De Labadie tried in vain to

effect a merger with the followers of de Bourignon and Gichtel. In 1670 the generous Princess Elizabeth, daughter of the
unfortunate Elector Palatine Frederic V, granted the Labadists
a refuge in Herford. This they soon afterwards abandoned to
go to Altona, and de Labadie died there in 1674. They settled
finally at Wieuwerd in Friesland, where the three sisters van
Sommelsdijk, all enthusiastic Labadists, owned a castle. There
the sect expired about fifty years after the founder's death. The
early freedom and deliberate repudiation of external forms and
ceremonies vanished as Yvon, de Labadie's successor, subjected the community to a closer organization and a more
rigorous discipline. Under his oppressive rule it lost its spon-
taneity, which was the only thing that justified its distinct existence. The daughter congregation in Surinam (Dutch Guiana)
likewise succumbed to the forces of dissolution. Not long after
the commencement of Penn's "holy experiment" in Pennsylvania, the Labadists purchased a sizable tract of land at Bohemia
Manor. Here Peter Schlüter, a martinet like Yvon, exercised
an absolute authority, part of which he delegated to his wife,
who presided over the female portion of the establishment.
Beissel came just in time to inspect this community. Shortly
after Schlüter's death in 1722 it vanished.

Certain features of Labadism find parallels in Beissel's foundation; to others nothing in the Ephrata settlement corresponds.
The Labadists practised community of goods and obedience,
maintained workshops, and engaged in commercial enterprises.
The plan of life was essentially monastic, and its discipline was
designed to tame the human will. The initiates, or fully qualified members, formed only a part of the community; there
was, besides, a body of postulants or probationers. There were
common meals, and the most private matters of life, including
dress, were severely regulated. In all these respects the Labadists
bore a close likeness to the religious of Ephrata. The agreement,
however, was not complete. The Labadists held marriage in
high esteem and baptized their children. They did not suspend
their labors when Sunday came. Their practice with regard to

these matters differed materially from that of Beissel and his followers.

Beissel made his way back to Conestoga and resumed the life to which both circumstances and his proclivities had inclined him. Isaac von Bebern had returned with him, and Stiefel attached himself to the little company. The venture excited the curiosity and suspicion of the backwoods folk in the neighborhood, who plagued the hermits unceasingly with their questions. Beissel and his associates probably welcomed a certain amount of prying and embraced the opportunity to instruct their visitors. These gullible pioneers approached the anchorites with mixed emotions, half in awe of their self-denying sanctity and half in terror of the baneful techniques they might possess. Beissel's increasing reputation had doubtless, even in these early days, brought him a nucleus of credulous devotees, whom he might have exploited if he had been disposed to do so; but, apart from the longing for inward repose and release from the vexatious distractions of ordinary life and notwithstanding his sometimes overweening confidence in the correctness of his own judgment, he was still exploring his own soul and was not prepared to advance extravagant claims for himself; and besides, most of his neighbors were probably astute enough to be skeptical about prophets. His response to the excesses of Matthias Baumann, a less scrupulous enthusiast, exhibits the fundamental balance and wholesomeness of his own spiritual life.

Baumann preached the doctrine of the new birth. He announced to all who would listen that he had undergone a complete regeneration, with the happy result that he simply could not sin. This transformation had occurred in the course of an illness at the beginning of the century, and now, more than twenty years later, Baumann's ludicrous utterances, though diverting to most people, were seducing a few. His lucubrations on his amazing experiences and the conclusions to be drawn from them were printed in the *Geistliche Fama*. Though mildly mad, they are remarkable as the work of a man who had been merely "a workman and small farmer" at Lamsheim in the

Palatinate. Pietism, like other enthusiasms, often made an untrained tongue articulate and even eloquent. Baumann declared his willingness to walk across the Delaware in order to demonstrate the truth of his teaching, but there is no record of his success. His doctrine of the spirituality of sin, as the *Chronicon* observes, scandalized his auditors, because it implied that carnal sins might be committed with impunity, except for the penalties imposed by the law of the land. His blasphemy, however, was even more objectionable. One or two examples will suffice. "God dwelt in Christ," he asserted, "and He dwells in me too, wherefore we are completely equal, for we are brothers." "Christ took away no sin, but God spoke through him, not otherwise than as He speaks through me." It would be unprofitable to explain the premisses of a theology that leads to such startling conclusions. Beissel's coarse but devastating reply to these preposterous simplicities is reminiscent of Dr. Johnson's refutation of Berkeley's idealism. He invited Baumann to inhale the odor of his own dung and reconcile it, if he could, with the new birth. The Baumannites made a venomous answer and took their leave.

The early promise of Beissel's pious undertaking was not fulfilled. Even those who aspire to be angels on earth must eat and drink, and few had the fortitude to live as abstemiously as Beissel did. His gifts were those of a hermit in the literal sense of the word, and he showed almost no comprehension of the obligations social life imposed upon him. He lived in wellnigh complete abstraction from the duties and preoccupations of mankind and could not be trusted to carry out satisfactorily any task assigned to him. He did not mean to be slack or rude. He was simply blind to the forces that govern human relations, and this congenital obtuseness was a lasting impediment. His little fraternity was merely a fortuitous aggregation of fallible and angular human beings. It would never become a community until every member of it learned to make the sacrifices that are requisite to the success of a common life. When chores were allotted to Beissel he performed them with his mind in heaven. Naturally, his negligence irritated his fellows. The fault was not wholly Beissel's. The religious life bristles with intricate and baffling problems, and only a person who possesses rare social insight himself or has inherited a rich traditional wisdom knows how to cope with them. It was an admirable school for Beissel, but its lessons were wasted on him. His periods of service in the kitchen were a grievous trial to the ravenous appetites of his companions, who felt that they required and deserved substantial victuals. They remonstrated with him and received nothing for their pains but a homily on self-indulgence. Beissel's Sabbatarianism was another cause of friction. It was not long before all save Beissel were surfeited with the monotony and rigor of the asceticism in which he alone found solace and profit. He luxuriated in self-denial as other people bask in the warmth of plenty. Stiefel was the first to fall away. Von Bebern followed him, his boredom and aversion from the austerities urged upon him by Beissel winning the day against a deep affection for the man whose spiritual endowments far surpassed his own. Stuntz had been wondering for a long time about the repayment of his loan to Beissel. At last he decided to reimburse himself by selling the cabin. He was entirely within his rights, but Beissel felt himself unjustly used. His resentment suggests a frank, bold question. Beissel fasted, prayed, and gave alms; but was he honest? Perhaps the exalted virtues that adorn such characters as his crowd out the lowlier graces that merely enable men to live together. Beissel's raptures left no room for common integrity. His faults were lamentable, but he must not be judged by canons that are not strictly applicable to persons of his high degree. The actions of saints and men of genius fall, for the most part, outside the frame of ordinary ethics. If Beissel had been a farmer or a trader, he would have been greatly to blame for his failure to meet an obligation. As it is, his conduct is not wholly defensible; but allowance must be made for an underdeveloped sense of property rights. Beissel, possessing nothing himself, and regarding all ownership as a hindrance to salvation, was, on the basis of his own principles, justifiably unmindful of other people's claims. His naïve stupidity with regard to the things he did not understand is merely the inevitable concomitant of the extraordinary soundness of mind and certainty of touch he displayed in dealing with matters that lay within the confines of his gifts and interests. The *Chronicon* observes that he ultimately alienated many who at first were strongly attracted to him. People were drawn by the apparent light of his spirituality only to discover that it was a consuming flame. They craved a share of his interior poise and peace, but recoiled when they learned at what cost these things had been purchased.

For the moment, Beissel was left to enjoy his transports alone. He contrived to build a cabin at Swedes' Spring, approximately a mile from the old hermitage on Mill Creek. Here he gained his first devoted male adherent, Michael Wohlfahrt, who had visited Beissel and his companions before the disintegration of their common life and now returned from Carolina to become the second member of the new community. Wohlfahrt's zeal had grown tepid in the course of his prolonged wanderings. However, his unrest is to be ascribed as much to the distractions of sectarianism as to a diminution of fervor. He confessed the state of his soul to Beissel, who, none too confident of the acceptability of his own life at the moment, could not deny the request of so humble a postulant, and welcomed him to the hermitage. They contracted a friendship that endured, without a serious rift, until Wohlfahrt's death almost twenty years later. Wohlfahrt's temperament was passionate and aggressive. Like many of his contemporaries, he set greater value upon the cultivation of the type of spirituality he preferred than upon membership in a sect. His ardent Inspirationism, therefore, does not presuppose outward communion with Rock's band of prophets. His experience, probably, had run parallel with Beissel's, and their common distaste for, and independence of, all the sects they knew was a close bond between them. Wohlfahrt was slightly older than Beissel, but he accepted the position of a disciple at the outset, and there was no ambiguity in their relations. If Wohlfahrt was not the first person to suggest Seventh Day Sabbatarianism to Beissel, he fortified the latter's convictions regarding the Sabbath by endorsing them loyally and placing his facile pen and his knowledge of English at his master's disposal. As Michael Welfare, he was well known to the English-speaking settlers, who had seen him invade Quaker meetings or stand up to publish the truth to the crowds in the market place at Philadelphia. Benjamin Franklin mentions him with approval in his *Autobiography*. The passage will enable the reader to contemplate Wohlfahrt and his co-religionists, for a moment, from Franklin's tolerant and emancipated point of view.

These embarrassments that the Quakers suffer'd from having establish'd and published it as one of their principles that no kind of war was lawful, and which, being once published, they could not afterwards, however they might change their minds, easily get rid of, reminds me of what I think a more prudent conduct in another sect among us, that of the Dunkers. I was acquainted with one of its founders, Michael Welfare, soon after it appear'd. He complain'd to me that they were grievously calumniated by the zealots of other persuasions, and charg'd with abominable principles and practices, to which they were utter strangers. I told him this had always been the case with new sects, and that, to put a stop to such abuse, I imagin'd it might be well to publish the articles of their belief, and the rules of their discipline. He said that it had been propos'd among them, but not agreed to, for this reason: "When we were first drawn together as a society," says he, "it had pleased God to enlighten our minds so far as to see that some doctrines, which we once esteemed truths, were errors; and that others, which we had esteemed errors, were real truths. From time to time He has been pleased to afford us farther light, and our principles have been improving, and our errors diminishing. Now we are not sure that we are arrived at the end of this progression, and at the perfection of spiritual or theological knowledge; and we fear that, if we should once print our confession of faith, we should feel ourselves as if bound and confin'd by it, and perhaps be unwilling to receive further im-

provement, and our successors still more so, as conceiving what
we their elders and founders had done, to be something sacred,
never to be departed from."

This modesty in a sect is perhaps a singular instance in the
history of mankind, every other sect supposing itself in possession of all truth, and that those who differ are so far in the
wrong . . .

Franklin's contempt for Keimer, whose previous life bears a
a close resemblance to Wohlfahrt's, accentuates the sincerity of
this tribute. Keimer, who, like Wohlfahrt, was a Seventh Day
Sabbatarian, "had been one of the French prophets, and could
act their enthusiastic agitations. At this time he did not profess
any particular religion, but something of all on occasion; was
very ignorant of the world, and had, as I afterward found, a
good deal of the knave in his composition." Keimer had not
discovered a Beissel.

Despite the rigor of his penance, Beissel was still not completely mortified. He broke the enclosure of his retreat from
time to time and sought relief from the monotony of his almost
solitary life in missions of instruction and exhortation, which
interrupted his eremitic seclusion for days at a stretch. Perhaps he realized that his motives were mixed and that his occasional lapses from complete detachment were a proof of his
inability to live permanently in the state for which he had
longed. A hermit's exemptions from the good and evil chances
of society might serve him well if they opened the way to an
active life, but, apart from such an objective, they were a
blind alley. The hermit becomes a specialist in austerities and
is often betrayed into parading his dominion over the flesh and
neutralizing, by his display of pride, the gains he may have
made in the performance of his ascetic feats. Beissel fell a prey,
in some measure, to this temptation. Often, when he was a
guest in some farmhouse, he refused food for three days at a
time, and his hosts were displeased. A more gracious acceptance
of hospitality at such times could not have endangered his soul,
and he would have been both humbler and more courteous if

he had eaten with and like the rest. His abstinence was boorish, and simple folk who saw nothing wrong in sitting down to a hearty meal after an honest day's work must have found his aloofness repellent, for it was an unspoken sermon on self-indulgence and implied a supercilious unwillingness on Beissel's part to be subject to hunger like other men. Such renunciations are best made in private. Beissel, reflecting on the sterility of his life as such experiences made it increasingly evident, concluded that he would have to mingle with mankind or run the risk of defeating his own efforts. He retained enough reverence for Christian tradition to feel that baptism was indispensable. An abortive experiment in self-baptism made him very uneasy, and, when the German Baptists came to convert the backlands, he did not view their arrival with indifference.

IV

THE INVASION OF PARADISE

Beissel had barely accustomed himself to the amenities of solitude, varied with evangelistic interludes that refreshed him without imposing upon him the onerous responsibility of a regular cure of souls, when he was catapulted, with disconcerting violence, back into the maelstrom of society. A soft haze of pious rationalization obscures this period of his life. At bottom, because he was a shrewd peasant, he could not be blind to the advantages bestowed upon him by the establishment of a German Baptist congregation in Conestoga and his own elevation to the dignity of pastor. It is indisputably true that he was drafted into active service, but it is probably not less true that, in devious and subtle ways, he invited the call, even while shrinking from the danger and perturbation that were inseparable from it. Beyond doubt his new authority gave him an opportunity, as virtually nothing else could have done, to widen and consolidate his influence. It was the making of Beissel as a spiritual force, but, at the same time, it could too easily be construed as a defection from his professed ideals. This aspect of his change of habit and interest required an explanation that would be palatable to his own conscience and convincing to his critics. He accounted for it by assuming a conventional pose. Many before him had forsaken the ascetic life—or, at least, consented to modify their practice of it—in response to the importunate pressure of the Church. It is always possible, in such a situation, to plead a divine summons or an imperative practical need as an excuse for the assumption of duties that entail abandonment of seclusion and a return to the multifarious concerns and distractions of the world. For some this has not been a sacrifice at all, though they made it appear so by simulating a reluctance they did not feel; for others it has meant the immolation of their most cherished tastes and inclinations. It is hardly possible to place Beissel ex-

54

clusively in either category. His motives, like other people's, were snarled and confused, and, while he displayed an astonishing insight into the self-deceptions of the human mind in general, he often failed to disentangle the matted strands of his own desires and affections. Intellects like his are sharp, but not clear.

Beissel errs when he connects the revival that occurred in Pennsylvania at this time with the Great Awakening, which began a decade later; yet he deserves an ample meed of credit for the work he did in preparing for and furthering the earlier movement. His valiant witness to the reality of religion aroused the interest of many and made them receptive to the appeals of the Baptist missionaries. His earnest and sagacious admonitions helped to fortify and regulate the first impulses towards a renewal of the Christian affection that had proved too feeble to withstand the strain of a tedious voyage. By the fall of 1722, Peter Becker was ready, with two companions, to make a survey of his dispersed co-religionists with a view to reconstituting the disrupted congregation. Their itinerary embraced, among other places, Skippack, Falckner's Swamp (roughly eight miles east of Pottstown), and Oley (about fifteen miles west of Falckner's Swamp). The journey would not have seemed extensive to a pious vagabond like Michael Wohlfahrt, but for men of sedentary occupations it involved mild hardship and not a little inconvenience, in addition to the risk of economic loss. Throughout this tour, Becker and his associates declared their willingness to forget the disagreeable past, and their sincere longing for a restoration of the congregation's shattered solidarity. Upon their return to Germantown, they held services in Peter Becker's and Gomorry's houses as long as the weather permitted. Since it was the season, and not a new breach, that caused the suspension of the meetings, it is reasonable to conclude that many of the worshippers lived in distant places. The effect of Becker's zeal and tact had been widely felt.

During the late summer of the next year it was bruited about that Christian Liebe was in Philadelphia. If this rumor had been true, it would have grieved Becker, who had not forgotten that several years before, in Krefeld, his close friend Häcker had been excommunicated by a faction of Baptists under Liebe's leadership. The report was false, but it drew a number of recent converts in the Schuylkill valley to the metropolis, for Liebe was a renowned confessor. They were prevailed upon to attend the Baptist services in Germantown and were so deeply impressed that they came again after a short time. A month later the Germantown Dunkers made a trip up the river, and the relations between the two groups became very cordial. The upshot of these pious excursions was that the neophytes implored the Germantown congregation to baptize them. It was a perplexing demand; Becker and his followers were not sure that they had the requisite authority. Nevertheless, they argued away their scruples, and the baptism took place on Christmas Day in the frigid waters of the Wissahickon. On this occasion the Dunkers united in a love feast for the first time since their arrival in Pennsylvania. Spring ushered in a fresh revival, which eclipsed its predecessor and continued unabated until the fall, with a pronounced effect upon the young people. An account of these gratifying achievements was dispatched to the mother congregation abroad.

Carried along by this spate of success, the elated Baptists, on the twenty-third of October, began a long missionary junket, in which, no doubt, social motives were mingled innocently with evangelistic zeal. They contrived to see a great deal of the country before they returned. Following the customary route through the German settlements visited by Becker in his first tour, they reached, at length, the remote dwellings of the six who had been baptized at Christmas. Here baptism was administered again, and the infinitesimal community gained two members. Learning that they had some prospect of obtaining adherents in Conestoga, they ventured into that district, calling on Beissel, and presently establishing their headquarters under the roof of a settler named Heinrich Höhn, almost three weeks after their departure from Germantown. They went to work promptly, and at a service held the next day Beissel saw five converts offer themselves as candidates for baptism. This time Becker did not hesitate, but performed the ceremony at once. An irresolute sister conquered her timidity at the last moment and went down into the chilly stream after the rest. Beissel stood on the bank in the throes of a sore conflict. He acknowledged an obligation to submit to a rite of divine appointment, yet the spirituality of these people was patently inferior to his own, and he dreaded the ruin that might ensue if he committed himself wholly to them. He remained in the grip of this painful indecision until it occurred to him that Christ had not disdained John's baptism. This seemed to settle the question. With a humility that was hardly to survive the moment he waded into the water at the end of the line and was incorporated into the Baptist fold by immersion.

A love feast brought this strenuous day—and, one regrets to observe, the harmony that had hitherto reigned—to an end. During the remainder of their sojourn in Conestoga, the missionaries had grievous differences of opinion. Some of the settlers, the bellicose Michael Wohlfahrt among them, upbraided them with their former want of charity. After a meeting held in Sigmund Landert's house, the host and his wife were baptized very unimpressively in filthy water. The force that had animated the venture at the outset had been lost beyond recovery, and the evangelists prudently retired, but not until they had hastily and impulsively granted their converts a measure of independence that verged upon unbounded autonomy. On the way home they had misgivings about their generosity, chiefly because Beissel was known to be a Seventh Day Sabbatarian. It was suggested that an overseer be appointed to regulate the first steps of the infant congregation, but everybody knew that such interference would precipitate a clash. The discussion was inconclusive, and, in the absence of an effective means of retrieving the control they had so lightly waived, they were helpless. The sole immediate result of the affair was that Becker's painstaking reclamation of his derelict charges was hampered by the resentment they harbored against him for his alleged blunder in giving the Conestoga Baptists too free a hand. For those who were conversant with the stormy past of the contentious Dunker sect, a forecast of what would speedily befall its newest outpost presented no difficulties. The mordant suspicion felt by the Germantown group at the very inception of the enterprise presaged a schism and helped to bring it about. Nor did Beissel study to avert a division; true to his refractory self, he was glaringly devoid of loyalty to the Germantown leaders and at no time looked upon himself as their subordinate. Before the close of the year he was chosen to be head of the newly founded congregation. He submitted to no ordination, accepted no commission defining his duties and jurisdiction. He simply took charge and ruled in accordance with his own autocratic notions.

In the tortuous history of Beissel's rivalry with the Germantown Baptists there are, for one who adheres to the Germantown party, three leading causes of offense: Beissel's Judaistic doctrines and customs, his scorn for marriage, and his proselytizing incursions into territory of which the Germantown brethren deemed themselves the rightful owners. The acrimonious wranglings that took place with deplorable frequency, at times sinking to the level of an open brawl, do not alter the issue, and it is clear that there was a preponderance of guilt on Beissel's side, for he exploited his position to the full and never made a serious attempt to establish organic union with the parent church.

Early in 1725 Beissel, accompanied by two fanatics, whose observance of Jewish customs was more scrupulous than his own, set out on a pilgrimage to the Baptists on the Schuylkill and to Germantown. The conduct of these two zealots seemed to confirm the Germantown Baptists' worst apprehensions concerning Beissel. His fellow travelers had to satisfy themselves, before eating, that the pots and pans in which their food had been prepared were ceremonially pure. Such rudeness, intolerable in a guest, was not reassuring to people who had been expecting aberrations of the sort to be revealed at any moment. In justice to Beissel it must be observed that he did not countenance the preposterous lengths to which his disciples sometimes carried their reversion to the Old Testament. His own practice was mild enough: he kept the seventh day as the Sabbath, though not as yet making it a matter of obligation for others, and abstained from pork, because he had a theory—not wholly unscientific—that heavy dishes induced spiritual torpor and grossness. He seems to have offered no objection when some of his adherents declared themselves in favor of the prohibition of goose flesh, on the ground that the comforts of a feather bed were a peril to the soul. He did, however, administer a rebuke to a pair of crackpots who circumcised each other and reviled St. Paul for abolishing circumcision. Beissel's convictions with regard to the Sabbath ripened slowly, and he was probably forced at last to take an unequivocal stand by certain hot-heads in his own group. Not until Bradford printed his book on the subject was he irrevocably committed to the doctrine. While his views were maturing, the congregation retained Sunday as a day of worship and kept Saturday by abstaining from work. The fact that Beissel was, on one occasion, threatened with excommunication because he labored on the Sabbath indicates that some of his co-religionists had gone far beyond him in their devotion to a practice that was common among the sectarians of the time. Ultimately, when Beissel announced his opinion clearly, his Sabbatarianism became the principal outward point of difference between his group and the other Dunkers. Even after he had declared his position, he remained aloof from the altercations that ensued. This discretion was calculated. Nobody, except those directly concerned, minded how much he fulminated against the Germantonians in purely religious disputes, but his type of Sabbatarianism ran counter to the laws of the colony, which prescribed a strict observance of Sunday. The English Baptists had made the concession of keeping Sunday, as well as Saturday, out of respect for the civil government. Beissel's followers declined to yield, and some of them were haled into court for their defiance.

Beissel's tract on the Sabbath, entitled *Mystyrion Anomias*, is his earliest published work. It appeared in German in 1728. The German edition has perished, and Michael Wohlfahrt's English rendering, which was published in 1729, is the only extant form of this brief polemic. There is no reason to suspect the translator of material infidelity to the original.

It is, of course, impossible, in the absence of the German text, to prove that Wohlfahrt's version is literal. His own tract in defense of the Seventh Day Sabbath, *The Naked Truth* (1729), is roughly one-third the length of the *Mystyrion*. If Beissel's pamphlet is to any extent the creation of Wohlfahrt's pen, it is difficult to understand why Wohlfahrt advanced most of his arguments under another man's name. Still, he was inclined to efface himself, and such a sacrifice is conceivable, if it had any point. However, a trivial difference between the two tracts solves the problem in part. In Wohlfahrt's tract a reference ordinarily accompanies a quotation from Scripture. There are almost no references in Beissel's, if we restrict our observations to the work proper. This indicates that Wohlfahrt handled Beissel's text with conscientious respect, for it was Beissel's lifelong custom, in his writings, to quote Scripture without reference.

This maiden effort furnishes conclusive evidence of Beissel's aptitude for controversy. The arguments are presented with skill and cogency. If the author lapses from time to time into prolixity, it is merely because he delights, like many of his contemporaries, in copious expression. The apparent digressions prove, upon close examination, to be entirely relevant to the main sequence of reasoning, which is maintained with unswerving firmness to the end. With a remarkable command of his own kind of logic, the writer shows how his doctrine of the Sabbath is related to his theology of redemption and salvation. The pamphlet adumbrates some of the principal features of the thought Beissel expounded more elaborately in his later writings.

The title-page, in the manner of the day, presents not only the title of the book, *Mystyrion Anomias: The Mystery of Lawlessness*, but also a résumé of its contents. The second page contains six adroitly chosen quotations from Scripture, all of them calculated to prove the abiding character of the Law, which is the general truth upon which the specific point of the Seventh Day Sabbath is made to depend. "My covenant will I not break, nor alter the thing that is gone out of My lips" (Psalms 89:34) is particularly telling.

There follows an address to the reader, in which Beissel and Wohlfahrt enunciate the principle that doctrine is to be proclaimed by word of mouth, in accordance with the example of the Apostles, before it is disseminated in written form—a rule with which they have invariably complied. For "some years" they have been urging their hearers to observe the Sabbath on the seventh day of the week, and have encountered opposition. They are loth to add to the unseemly wranglings that already prevail, but the end is near, and they will not incur the punishment of the prophet who fails to deliver the message committed to him. They are careful to state, not quite superfluously, that the keeping of the seventh day is not in itself an indubitable proof of sanctity.

The work proper begins with a brief introduction, in which the three chief views concerning the Sabbath are summarized. (1) The first belief, which is the author's, as the argument subsequently proves, is that the Sabbath was instituted "as a distinction between holy and unholy." It is a gift of divine love and does not originate in sin. It abides necessarily until the whole created world is liberated from the penalties of sin. (2) Against this, some maintain that the observance of the Sabbath on the seventh day stultifies the Passion of Christ, Who "came to deliver us from the Curse of the Law." Every day should be kept as a Sabbath. This belief, in all likelihood, was held at least by individuals in Pennsylvania, where so many shades of religious opinion found shelter. Outside Pennsylvania, it was to be found among the Labadists, whom Beissel had visited, and among the Rogerene Baptists (a sect that sprang up about 1674 in New London, Connecticut), one of whose tenets was that "all days are alike since the death of Christ." Wohlfahrt perhaps possessed some knowledge of the Rogerenes. (3) Finally, most people keep the first day of the week, presumably without a valid reason for doing so.

The tract soon resolves itself into a dialogue between a son who, on the verge of conviction, still has a few obstacles to surmount in the arguments of those who reject the Seventh Day Sabbath, and his father, who demolishes these arguments one by one. This literary form lends itself admirably to the presentation of Beissel's case, and Beissel was alive to its advantages. Nevertheless there is a deeper reason for his choice: by placing his vacillating self beside his resolute self, and bringing about the triumph of the latter, he purged himself of doubt. The son's account of his perplexity reflects Beissel's own former hesitancy. For a time, although he kept the Seventh Day Sabbath himself, he had not been sufficiently sure of his ground to demand that his followers observe it.

The son opens the dialogue by declaring that, after a long and agitated quest for assurance, he has reached the conclusion that the Seventh Day Sabbath was given man out of love and the other days of the week are under the curse of sin. The father, in reply, says that he is surprised at the son's wavering at all. The son explains his misgivings by reviewing the arguments advanced by his opponents. (1) The position adopted by some is that Christ emancipated men from servitude to the Law, and therefore to keep the Law is to deny the reality of Christ's redemptive labors. (2) Others contend that the Sabbath is a feature of the Old Dispensation. Christ has abolished it, and it remains only as a type. (3) St. Paul's words: "Unto the righteous is no law given" (I Timothy 1:9) are quoted in defense of the view that Christians may follow their inclinations without scruple. (4) Another proof text used by his adversaries is Romans 13:10: "Love is the fulfilling of the Law." (5) It is maintained that Christ's purpose in directing the man He had healed on the Sabbath to take up his bed and walk (John 5:8) and in curing blindness on the Sabbath (John 9:6, 14) was to indicate that the law governing the Sabbath was no longer binding. Two more proof texts are sometimes employed: (6) "Let no man therefore judge you in meat, or in drink, or in respect of an holyday, or of the new moon, or of the sabbath days" (Colossians 2:16); and (7) "Behold, the days come, saith the Lord, that I will make a new covenant with the house of Israel and with the house of Judah . . . I will put my law in their inward parts and write it in their hearts . . ." (Jeremiah 31:31–33).

The father confutes each opinion as the son presents it. (1) He meets the first with the assertion that the Sabbath is a blessing, not a curse, for rest has its roots in God. (2) Against the second he reasons that the Sabbath is more than a type. It is what it represents. Christ is the end of the Law only in the sense that He alone fulfilled the Law, rendering inward obedience—which was beyond the power of others—as well as outward conformity. It is sin, not the Law, that is annihilated. Christ came to fulfill, not to destroy. (3) The third view admits of a ready reply. The father refers those who entertain it to the context of the verse they have quoted and bids them remember that a man who does things prohibited by the law thereby proves his unrighteousness. (4) His retort to the fourth argument is evidence of his spiritual alertness and sanity. Everybody professes a love for God, but works are the criterion by which these facile claims may be tested. "By this we know that we love Him, because we do keep His commandments" (1 John 2:3). "If ye love Me, keep My commandments" (John 14:15). "For if one loveth God, whatever he doth he doth it willingly, and with Heart's Delight, yea rather more than is commanded, if he doth but know that it pleases God." (5) His answer to the next argument is that Christ did not profane and therefore did not intend to annul the Sabbath. The Jews accused Him of violating it, but they made other accusations against Him, which we do not believe, and why, then, should we regard the charge of Sabbath-breaking as sound? He reminds the son that Christ's answers to these complaints imply no disrespect towards the Sabbath as an institution: "Doth not each of you on the Sabbath loose his ox or his ass from the stall, and lead him away to watering?" (Luke 13:15); "Have ye not read in the Law, how the priests on the Sabbath days in the temple profane the Sabbath, and are blameless?" (Matthew 12:5); and "Is it lawful to do good on the Sabbath days, or to do evil? to save life, or to kill?" (Mark 3:4). The remaining objections are easily disposed of. (6) St. Paul means, not the Seventh Day Sabbath, but "the many feasts and sabbaths of the Jews, according to the ceremonial law, of which, as of Shadows, we certainly now are freed and delivered." (7) The establishment of the new covenant is not the abrogation of the Law. It is rather the fulfillment of the Law in a new spirit of love and willingness, made possible by Christ's work.

The transition from Jeremiah's prophecy to the labyrinth of the Apocalypse, where Beissel wandered with ease and assurance, is not difficult. The son inquires about the Seventh Time (Revelation 10:7, 11:15, 16:17). The father's answer is that they must first discuss the Wedding Day of the Lamb (Revelation 19:7–9). In response to further questioning, he assigns this event and the Seventh Day Sabbath to the Seventh Time. Originally Adam and Wisdom inhabited one body. The bond was dissolved when Adam fell. At the Wedding this union, the "pure image of God," will be reconstituted, but the Sabbath will not as yet embrace the entire universe; only to the Bride and her companions will its delights be vouchsafed. The son declares his conviction that the time is near. The Jews will be converted. The father discourses upon this point. The Gospel illuminated the Jews for three hundred years, and at this period the Seventh Day Sabbath was observed. Then the true sabbath

was rejected. Corruption among Christians ensued; infant baptism was introduced and hatred prevailed. This failure on the
part of Christians gave the Jews a pretext for refusing to embrace the Gospel. Nevertheless at the restoration of the true
Church the Jews will be converted. One may keep the first day
in addition to the seventh, but not in its place. God "never
commanded us, neither by Christ nor his Apostles to keep the
first." God abandoned His rest and fashioned the world in six
days. Man was made just before He returned to His rest on
the seventh day. Man through his carnal desires has fallen into
the six days of fleshly unrest, but God has given him the Sabbath to remind him of the eternal rest that is in store for him.
The Sabbath was observed from the beginning until people
neglected it, and God preserved it from disuse by electing the
Jews and entrusting it to them. God could not make people
understand what His rest was until He had labored. In like
manner, we cannot attain to the rest of eternity without spiritual struggles. It is appropriate that the day of rest should
come at the end of the week, not the beginning, because we
rest after labor and not before it. Nowhere in the Bible are we
told that any but the seventh day is the Sabbath. Christ's cures
on the Sabbath prefigure the cessation of our infirmities in the
Great Sabbath. "Because Christ with his bride shall keep wedding on the 7th day, he has given her the 7th day . . . and because Antichrist with his bride the Whore shall keep wedding
on the 8th day, he also has given her here an 8th day."

The last paragraph of the father's closing discourse merits
quotation:

Moreover, It is admirable, that Antichrist hath exalted himself
so high, in the 6th Number, until that on[e] six is encreased
into Three, and these three Sixes are very equal and alike to
one another in those three Head Sects, and especially in reject-
ing of the Lord's Sabbath for they all living in the 6th Number,
and so every Sect produceth a 6, which makes together 666,
Six hundred sixty six, the Number of the *Beast*. These 3 Sixes
now multiplied by 3, make 18, but by Addition make 9, which
are the Nine Commandments, for they have rejected the 10th,

the Lord's Sabbath. And this indeed is in him a right Figure, because he doth not belong to the 10th Number, for in the 10th Number the End findeth its beginning again; but the Ninth Number is the highest Number in Division, wherein *Babylon* shall be destroyed, when she is come to her highest Degree; for she doth not reach the 10th Number, where 1 and a 0 stand together, which 1 as the Beginning, carryeth the End of all things into that great Circuit or Rest of God again, which that 0 in the 10th Number demonstrates as 10, and is the eternal Rest of God.

The tract ends with the quotation of Revelation 14:8–12 in full.

To what extent was Beissel indebted to his predecessors for the substance of this work, and to what extent did he devise proofs of his own? His booklet was written in support of a doctrine to which many theologians and many who could pretend to no remarkable attainments in divinity had subscribed. The question had been discussed for hundreds of years. If the materials for a complete and systematic inquiry could be assembled, the findings of such a study would almost certainly be that, while Beissel made no startling contribution to the defense of this ancient theological position, his presentation of the thought of earlier writers indicates that he had digested their discussions and appropriated them in such a way that he could reproduce them with a real measure of originality.

How were these teachings transmitted to Beissel? If the writers of the *Chronicon* knew, a desire to magnify Beissel made them suppress the facts. Their thoughts ran thus: If the Vorsteher obtained his precious doctrine of the Sabbath from no human instructor, its heavenly origin is evident. This is enough for Beissel's admirers, but not for us. We may freely acknowledge that in his mind Sabbatarianism coalesced with Böhmism to the enrichment of both. Perhaps this fusion was his own work. He had a profoundly spiritual reverence for the Sabbath as a pledge of the repose and peace that the blessed would ultimately enjoy in their union with God. Nevertheless, with Seventh Day Sabbatarians all about him, he stood in no need of an independent revelation.

Morgan Edwards traces Beissel's Sabbatarianism to the remnant of the Keithian Baptists, and credits Thomas Rutter with the principal part in his conversion. An amplification of this statement will give the reader a glimpse of the tradition behind the celestial Sabbath of Ephrata.

Seventh Day Sabbatarianism in England has an almost continuous history from the first years of the sixteenth century to Beissel's own generation. With its later phenomena we have no concern. Many books were written to demonstrate that the Old Testament command to observe the last day of the week was still in force. Some of these books were highly ingenious.

In 1671, at Newport, Rhode Island, Stephen Mumford organized the earliest congregation of Seventh Day Baptists within the present limits of the United States. In Penn's colony, the first preacher of the doctrines of the Seventh Day Baptists was Abel Noble. He reached Pennsylvania at an uncertain date, probably 1684. Seven years later the Keithian schism among the Quakers occurred. The uproar occasioned by this separation subsided in the course of the next few years, but a lonely group of schismatics remained. They ransacked the Scriptures for sound doctrine and "began to find water in the commission; bread and wine in the command; community of goods, love feast, kiss of charity, right hand of fellowship, anointing the sick for recovery, and washing the disciples feet in other texts; and therefore were determined to practise accordingly." They had four congregations. The most zealous of these was the one at Upper Providence. It was incorporated in 1697, and in 1700 some of its members, converted to the keeping of the seventh day by Abel Noble, parted company with those who observed Sunday and set up a society of their own at Newtown. Thomas Rutter presided over the Keithian Baptists of Philadelphia. He baptized John Hart, who became the pastor of the congregation at Southampton, in Bucks County. A dispute about the Sabbath divided the society at Lower Dublin, and the Seventh Day Sabbatarian party built a chapel in Oxford Township in 1702. Besides the societies that arose among the Keithian Baptists, there were, at Nottingham and French Creek, Seventh Day Sabbatarian Baptist congregations without Keithian antecedents. It is interesting to observe that the beginning of the society at French Creek antedates the appearance of Beissel's pamphlet on the Sabbath by three years. Beissel may have derived his Sabbatarianism in part from these people. The only English Seventh Day Sabbatarians mentioned by name in the *Chronicon* are Abel Noble, some people named Welch, and Ritter, who is probably Rutter.

All the congregations named thus far were in Pennsylvania. Abel Noble's influence extended to New Jersey, where, in all likelihood, though there is no proof, he was the earliest proponent of Sabbatarianism. Edmond Dunham arrived, through his own studies, at the conviction that the law of the Sabbath was still binding, and founded a society at Piscataway in 1707. The third minister of this congregation was Nathan Rogers. "He has preferred," writes Morgan Edwards in a sketch of his life, "a single life hitherto; which preference he obtained (perhaps) while he lived with the Tunkers of Ephrata. However that be, it is hoped that he learned from the Tunkers to be a meek, harmless, and a bible-christian; for I know of no better patterns." The congregations at Shiloh (1737) and Squan (1745) came into existence too late to affect Beissel's development. The first pastor at Squan had belonged to the Keithian schismatics and owed his conversion to Abel Noble.

The conclusion to which this review of Sabbatarianism leads is that Beissel might easily have borrowed his notions about the Sabbath from any of a number of societies, or members of societies, or from a roving Sabbatarian. A link between Beissel and the German Jews who lived at Schaefferstown, eighteen miles from Ephrata, early in the eighteenth century, is not required to account for the Sabbatarian element in the Vorsteher's theology.

If Beissel proceeded warily in the publication of his Sabbatarian teachings, he promulgated his doctrine concerning marriage with the audacity of immutable conviction. He had formed a clear opinion of the relative merits of wedlock and virginity early in life and needed no Wohlfahrt to stimulate his growth in this direction. The Dunkers had cherished much the same views at the beginning of their history, only to relinquish them for reasons that doubtless seemed to them sufficient. The intensity of their opposition to Beissel is to be ascribed, in part, to the lingering sense of guilt they felt at the recollection of their own weakness, however certain they may have been, in their conscious minds, that they had been justified in abandoning an impracticable ideal. Beissel had the fortitude to persevere. Though he steered a blameless course through the perils that surrounded him in his necessarily intimate relations with the women who accepted his direction, he did not entirely escape the attacks of malicious tongues. His intrepid devotion to the cause of celestial Wisdom, notwithstanding the torrent of slander that assailed him, is the most praiseworthy trait in his very uneven character. In his cunning way, he foiled the designs of his calumniators and even made capital of their attempts to ruin him.

It is a pity that not a single copy of Beissel's brochure on marriage, entitled *Die Ehe das Zuchthaus fleischlicher Menschen*, is known to have survived the vicissitudes to which all such books are exposed, but the views propounded in this work (issued in 1730), which was inspired by a trying experience Beissel underwent in court, may be inferred from discussions of the subject in Beissel's extant writings. He stated his position boldly: The only merit to be found in matrimony was the salutary discipline it provided for the natural man, to whom it was a safeguard against illicit connections. Beyond that, and in spite of it, conjugal relations were an abomination, revolting to God and unworthy of anybody who had a serious interest in religion. It would serve no purpose to pause and expound these teachings elaborately here. Beissel's doctrine as a whole will be examined in detail at the end of the present work, and the philosophical underpinnings of his misogynism will then be subjected to a close scrutiny. This metaphysical groundwork is entirely distinct from the impression Beissel's tenets made upon his astounded fellow settlers. Some were captivated: others, infuriated. Many were all too familiar with the antics of the hermits in Germany, and had resolved that such nonsense should not be revived in Pennsylvania. In his retirement Beissel had seemed remote enough to be harmless, but when he appeared in the rôle of preacher he became a malevolent intruder whose covert design was to sever all natural bonds, and his potent harangues were all the more sinister in the eyes of the simple backwoodsmen of Conestoga because few of them had even a nebulous comprehension of what he was about. Beissel exacerbated this mistrust by mystifying, to the full extent of his considerable ability, all those who ventured to attend his services. If he hoped to disarm and conciliate the inimical part of the community by leaving his hermitage and moving into a cabin built for his accommodation on a friendly farmer's land, he showed an almost presumptuous indiscretion in receiving two young women as aspirants to the solitary life and admitting them to an intimacy that scandalized his neighbors. Fathers and husbands lived in acute terror of Beissel's uncanny power with women. An anxious householder threw his arms about his wife and implored her not to forsake him. The remonstrances of carnal and unimaginative husbands were of little avail with infatuated women who had felt the spell of Beissel's austerity. Christina Höhn solved the problem by remaining under her husband's roof as his platonic companion, until his death released her and she joined Beissel, who by that time had founded the community at Ephrata. Others were less patient. Maria Sauer deserted her husband Christopher and maintained herself as a recluse, later entering the convent at Ephrata, where she became subprioress. In this instance, however, Beissel was finally defeated, for Maria's son persuaded her to end her life in his father's house.

The unsavory tales circulated among the housewives of the district brought Beissel and his mixed community into grave disrepute. It was noised about, at last, that he had begotten an illegitimate child. An unwary magistrate had the temerity to order the arrest of Beissel and the woman who was charged with being his partner in sin. Irritated at being obliged to appear in court on the Sabbath, Beissel brought the proceedings to a sudden end by calling for witnesses, and, when none could be produced, rebuking the judge severely. The chagrined official promptly conducted an investigation and discovered that the report had its source in somebody's misinterpretation of a casual remark.

Beissel's exculpation was not a difficult matter, but it was less easy to explain the deplorable lunacy of Brother Amos, who lost his wits in the intense pursuit of heavenly Wisdom. One night he undressed and walked in the nude to a near-by cabin, where, omitting the formality of asking permission, he crept into the bed occupied by the mistress of the house. He was apprehended, but the law, perplexed, returned him to the congregation. He subsequently added to his reputation by clambering to the belfry of the court house in Philadelphia and addressing a concourse of hearers. One is surprised at the compassion Beissel had for the poor, demented wretch. He welcomed him back and helped to restore his self-esteem by making him the baker of the community. Amos, though never free of certain foibles, outlived his benefactor and died, after long usefulness, at the age of eighty-one.

At least one outraged husband conceived an implacable hatred for Beissel and made a murderous assault upon him. This man, whose name was John Landes, had briefly held the office of teacher in the church at Falckner's Swamp. His wife, despite his manifest displeasure, made frequent and protracted visits to Beissel. The irate husband brought these absences to a close by dragging his truant wife back to the drudgery of the farmhouse. He even enlisted the aid of the law in an effort to vindicate his authority. Once privately and once publicly he laid violent hands on Beissel. After the second encounter, the woman was dismissed from the congregation, but when her liberty was restored at her husband's death she returned and spent the remainder of her life in spiritual company.

These manifold hindrances did not deter Beissel in his unflagging labors. As more and more souls submitted to his influence he brought the most devoted among them into his personal circle. Men and women embraced the rigors of the solitary life, and gradually Beissel became the revered patriarch of an earnest community. About the rude house on Nägele's farm huts were built to shelter the brides and bridegrooms of Wisdom. The regular portion of the congregation won an ascendancy over the secular and relegated it to a subordinate place. Beissel found himself in a delicate position between the rival groups. In time his work as a religious superior made such demands upon his time that he resigned his leadership and took up his abode in Ephrata, determined to free himself forever from responsibilities that had vexed him almost to madness. He was soon to discover, perhaps not entirely to his disappointment, that the burdens he had assumed could not lightly be shaken off. Those who could not follow him into the monastic life nevertheless had a claim upon him. His eccentricities had not prevented him from being an effective pastor.

Perhaps the best point of departure for an account of Beissel's dealings with the people to whom he preached as head of the Conestoga congregation is a summary of his *Mystische Und sehr geheyme Sprueche*. This devotional miscellany, published in 1730, consists of (1) a page of quotations from Scripture (Proverbs 3:13, 14; Wisdom 8:4, 8); (2) ninety-nine sayings (pp. 3–14) from which the book derives the principal part of its title; (3) sixty-two short pieces of verse (pp. 14–23); (4) a number of questions for use in self-examination (pp. 24–25) (5) a "submission" to this doctrine (pp. 26–27); and (6) a second lesson (pp. 28–32). The verse is tolerable but undistinguished. Beissel, like Zinzendorf, composed religious verse with prolific ease. His effusions are estimable, but soporific. The saws, though often banal, are a useful digest of Beissel's spir ituality. Many of them are commonplaces of the life of the soul. Others bear Beissel's distinctive stamp. Like many other celibates, he revels in sexual imagery. He describes marriage as a very delectable state, but it is the celestial wedlock, the union of the soul and Wisdom, that he presses upon his disciples. His conceits suited the taste of his period; for us they are artificial and tiresome. He supplies no interpretation—probably an indication that the maxims are designed for initiates. Only a person acquainted with his mind would apprehend the hidden sense of this dictum: "No unmarried man shall see the face of God, for he lives for himself and produces no fruit. But he who is in holy matrimony lives not for himself, for he seeks to please his wife, since he is fruitful in her."

The poems, though doubtless not all written at the same time, hang together remarkably well. They open with an admonition to the soul to detach itself from the world, and end by celebrating the glories and delights of the spiritual life. The most arresting of the couplets is the tenth, in which Beissel exhorts the soul to abandon multiplicity and make its way to the One. Both in the poems and in the sayings, "wisdom" is the spiritual life, and "the wise man" is the person who pursues this life. The first saying, "To know oneself aright is the loftiest perfection, and to reverence and worship aright the sole, eternal, and invisible God in Christ Jesus is eternal life," is, in part, a Christian adaptation of a familiar piece of Greek wisdom. This conception of the Christian vocation places Beissel in the fellowship of the Gnostics, who menaced the very life of Christianity early in its career, and allies him with that current of monastic thought which regards the ascetic life as the true philosophy. When he opposes the many to the One he speaks the language of Plotinus. An attempt will be made later to explain through what channels such ideas were transmitted to Beissel.

In the fourth section of the book Beissel shows how penetrating and uncompromising he can be when he undertakes to ferret out every lingering trace of self-regard in the soul, exposing its impure motives and camouflaged selfishness without pity. One question, "*Gott soll dein ein und dein alles sein, ists dann auch so?*," reminds us of St. Francis of Assisi's "*Deus meus et omnia.*" Beissel discloses his ripe knowledge of souls in the following observation: "When a person lives according to his human affections or corrupt natural property, he always requires of other people what he is himself bound to do. And with the eye with which he should contemplate his own mistakes and deficiencies, he contemplates other people's." It is neatly put and profoundly true. We punish others for our own delinquencies. Beissel was aware of it long before the psychology of our own day discovered it.

Such materials were Beissel's stock in trade, and his success in finding purchasers for these spiritual wares is a tribute to the force of his personality rather than to the skill of his methods. As a preacher, his most evident characteristic is a total lack of the platitudinous simplicity that is so highly esteemed in the sermons of the present day. In reply to a question concerning the ninety-nine maxims of his *Mystische Und sehr geheyme Sprueche*, Beissel attributed the number to inspiration. His preachments were derived from the same source. His chief purpose, apparently, was not so much to edify as to prove his complete independence of human assistance. He quoted the Bible from memory, both in his sermons and in his writings. Taking his place before the congregation with his eyes shut, he plunged recklessly into a swirling sea of abstruse doctrines, improvising a discourse that, besides being ungrammatical, violated all the laws of rhetoric and was gabbled with giddy haste. As he proceeded, he stumbled upon heavenly secrets that were new to him. His efforts to expound these arcana on the spot were as remarkable for their superabundant enthusiasm as they were for their complete want of perspicuity. From time to time his lively intuition warned him that some of his auditors were searching for a strand of thought in his chaotic verbiage. When this occurred, he shifted his ground at once and puzzled them by defending the opposite side of the question. His rambling

sermons often emptied the church, yet there were obviously
many who, so far from finding these dithyrambics absurd, felt
certain at the outset that Beissel was God's mouthpiece.

Within a year of the memorable meeting at which Beissel
had been baptized, his beliefs and methods were so fundamentally in conflict with those of the Germantown Baptists that it
was regarded as a transfer of allegiance to abandon the older
congregation and enlist in the more militant ranks of Beissel's
followers. When Jan Mayle took this step, it was easy to fore-
see a rupture, but the tenuous union was not dissolved until
several years later. Beissel went his way serenely, never giving
himself the trouble of consulting Becker. In May 1725, he baptized Michael Wohlfahrt, Rudolph Nägele, who donated the
land for a new monastic settlement, and five others. At Whit-
suntide 1726, in Becker's absence, Beissel presided over a love
feast among the Baptists on the Schuylkill. Eleven were baptized on this occasion. Becker's partisans looked askance at the
disorderly fervor of these meetings. More than a year later the
Germantonians made one of their frequent missionary excursions to Conestoga, and an untoward incident occurred. Stuntz,
whose cupidity had left Beissel without a roof over his head,
had been excommunicated for marrying within the prohibited
degrees. Two members of the Germantown delegation released
him from the ban on their own initiative and were punished by
Beissel's adherents for their presumption. The *Chronicon* does
not tell the story clearly, but it may safely be surmised that
Beissel, even though he did not approve of excommunication,
resented the action of these interlopers and gave his cordial assent to the severe penalty that was imposed upon them.

After a reconnaissance by Michael Wohlfahrt, Beissel carried out a raid upon the missionary territory of the Germantown Baptists at Falckner's Swamp, in the spring of 1728. Six-
teen were baptized, and one Andreas Frey became their minister. When the Germantown Baptists learned of this revival,
they felt constrained to inform the church at Falckner's Swamp
of the diabolical machinations of the Conestoga group. They

had several fresh grievances. The Conestogans had lately ex-communicated the two Germantown Baptists who had liber-ated Stuntz from the ban. One of the Schuylkill settlers had engaged in an altercation with Beissel about the lot of departed infants, and Beissel had asserted that their souls, despite their freedom from deliberate sin, would have to undergo some mode of purification. Subsequently this person had died, still out of charity with Beissel's party. By recounting these misdeeds the Germantonians built up a strong case for themselves, and the neophytes were deeply perplexed. Beissel's counterblast was a vitriolic letter, stuffed with recriminations. The Germantonians then adopted the strange expedient of making the converts at Falckner's Swamp the arbiters of the matter. Preparations were made for a trial, but it was never held, and when Beissel's depu-tation arrived its six members had little difficulty in reëstablish-ing their master's authority.

Beissel exercised this authority ruthlessly. He regarded the ministers of the congregation at Falckner's Swamp as his depu-ties, and appointed and deposed them according to his fancy. He had already become an almost insensate autocrat, unable to brook the slightest opposition. Three pastors were elevated and unseated in a short time. Michael Wohlfahrt was one of them, and only his passionate devotion to Beissel enabled him to live through the humiliation of his dismissal. With a certain slyness, the *Chronicon* often alludes in a knowing way to the misde-meanors of those who clashed with Beissel, without describing their offenses at length. Probably in most instances the culprit was merely unwilling to grovel abjectly before his superior.

Beissel's domineering and exacting ways with his followers grew as much out of his lack of sympathy towards ordinary infirmities as out of his undisciplined pride and overweening zeal. He could never have founded a large religious body, be-cause he had no room in his narrow scheme for a multiplicity of vocations. Nor could he guide people to sanctity gently and by degrees. The great pastors of the world are richly furnished with pity and tact. They are inclined to concede a point to human weakness whenever they can do so without condoning sin. They do this, not because they admire weakness, but because, knowing that in their delicate art enduring gains are slowly made, they shrink from the peril of retarding or terminating a penitent's spiritual development by encouraging a volatile eagerness at the beginning. They study to maintain a direct relation between the soul's fervor and the practices in which that fervor finds expression. They recognize that not all their spiritual children are called to the same degree—or, to put it more accurately, to the same exterior form—of perfection. Of such magnanimity and understanding Beissel had not the slightest touch. This grave limitation is the key to much of his folly. He was a trainer rather than a physician.

As the stale quarrel between the old Baptists and the new continued year after year and Beissel committed blunder after blunder, disaffection increased among his supporters, and ultimately the disgruntled members of his congregation outnumbered those who submitted uncritically to his will. The malcontents at last founded a church of their own. The Germantown Baptists fostered the schism. Michael Wohlfahrt brooded upon their wily designs to thwart Beissel until he had fanned his emotions to the point of incandescent fury. Ablaze with prophetic anger, he stormed into a service at Germantown and denounced the plotters to their faces. His impassioned diatribe widened the rift that was soon to end in open enmity. Brother Joel, one of Beissel's ardent supporters, invaded a meeting of the schismatics and delivered a vehement prophecy against them. These utterances were preserved in writing, but Beissel, despising them because they were not his own work, connived at the destruction of the written copies. It is clear that his objection was not one of conscience, for his own savage oracles circulated freely in writing.

Towards the end of the year 1728 Beissel determined to separate himself formally from the Germantown Baptists. He had an uneasy feeling that he was beholden to them for the baptism he had received and that, so long as his success could plausibly be attributed to the grace bestowed upon him four years earlier, his foes had a telling weapon against him. He decided to repudiate his baptism, and begin afresh. Accordingly, when Brother Amos had baptized him, he baptized Brother Amos and five others. The symbolic number, seven, was a pledge of the purity of this nucleus, around which he hoped to gather a congregation that would subscribe loyally to his views. This hope was not completely fulfilled; even in the new church an unreconciled faction remained, and there were several attempts at reunion with the Germantown Baptists. In 1729 Alexander Mack settled in Pennsylvania, and the next year he and Beissel had an inconclusive encounter at Falckner's Swamp. The two congregations were radically different, and a close fellowship was impossible, but a decisive break was equally impossible, and a measure of communication, if not of communion, was maintained.

The *Chronicon* presents only the extremes of opinion concerning Beissel. On the one hand, there is the virulent denunciation of his enemies: on the other hand, the immoderate adulation of his friends. The report of a disinterested observer strikes a balance between the two. Johann Adam Gruber wrote from Germantown, in 1730, that a new awakening was taking place in Conestoga. Beissel, "the well-known baker," is named as the guiding spirit of the revival. The "new Baptists" exert a strong influence, despise the world and their own wills, wear only such clothing and take only such nourishment as the body requires for the maintenance of life, and deny themselves superfluous property. They do not pass the time of day with the persons they meet out of doors, but walk straight ahead, soberly and silently. To all appearances, they are a united group. Both the men and the women hold services and love feasts almost every day. They observe the Seventh Day. Their lives are blameless, and they display great power and zeal. They have prophesied against the Dunkers and the Quakers in the meeting-houses of these two sects in Germantown. The Dunkers have opposed them. "What the future holds for them," concludes

Gruber, "time will tell." To one who had doubtless seen many sects rise and fall, the future of this movement must have seemed precarious; yet he felt bound, in justice to its manifest vigor and enterprise, to record its merits.

The congregation was about seven years old when Beissel impulsively gave up his office, designated elders to take his place, and left the church to its own devices. The religious community on Nägele's farm had prospered, and its works of mercy had done a great deal to counteract the effect of Beissel's absolutism. A few defections had occurred, but in the main there had been a steady growth of solidarity and zeal. Among his submissive monks and nuns Beissel would have an easier time than he could ever hope to have in his relations with the unruly housefathers of the secular congregation. Leaving the vexations of a pastor's life behind, he took up his residence at Ephrata. He looked for peace, but sore tribulations awaited him.

V

WISDOM'S HABITATION

It was divine providence, not human reckoning, that determined the scene of Beissel's remaining years, the arena that was to witness the supreme triumph of his prime, the most inglorious discomfiture of his career, and the quietude of his decline. At the time of his abdication, the kernel of Ephrata already existed in the form of a hermitage built and inhabited by Emanuel Eckerle, one of the recluses who spent their time emulating the feats Beissel had performed in the serene days of his first retirement. Nobody as yet had an inkling of the prosperous colony that was to spring up about this rude structure, nor had anybody reason to predict that one of Emanuel's three brothers would become the evil genius of the community. Cocalico, the district in which the cottage stood, was a few miles from the cabin in which Beissel had lived during his agitated incumbency as head of the Conestoga congregation. Traversed by a slender creek and teeming with snakes, it had a bad reputation among the farmers of the neighborhood, who thought ill of its soil. In the next few years its resources and advantageous position were to be exploited by the Brotherhood of Zion, but at the moment its desolation was its greatest virtue.

After divesting himself, for the nonce, of all dignities and cares, Beissel repaired to the welcome solitude of this retreat. With the generosity of unquestioning admiration, Eckerle made him a present of the cabin, and Beissel hacked blithely away at trees and bushes, reducing his stubborn patch of ground to subjection and exorcising the demons that infested the thickets, resentful of his intrusion. It was a wholesome, balanced life, half of it devoted to the cultivation of the land and the other half to the cultivation of Wisdom. There was, in fact, only one unruly emotion to mar the concord of this salutary rustication. Beissel's renunciation of power had not been wholly sincere, and he yearned to be cajoled back to his old position on his own terms.

For seven months everybody respected his privacy. The congregation fell a prey to litigation, and it became evident to Beissel that his pacifying presence was required. Accordingly he invited the most important members of the congregation to discuss the situation with him, and was soon involved in the old troubles as deeply as ever. He had taken the initiative, and, if he was to be harassed in the future as he had been in the past, his worries were of his own seeking.

Perhaps the readiness with which he renewed his relations with the secular congregation conveyed to the ascetics a hint of his willingness to suffer their presence. Before the year had drawn to a close, Samuel Eckerle, with two others, joined Beissel at Ephrata. The newcomers erected the second building of the colony. Presently Anna and Maria Eicher, whose spiritual friendship with Beissel had set many tongues in motion, applied for admission to the refuge. Beissel's companions felt misgivings about the propriety of granting this request, but he himself had a godly boldness in such matters, as well as, in the opinion of his devotees, a penetrating judgment that was equivalent to second-sight. Certain that no evil would ensue, he arranged for the accommodation of the virgins in a new house across the creek. If flowing water could serve as the token of adoption into the fellowship of Christ, it might be depended upon to protect chastity. The objections of his subjects were easily met, but the farmers round about could not accept the conclusions of Beissel's recondite logic. Whether they were Mennonites or lapsed Protestants, they found the pernicious monkery that had unexpectedly appeared among them a menace to hearth and home. The upper classes cherished the fantastic notion that the anchorites had some connection with the Jesuits. The countryside buzzed with speculation. No doubt the credulous settlers believed that Beissel and his fellow ascetics were hypocritical libertines. At any rate, they tried to burn out these eccentric strangers, but the wind shifted, and the fire consumed a barn.

Two years after the beginning of the enterprise, there was an influx of converts from Falckner's Swamp. The land surrounding Ephrata was gradually acquired by Beissel's adherents, and scriptural names were given to various parts of it. A company of recruits came from the Schuylkill. Beissel, with a retinue of eremites, went to Oley in pursuit of souls and captured a bride, who promptly deserted her husband and joined the virgins at Ephrata. Yet even these substantial gains were trifling compared with the sensational conversion of two men who had already begun to exhibit gifts and attainments that would later earn them at least local renown.

Peter Miller and Conrad Weiser had in common a German background, extraordinary intelligence, and a deep attachment to Beissel, but even in these things they differed greatly, and in other respects they were wholly dissimilar. Miller came to Pennsylvania in early manhood. He had been trained at Heidelberg and was ordained to the ministry soon after his arrival. He was a retiring person, amply equipped with the instruments of scholarship and fitted by temperament more for speculation and devotion than for the executive duties he was compelled to shoulder when he filled Beissel's place at the latter's death. His loyalty to Beissel was as staunch as Michael Wohlfahrt's. Weiser, in contrast, was only a boy when he accompanied his father to America, and circumstances denied him a university education. The opportunities that came his way demanded the exercise of practical aptitudes, with which he was abundantly furnished. Rebelling against his father's harsh rule, he ran away from home and, during the impressionable years of his life, had such close intercourse with the Indians that he accumulated a prodigious knowledge of their languages, customs, and psychological traits. His familiarity with the natives made him indispensable to the colonial authorities, who would have been at a grave disadvantage without his expert counsel. His reputation for integrity and his personal friendships among the Indians made him an acceptable emissary, and he conducted delicate and slow negotiations with untiring resourcefulness and perseverance. His association with the Seventh Day Baptists was merely an interlude between a romantic youth and a busy maturity. His interest in religion was genuine, but he passed too readily from one denomination to another, and merited censure for these frequent changes of faith. Though at first dazzled by the aureole that adorned Beissel's holy person, he later contemplated his ghostly father's vagaries with so critical an eye that he discerned faults to which others remained blind. Still, Beissel's ability to gain even a passing control of so powerful a mind proves that he was more than an irresponsible ranter. He gathered Weiser and Miller into his fold with consummate dexterity. Never, at any time, was he obsequious, nor did he court the favor of the great; yet it gratified him to know and, as sometimes happened, to influence people who belonged to a higher social or intellectual level than his own. He was not a snob, but, at the same time, he was not totally unmindful of worldly differences.

Peter Miller's life, after his conversion, was intertwined with Beissel's, and, if he was not the most brilliant of the master's satellites, he burned with a faithful and steady glow to the end. He will appear constantly in the rest of this narrative. Weiser's sojourn was relatively brief. He was not really at home in the world of sectarian contests, and his services were required in a more congenial sphere. In obtaining so lasting a hold upon Miller, Beissel may seem, at first sight, to have bridged a wide chasm and to have employed unwonted tact. Miller had been favored with much that Beissel coveted for the furtherance of his work, but the disparity between the two must have made Beissel uneasily aware of his limitations. Did he not show unexpected graciousness and self-forgetfulness in the warmth with which he received this convert into his community, knowing that the proximity of so accomplished a person would accentuate his own want of schooling? In reality, the situation demanded no such sacrifice of Beissel. Miller was a diffident man, and it is highly probable that the primitive life of a backwoods parish bristled with painful experiences for so tender a nature.

His flight to Ephrata, if this interpretation is correct, was not the renunciation of a position to which he was attached, but an escape from trials that his sensitive temperament could not bear. He craved the protection that Beissel's indomitable self-confidence could afford. The last thing he purposed to do was to challenge Beissel's supremacy. He was a disciple whom no conceivable turn of events could transform into a rival. These things were not true of Weiser. Habituated to self-reliance, he found Beissel's ruthless despotism repugnant to his common sense, which was strong despite the temporary abnormality of his emotions. He did his utmost to conform, but he was incapable of the servility that Beissel required. He baffled and resisted Beissel, and Beissel abominated him with the deep intensity of a frustrated tyrant. When Weiser was offered an honorable post in the colonial government, Beissel accelerated his departure with an eagerness that discloses the depth of his chagrin.

In the light of these observations, the success of Beissel's foray into Tulpehocken becomes comprehensible. When he first surveyed this community, an apparently impregnable fortress of Protestantism, he must have felt disheartened. It had been founded a few years before by Weiser's father, who had led a company of Germans from Schoharie in an arduous trek to the Susquehanna and thence up the Swatara and into the Tulpehocken valley. Conrad Weiser, then thirty-three and happily married for almost a decade, joined the settlers at Tulpehocken a year or two before Miller took charge of the congregation. The inhabitants were solidly hostile to sects and separatists and had determined to shut them out and keep the settlement free of their perpetual broils. It is doubtful whether such vigilance could ever have attained its end in Pennsylvania. The spirit of separatism was an insidious force that silently worked its way under or around every obstacle. Perhaps Miller was already tainted with it when he came to Pennsylvania at the age of twenty. If so, he communicated the infection to Weiser, for the two quickly became fast friends. The new pastor appears to have been on cordial terms with the Seventh Day

Baptists from the outset. He must have listened often to accounts of their progress as he went his rounds, for he served three congregations in addition to the one at Tulpehocken, and one of these three met in Beissel's neighborhood.

Beissel's interest in the two young Reformed clergymen of the colony, Miller and his colleague, Bartholomew Rieger, was very keen. Both of them had been students at Heidelberg, for which Beissel retained a nostalgic regard. Beissel kept them in mind, fervently beseeching God to grant him one of them for the more effective propagation of his doctrines. As he pondered the prospects of the congregation he had founded, there were moments when his belief in his own adequacy ebbed, and other moments when he reflected that the accession of a real cleric to his obscure band of enthusiasts would lend prestige to an endeavor that could too readily be stigmatized as the visionary project of a misguided autodidact. Rieger's marriage rendered him unfit for Beissel's purpose, but Miller remained free of matrimonial entanglements.

There must have been some preliminaries to Beissel's first appearance in Tulpehocken. They served as a pretext for a solemn visit of state. Beissel had provided himself with the customary entourage. Miller and the elders, of whom Weiser was one, welcomed their callers graciously and with a degree of ceremony. When Beissel and his party started on the homeward journey, their hosts attended them politely until they were six miles on the way. We are not told what Beissel said in the course of this visit, but he must have used every art at his command, for Miller, his elders, and some members of the congregation dissolved their connection with the church. For a time they drifted, in a quandary as to what direction they should take. Beissel's guidance was sought, and in subsequent visits he strengthened his influence. The convulsive tremors of an awakening shook Tulpehocken as they had shaken other communities. It was not necessary for Beissel to wear himself out with preachments and other exhortations; the task performed itself. Beissel controlled Weiser, and Weiser controlled the awakened portion of Tulpehocken. The situation called only for a little deft management. When Weiser and Miller, accompanied by many of their fellow converts, journeyed to Ephrata, Beissel pressed the pastor to submit to baptism. Miller yielded, and his new life began in the spring of 1735, less than five years after his coming to America. The church at Tulpehocken lost ten families. Miller, for the present, resolved to lead a solitary life, and a cabin was built for him in Tulpehocken. A few of his adherents joined the community at Ephrata, and the rest established a congregation at Tulpehocken. Those who had the hardihood to minister to this charge found that it overtaxed their resources. Wohlfahrt repeated his earlier failure. Emanuel Eckerle then exposed himself to the perils of the pastorate and was soon vanquished. After his retirement, Weiser ventured to assume the dangerous office. His presumption was almost his undoing. The *Chronicon*, with its usual stilted piosity, leaves the uninformed reader in doubt as to what the actual trouble was, and at least one historian has misunderstood the story. What really happened was that Weiser had great difficulty in accepting Beissel's teaching with regard to marriage, and the constant sight of his wife tempted him to resume sexual relations with her. The studied vagueness of the *Chronicon*—perhaps prudish, perhaps malicious—is open to serious misinterpretation, for it contains no explicit statement that the woman in question was his wife. To the readers for whom it was intended this cryptic language was, one may suppose, readily intelligible: to our own outspoken generation it is perplexing. Whether it was delicacy or ill will that motivated the authors, they are just enough to admit that Weiser struggled manfully, even when they suggest that he might have exercised greater care. He grappled valiantly with the temptation, confiding his distress to Beissel. At length his wife was baptized, and for a time the torment ceased.

With an earnestness at which he must have marveled when he had shaken off Beissel's spell, Weiser strove to accommodate himself to the bizarre life at Ephrata. He accompanied Beissel on an evangelistic tour, and his flowing beard, measured gait, and decorous bearing made him a deplorable spectacle in the eyes of those who had known him before this curious enthusiasm turned his head. It was a pity to see a man of such extraordinary parts frittering away the best years of his life in a perverse quest for contentment among uncouth bigots who fettered his mind with their execrable nonsense. Imperceptibly Weiser himself gravitated towards a similar conclusion. He observed certain things that had escaped him at the beginning. The conventual life induces a gradual and irreparable solidification of character. If a man does not reach sanctity by it, and sometimes when he does, oddities of every sort—prejudices, automatisms, phobias—take possession of him. It began to dawn upon Weiser that, if he remained, he would have to settle down to a life of growing eccentricity. Besides, Ephrata could not house two masters. Even a subordinate, assigned to a distant place, was promptly taken to task for the slightest independent action. Beissel's imperious nature reduced virtually all his subjects to drudges. Those who withstood him forfeited his interest and regard. If nobody had thwarted him, he would never have relaxed his dictatorial grip. In such a community, only a single martinet could flourish. Piety might blunt Weiser's mind temporarily, but eventually he was obliged to acknowledge these truths. His acumen penetrated Beissel's affected lowliness and synthetic charity.

The Governor was one of the many who lamented the misdirection of Weiser's abilities. He made up a party of gentlefolk from Maryland and Virginia and took them out to Ephrata. The religious were courteous and showed him about the place, but Beissel remained sulkily in his own quarters. The urbanity of these well-bred people must have been refreshing to Weiser after a long experience of Beissel's rough manners. Perhaps he was not altogether surprised when the Governor, before leaving, expressed a wish to make him a magistrate and urged him to accept the appointment. Weiser himself had no scruples about the matter but felt that it should be referred to the community. The prevailing view was that such a step was inconsistent with his profession. It was, of course, repugnant to the entire tradition of Anabaptism and separatism, and the elders of the congregation rendered the only possible decision; but Beissel was too astute to miss an opportunity to rid himself of Weiser. Besides, it suited his inclinations to overrule the verdict; his murky intellect detested the lucidity of a definite statement, and he preferred to dispense with formularies and rules. Any semblance of a creed or constitution would have shackled him and curtailed the play of his fancy and the obdurate selfishness of his will. What authority, he demanded, had the elders to coerce Weiser's conscience? There was no reply to this, for the inchoate authority that existed at Ephrata was concentrated in Beissel's hands. The Governor obligingly made concessions to Weiser's religious beliefs, and there was now nothing to hinder his acceptance.

A bearded Seventh Day Dunker in the seat of justice was an arresting sight. As the business of the bench required more and more of Weiser's attention, he grew cool towards Ephrata and Beissel. Renewed converse with normal people revealed to him absurdities that had formerly escaped his notice. Beissel asserted that the intensity of his prayers in behalf of a departed member of the community had squeezed blood out of his finger nails. This suggested to Weiser that Beissel was placing himself on a level with Christ—a clear sign of megalomania. Beissel's freedom of access to the convent, which by this time had been erected to shelter the virgins at Ephrata, made Weiser suspect that something was amiss. Perhaps the Vorsteher, as Beissel was now called, did not limit himself to spiritual conversations during his frequent visits. He ordered Beissel peremptorily to stay away. It was unfortunate for the latter that Anna Eicher, one of the very first to adopt the solitary life, selected this time to carry out a plan that was the result of long cogitation. Her mind was slightly disordered after years of familiarity with Beissel, and she asked him to marry her. The Vorsteher could not bring himself to accept this proposal. Anna then suggested that he permit her to call herself Frau Beissel. Conrad would have none of it. Her sister's appointment as abbess transformed her passion into a desperate desire to pay Beissel back for his supercilious rejection of her advances. She hurried to Weiser and accused Beissel and herself of infanticide, declaring that she was the mother, and Beissel the father, of the victim. Weiser transmitted the information to the Governor, but, when two of the hermits entreated him not to punish an innocent man, he was sorry that he had been so precipitate. In the end the woman, discovering that the scaffold was as real a possibility for her as for Beissel, withdrew her confession. She married somebody else and promptly died. Beissel was vindicated.

Weiser essayed a written refutation of Beissel's doctrines and prepared a stern denunciation of the oppression to which the secular members of the congregation were subjected. The housefathers undoubtedly were exploited, and this was a sore point with Weiser, who had made a liberal contribution to the funds of the community. His efforts to reform the Seventh Day Baptists won no support. For many years he consecrated his energies to Indian affairs, and the Brethren forgot him. Once he returned to the settlement for a brief visit and participated in a love feast. His subsequent vacillations in religious matters have no bearing upon the present narrative. He was intimate with some of the Moravians, who availed themselves of his unique knowledge of the Indian. In his latter years he appears to have had no exclusive convictions. The size of Reading permitted the Lutherans and the Reformed to maintain distinct congregations. Weiser held official positions in both these churches, perhaps simultaneously.

If Beissel had not already adopted the year of his conversion as the commencement of a new era, it is not improbable that he would have dated all subsequent happenings from the year of Peter Miller's baptism. In that year Beissel gained his two most distinguished converts, Alexander Mack's death closed an epoch in the history of the Dunkers, Kedar was built, and the recluses abandoned their hermitages and sacrificed the consolations of seclusion for the advantages of the cenobitic life. In a few brief months Ephrata was transformed.

The new trend manifested itself most conspicuously in a frenzy of building. Kedar was provided with a great *Saal* for services, special rooms for the love feasts, and cubicles to serve as the bedchambers of the religious. Four women inhabited the second story, and below them were four men. This arrangement, though fraught with possibilities of evil, seems actually to have led to no misconduct—indeed, close contact took the sting out of sex. Nevertheless, certain members of the community, not to mention outsiders, were willing to think the worst. When Sigmund Landert offered to bear the expense of erecting a cottage for the Vorsteher and a building for the use of the congregation, in order that Kedar might be reserved for the Sisters, Beissel consented readily. Four years later he astounded his followers by ordering the second meetinghouse to be pulled down. In due time, he found the means to build a monastery for the male religious on Zion Hill, where there was already a house sheltering four brothers. The funds for this undertaking were furnished by a Swiss convert. The next year a third meetinghouse was constructed. It remained standing almost forty years, falling into disrepair at last after it had housed several hundred wounded Continental soldiers during the Revolution. It was a gift to the brothers, but the congregation was permitted to hold services in it for a time. A year later the completion of a fourth meetinghouse, Peniel, gave the congregation a sanctuary of its own. All these things were accomplished in the space of four years.

The vibrant life that animated these buildings will be described in a later chapter. The reader, contemplating a precariously balanced distribution of authority and privilege in a society isolated from the ordinary concerns of human existence, will at first be lost in admiration of the placid tenor of this life and its sober, sustained productivity. He will wonder how human beings could accept its privations with such equanimity and do superbly for the love of God what common mortals do indifferently from less supernatural motives. He will see the ponderable results of a severe spiritual regimen, the concrete manifestations of a serene vitality, and it will seem to him that this fertile discipline must draw its strength from an extraordinary sanity. Yet, with further study, he will become conscious of other things, and will find the life of Ephrata deeply human. He will hear the shrill voice of contention lifted above the dull drone of routine. In the middle of the intricate social web that had grown out of his simple desire to rid himself of the world, Beissel sat, a few flimsy strands of power in his hands. One by one these threads were broken by wills that could rival his own. To inquire into the scheme of life that governed Ephrata is to examine an ideal and to see the community, so to speak, on parade. On a given day, there might have been no intimation of an attempt, on the part of a single member, to turn this hallowed life to his own advantage; but the tale as a whole is the usual sordid one of a contest for supremacy. Against a background of prayer and mortification, the dogged fight went on, to the ultimate loss of a sublime ideal that had been realized for a time.

Of course, at the present point of this narrative, such remarks are premature. Beissel was still feeling his way to the summit of his glory, and, as his reputation increased, he seemed close to eminence. Blocked again and again by prejudice, hatred, or sincere dissent from his views, he overthrew his adversaries by the weight of his persistence. He was invincible because he was stubborn.

The attention of the countryside was riveted upon Kedar during its erection. Beissel reasoned that a love feast would conciliate the unsympathetic. Invitations were issued to all the settlers, but not many accepted. One pioneer delivered a pointed reply at midnight; though not a word was uttered, and Beissel could not identify his assailant, it was impossible to misapprehend the meaning of the brawny blows showered upon him in the darkness. When Beissel had been in Ephrata five years, the neighborhood still contained a few stalwart infidels, lax Protestants, and decayed Mennonites who were alarmed at the amount of real estate that was falling into the hands of the Seventh Day Dunkers. They would have been overjoyed to see the outlandish fanatics harried out of the country, and, when six monks gave them an opening, they hastened to improve it. These six maintained that they were entitled, because of their good works, to exemption from taxes and declined to make the payments enjoined by law. They were arrested, but the magistrates were not disposed to be harsh, and one of them furnished bail for their liberation when they agreed to stand trial at the next session of the court. The court convened, and the accused, in reply to questions addressed to them, averred their willingness to serve the King of England so long as his commands did not clash with those of the sovereign Lord of heaven and earth and, while they did not budge from their refusal to pay taxes, declared that, if the law would respect their spiritual character, they would bear their just share of the expenses of the province. Upon these terms the law and the Dunkers reached a lasting agreement, and the question of taxes never vexed Ephrata again. Its enemies, worsted, decamped to more profane parts of the colony.

The extension of Beissel's contacts with groups of Dunkers that owned his sway or seemed inclined to submit to it kept pace with the development of Ephrata. From time to time Beissel led a carefully chosen train of co-workers off upon a missionary tour. Weiser took part in a trip that embraced New Jersey. The visit may have included some exchange of courtesies with the congregation at Piscataway, but one may venture to guess that Beissel's primary aim was to establish friendly relations with the Dunkers who had quitted Pennsylvania in 1733 for a new home at Amwell, New Jersey. Such fatiguing tramps were not disinterested; Beissel aspired to dominion over all the German Baptists, if not the English as well. Sometimes his part was largely passive. In 1736 some of the Germantown Baptists journeyed to Ephrata. Beissel was expecting them, but had been called away, and some of his less stable subjects used the opportunity to indulge in a little spiritual flirting with the visitors. A reproof set things right again, and Beissel had the comfort of knowing that the visit had made a favorable impression on one of the Germantonians. Not much later he triumphed over his old foes far beyond his expectations.

It was, as always, a revival that led to Beissel's victory, and his biographers would have us believe that he did not lift a finger to bring a single convert within the pale of the Community. It may be granted that he took no direct action and that, as a result of the trials to which the brethren had been subjected by the disgruntled Germantown Baptists who had passed over to the "Seventh Day people," there was a decided sentiment against the admission of other postulants from the older congregation. Against this trend towards a complete dissolution of an already strained bond, certain factors worked very vigorously. Personal relations between individuals in the two congregations continued in spite of the rupture, and Beissel was never indifferent to a turn of affairs that could be manipulated to his own gain. In 1739 the religious of Ephrata published a collection of hymns, called *Zionitischer Weyrauchs Hügel*, at Christopher Sauer's press in Germantown. The necessity of supervising the production of this work kept a few of the most important members of the community in Germantown, one may easily imagine, for several days at a time or longer. They would have been false to themselves if they had failed to utilize their leisure for the propagation of their own strain of Dunkerism. It was not unknown to them that a handful of earnest Germantown Baptists had conceived a violent distaste for the formalism into which their sect had lapsed. This zealous little circle, taking Ephrata or the archetype of all Pietistic hermitages as a pattern, had embraced the solitary life and was exhausting its energies in an attempt to recover the primitive and unadulterated spirit of the Schwarzenau awakening. There were, in all, four solitary brothers. They gave rise to a movement that finally swept a goodly portion of the Baptist congregation into Beissel's settlement. The reader, by this time, is familiar with the stereotyped phenomena of an awakening and may be spared an elaborate account of the extraordinary things that happened. It is enough to note that Beissel's agents worked diligently and with brilliant success. Beissel was accepted by many of the most pious Baptists as the guardian of the original revelation.

Similar results were achieved at Amwell, in less covert fashion. Here Beissel appeared in person and, with his wonted skill, drove a wedge into the congregation and won a part of it for his cause. He commissioned Emanuel Eckerle to minister to the Seventh Day faction, but Eckerle's innovations, thrust immoderately upon the people, ended in his humiliation. He was forced to relinquish his position, and those who had sided with him hurried after him to Ephrata, where they were warmly welcomed.

Beissel inhabited a celestial world in which there were many mountains, and the loftiest of these, a giddy, isolated peak, was reserved for him. It was his private high-place, a temple designed for self-adoration. Here the Narcissus of Conestoga was both votary and god. The bracing gales that swept about this summit were free of the heat and dust of human life, and, if Beissel had been suffered to live there undisturbed, he would in time have forgotten his limitations, and his untrammeled ego would have enjoyed a complete apotheosis. Exalted to such an eminence, he might have found the courage for some hardy and far-reaching enterprise that would have carried his name beyond the boundaries of Pennsylvania: he might have founded a theocracy in the unexploited wilderness across the mountains or schemed to overthrow the colonial government. These, however, are remote chances, and the only reason for mentioning them is that fanatics of far less spiritual depth have accomplished such things. Beissel was not a militant prophet, and the tradition upon which he drew did not sanction the use of violent means for the propagation of true Christianity. Even in the complete absence of opposition, he would have been content with the groveling subservience of a small, but wholly devoted following.

Luckily for the men and women whom he had subjugated to his will, there was always somebody to thwart him, some adversary possessed of sturdy good sense who punctured the distended bladder of his self-love. Of all his opponents, the most stalwart, honest, and outspoken was Christopher Sauer, a man whose piety, quite as genuine as Beissel's in its own way, belonged to a totally different category. Sauer had the strongest reason in the world for detesting the Vorsteher: his wife, caught in Beissel's net, had forsaken him. Sauer had nursed his outraged emotions for a long time. His opportunity to retaliate came when his press was busy with the publication of the bulky hymnal compiled by Beissel and his associates. He displayed a self-control that contrasts strikingly with Beissel's spiteful vituperation. Sauer coöperated cordially with the Ephrathites in the project because he was convinced that such a work was greatly needed. Nevertheless, certain effusions contributed by the Seventh Day Dunkers were not to his taste, and one of them, written by the Vorsteher, was uncommonly nauseating. It dilated upon the perils of the Christian life under the familiar figure of the forty years' passage of the Chosen People from the servitude of Egypt to the comfort of the land flowing with milk and honey. There was nothing save a dreary triteness to offend Sauer in the earlier stanzas, but when Beissel introduced himself as a mediator Sauer found the composition disgusting, and said so. Certainly Beissel depicted himself in language that was susceptible of a startling interpretation. His colossal self-esteem appears very patently in the following lines:

> For thou stiffly didst oppose
> Him whom God picked out and chose,
>
> Mocking him with raillery loud,
> Like the evil, sinning crowd,
> Who God's majesty despise
> And His teaching do not prize.

He who for thee suffering bore
In full many a combat sore
Thy derision hath to bear
While things seem not what they are,

He who, still, thy burden bears,
With small respite from his cares,
And pleads for thee at th' assize,
When God's anger doth arise.

.   .   .   .   .   .

Gaze and gaze and gaze, and then
Gaze once more upon the man
Who exalted is of God,
For he is our Christ and Lord.

Ever in our sight he says,
"Come and follow in my ways,
For I am your portion best,
Through whom ye can all be blest."

Sauer asked questions about the meaning of this hymn and satisfied himself that he had not misunderstood it. A spirited exchange of letters followed. Although he did not mince matters, Sauer far surpassed his antagonist in courtesy and restraint. Beissel did not deign to answer him point by point, but merely sent a virulent, haughty, and unsigned reply. Sauer published the correspondence under the title *Ein Abgenöthigter Bericht* (1739). This little work is exceedingly valuable to any person who undertakes to arrive at a dispassionate appraisal of Beissel's character and work. In the warmth of his choler, Sauer tells us more about Conrad than the official biographers convey in many pages of turgid prose. His presentation of the truth about the Vorsteher lacks the seasoned deliberation of a portrait. It is an incisive caricature, in which a few bold, sure strokes produce a living picture.

Sauer's main gravamen was that Beissel had the effrontery to portray himself as Christ. The *Chronicon* does not deny this charge. On the contrary, it confesses without shame that some of Beissel's followers were prepared to rank him as divine or almost divine. The doctrine that other Christs might follow the First had gained some currency, and this teaching might have opened the way for a proclamation of Beissel's messiahship. As always, he shrank from a definition. Forthright assertions were not for him. He was congenitally incapable of making a clear and honest claim. It was better to suggest the notion to his sectaries and let them draw their own insane conclusions in the surcharged air of Ephrata. The rambling and nebulous hymn that irritated Sauer contained as clear a statement as Beissel would, at any time, have ventured to make. It was lucid enough for those who had a mind to put a blasphemous construction upon it. If he only versified sentiments communicated to him by others, his willingness to accept such an estimate of himself shows that he was inordinately egotistical. It would have been easy for him to check the growth of the mad speculations about his person that led his most bewitched adherents to regard him as belonging to a plane higher than that of ordinary humanity. Not only did he neglect to stifle these witless vaporings, but he actually stimulated and encouraged them. As mere poetry, the language he employed, emanating from some other person, would have been tolerable, for penitents of many persuasions, in the fervor of gratitude towards those who have represented God in their redemption from sin, have been as immoderate as the Ephrathites were. A healthy and humble spiritual father would have had little patience with such tommyrot. Beissel devoured it, not knowing quite what it meant to him or to those who heaped it upon him so fulsomely. If this abject worship had continued he might have lost his reason. To be sure, it stopped short of this hazardous point, and, when every aspect of the question has been scrutinized, one is constrained to admit that there is no indubitable proof that he was convinced of his divinity. This, so far from mitigating his guilt, increases it. He trifled with an idea that contained enough energy to blow him and his congregation to atoms.

Sauer generously grants that Beissel had been endowed by nature with a multiplicity of gifts, admirably balanced. With a few dexterous touches he presents a brief and accurate characterization in the form of a horoscope. All the planets have influenced Beissel's temperament. When people first make his acquaintance, he is gracious and indulgent, like Jupiter. To those who accept his yoke, he manifests the affection of Venus, the intellectual penetration of the Sun, and the quickness of Mercury. To backsliders he exhibits Saturn's sternness. He thunders like Mars when his pride is wounded. The phases of the moon are reflected in his frequent changes of mood and attitude. It has not escaped Sauer that Beissel is Ephrata and Ephrata is Beissel. The Vorsteher cannot endure the slightest diminution of his power. If he cannot be the unchallenged lord of Ephrata, he will be nothing at all.

Sauer knows the sources of Beissel's teaching: it is a farrago of "Moses, Christ, Gichtel, and Conrad Beissel." He twits him with the mention of his four baptisms. He delivers his most telling stroke when he discovers the number of the Beast (Revelation 13:18) in Beissel's name. One has only to spell it out in this fashion: CVnraDVs BeIseLVs. The total of the numerals found in this form of the name is 666 (DCLVVVI).

Of the numerous picayune wrangles that vexed the settlement at Ephrata and impaired the celestial serenity that had prevailed for a time among its inmates, the dispute concerning Beissel's name affords perhaps the clearest illustration of the ludicrous solemnity with which these grave Sabbatarians studied and debated matters of small importance. A person's name is an inseparable part of his individuality. In order to divest themselves completely of the past, the members of the congregation exchanged their old, profane names for more spiritual ones. Beissel was not satisfied with the name Brother Conrad and requested some of the housefathers to select a more fitting appellation. They racked their brains with no success, and at last Beissel, who had been ruminating upon the question with more concentration than such a trifle deserved, secured their approbation of the name Brother Friedsam. The celibate brothers, not having been consulted in the choice, were indignant that Beissel should be known as a mere brother. They resolved to call him Father, and Beissel acquiesced. This action gave rise to further spirited deliberations, and, although it was settled at length that the religious should salute the Vorsteher as Father and the seculars should greet him as Brother, this rule was loosely kept.

John Hildebrand, one of the firebrands of the community, renewed the altercation by setting forth, in a lengthy communication to Beissel, his objections to the distinction conferred upon the Vorsteher by his papistical disciples of the Zionitic Brotherhood. Beissel appeased the offended housefather with a mild reply, but a little later Hildebrand's scruples were revived and he prepared a second missive. Beissel summoned two seculars and, with these witnesses to protect him, permitted Hildebrand to read his labored prose. If Beissel had made an unambiguous declaration of his position, no doubt the discussion would have been brought immediately to a close, for not many would have ventured to withstand his patriarchal authority. Instead, he elected to play the part of the spectator who cheers both sides impartially. First he egged on the religious to vindicate his claim to the title and then, when, momentarily, they seemed to have vanquished their opponents, he took the housefathers to task for their failure to second Hildebrand. In the end, a council of the entire community was held, and the conclusion of the affair was that the monks and the nuns, as well as the seculars who were so disposed, were permitted to call Beissel Father. The few dissident members of the congregation were granted complete freedom.

Although Weiser had become estranged from Beissel when serious occupations claimed his energy, and Sauer's seething anger had pilloried the wizard of Conestoga as an impudent humbug, it was always possible for Beissel to stare or shout such adversaries down, or else to freeze them out of his minute world. If he could not vanquish them, he could ignore them;

and, for all the provincial glory they enjoyed, they were still not his social betters. He had reached the apex of his career —indeed, he had already begun to slip down the gentle declivity that led to defeat—when he found himself menaced by an enemy whom he had not the spirit to face. Count Ludwig von Zinzendorf made the tiresome journey to Pennsylvania with no hostile design. He came attired in the garb of friendship to infuse a measure of apostolic sanity into the embittered roil of colonial religion. Beissel declined to encounter him in open combat and carried on a vitriolic struggle with him through certain members of the community. In the end Beissel was worsted, and when the Count's party branded him as a diabolical lunatic he received a stigma in which even he, with all his contumelious inattention to other people's opinions, could take little pleasure.

Zinzendorf had drifted, step by step, into a curious and not altogether comfortable position. With a warmth that was common among the devout noblemen of his day, he had admitted to his estates the residue of the Unitas Fratrum, or Moravian Brethren, whom persecution had reduced to the most wretched ignominy and impotence. This church, which had arisen among the adherents of John Huss sixty years before the Reformation, had retained the episcopate in a modified form. It cherished its apostolic constitution, and Zinzendorf was certain that its polity was superior to that of the Lutheran Church. His exertions in behalf of his guests had brought him misunderstanding and misery, but with dogged courage and unflagging enthusiasm he labored, notwithstanding a natural unfitness for the work, to rally all evangelical Christians about the venerable Unity, in which, to his mind, there was a perfect blend of Lutheran doctrine and apostolic discipline. In order to carry out this enterprise, he took orders in the Lutheran Church, and subsequently became a Moravian bishop. In this anomalous dual character, with a reputation among his opponents for greedy proselytizing, he arrived in Pennsylvania, determined to execute his plan among the tractable inhabitants of the land.

There was no need to dread a clash with the civil power. Governor Thomas described the situation in words that will bear quotation: "nobody who recognizes a single, almighty God, the Creator, Sustainer, and Ruler of the whole world, and regards himself as in duty bound to lead a peaceable life under the civil government is in the least molested or suffers any damage, either in his person or in his property, on account of matters of conscience. . . ." Pennsylvania seemed replete with promise; yet, despite the benignity, or indifference, of the government, the project was to fail, for the colonists were not so amenable to reason as Zinzendorf had expected them to be.

Such efforts were not an innovation among the Moravians. In 1570 the Synod of Sendomir, in Poland, had joined the Moravians, the Reformed, and the Lutherans in an evangelical federation, the constitution of which, while encouraging the people of each group to frequent the churches of the other two for sacramental ministrations and preaching, provided for the preservation of the three distinct modes of worship and discipline employed by the members of the federation. In Bohemia, after the collapse of the Polish scheme, the three confessions entered into a similar agreement. The principles upon which these two instruments of union were founded governed Zinzendorf's efforts. The reader has seen that he had only a mediocre success when he tried to draw Rock and his Inspirationists into such a partnership.

During the first half of the year 1742 Zinzendorf held a series of seven synods—in imitation, one may suppose, of the seven Ecumenical Councils—at various places in Pennsylvania. He was supported in this endeavor by Heinrich Antes, who addressed a circular to the denominations of the colony, inviting them to send delegates to the first synod. In this appeal he declares that earnest observers have been wondering for two years or more whether it was possible to bring the divided religious bodies of Pennsylvania together, "to discuss lovingly the most important articles of faith, in order to see how near people could get to each other fundamentally, and to bear with

each other in love, for the rest, in opinions that do not affect
eternal salvation. . . ." At the first synod, the representatives
of the religious bodies made a propitious beginning. They af-
firmed that members of the mystical Body of Christ existed all
over the world, even in the most unlikely places; that Christians were not under obligation to adhere to the same form
of church government, but, on the contrary, differences might
be permitted to remain so long as the groups tolerated each
other; and that all denominations were united in reality. They
envisaged a union in which all would subscribe to a creed to
be drawn up by the synod, each group continuing in the exercise of its own rights. This preliminary work completed, they
undertook to frame a formulary that would be acceptable to
all. In this task Zinzendorf's counsel was paramount, and he
imposed upon the synod, without evil intent or the use of
inordinate pressure, his own theological position, which consisted more of emotion than of ratiocination. His hand can be
discerned in the phraseology of the declaration issued by the
gathering. The gist of the statement is evident in the following
translation of parts of the German original:

"We believe and confess unanimously that nobody can release us from eternal death but our Lord and God, Jesus Christ
alone, with His Blood." "So long as a man has not been made
alive, he is under the judgment of condemnation to eternal
death, nevertheless it is not clear to him, but his conscience
is not at rest; as soon as he is awakened, he knows and recognizes himself as damned; but as soon as he believes on Him
who makes the godless righteous and believes that He has died
for his sins too (which no man can believe except through the
Holy Ghost), then the man is received into grace and is ab-
solved from sin . . . and has the privilege or right no longer
to sin but to become holy." Jesus is "not only the Saviour of the
faithful and the atonement for their sins, but also the atonement
for the sin of the whole world and the Saviour of all men."
The reception of grace brings with it a detestation of sin, and
the believer enters into an alliance with Christ against it. De-

spite the little sins that arise out of our infirmity, we carry the treasure of sanctification with us to the end. The visible proof of conversion is "that a sinner who has received grace does all that he does, in word or deed, in the name of the Lord Jesus." The synod was alive to the necessity of contriving some means of controlling its deliberations and attempted to secure this end by prohibiting fanciful and perverse interpretations of Scripture. This pronouncement boded ill for mystics like Beissel.

The official record of the proceedings of the first synod was signed by John Hildebrand of Ephrata. The notorious Prior of the Zionitic Brotherhood was also a deputy. The Beisselians had been familiar with the ethos and methods of the Unity for several years, and the relations between the two denominations had not precisely been amicable. Spangenberg and Nitschmann, on their way to the mission in the Virgin Islands, had met with a friendly reception at Ephrata. The fraternal good will manifested during their sojourn vanished before the suspicion and resentment that began to appear when a Moravian named Haberecht entered the Brotherhod. Anna Nitschmann, while a guest at Ephrata, prevailed upon him to return to the Unity. Another Moravian sister abused the hospitality of the convent, if the *Chronicon* is not in error, by circulating after her departure the falsehood that the Sisters of Ephrata were ready to abandon the religious life. The Prior, without the authorization of the community, invited the delegates at the first synod to hold their next meeting at Ephrata. The proposed invasion of the sacred enclosure did not commend itself to the Ephrathites, and Beissel, in withdrawing the invitation, asserted that he would take no part in the movement. Zinzendorf remained on good terms with the Prior and made a visit to the Settlement in an effort to come to some agreement with Beissel, but the Vorsteher was very churlish, and his rudeness made even a meeting, to say nothing of a conversation, impossible.

The second council was convened in Friedrichs Township, Philadelphia County, a fortnight after the first. Its minutes were signed by Hildebrand, and it is no doubt not an accident that he did not append the words "of Ephrata" to his signature. One of the matters debated at this synod was the moot question of the differences between the Beisselians and Moravians concerning marriage. "Is it true," ran the question, "that the Moravian Brethren have too high a regard for marriage and the people of Ephrata have no regard for it at all?" The answer follows:

It has appeared as though the congregation at Ephrata and the Brethren at Bethlehem in the Forks held directly contradictory views with regard to the question of marriage; but, when the Brethren publicly set forth the foundation of their views, the former said that they had no objection to it. Therefore we have herewith, on the one hand, recognized as unfounded the suspicion of a fleshly necessity for the sake of which marriage is exalted, until the opposite is seen and found; and, on the other hand, we absolve the congregation at Ephrata in future of the suspicion of diabolical teaching; and nobody who belongs to us is permitted to consider it a fault in them; and anybody who hereafter hears anything of the sort shall name the person who has said it to him and not blame the congregation. For the rest, we reserve this and like matters of principal importance for examination and for the joint public setting-forth of the opinions of all of us.

Final discussion was merely postponed.

Four members of the Ephrata congregation attended the third conference, at Oley, and laid before it their lucubrations on marriage. Zinzendorf, by this time, was so furious at the rebuffs he had received that he was no longer disposed to deal gently with the Ephrathites. He objected vigorously to their aspersions of the married state. He was assured that the Ephrathites did not repudiate this useful institution, and the deputies from Ephrata went so far as to volunteer the information that some families in the secular part of the community had a child annually, with great regularity. Zinzendorf exploded and declared that he was shocked at such laxity.

Beissel's people dissociated themselves from the synods at this juncture, but the Moravians did not relinquish their hope of a satisfactory adjustment until they had made a number of trips to Ephrata. These visits were not without result. The solitary were once about to commit themselves to a union with the Moravians, and Beissel had to intervene. This is the only occasion on which he appeared prominently in the course of this long, unseemly, and disorderly altercation. At last he terminated the controversy by directing a member of the congregation to write a denunciation of the Moravians. The first draft was revised, and appendices were added by the Prior and Johannes Hildebrand. The little work was published by Sauer in 1743 under the title *Mistisches und Kirchliches Zeuchnüss Der Brüderschaft In Zion.*

The Ephrathites had settled the argument in their own way, and now Zinzendorf and his adherents retaliated by dismissing them with a scathing condemnation. At the close of the series of synods those who had participated in them published a curious set of conclusions, in which they stated their findings with regard to each denomination. They delivered a severe verdict against Beissel and his congregation in the following words:

The congregation in Conestoga, which is improperly called the "Seventh Day People" because the seventh day is not a matter of ridicule, withdrew itself from scrutiny at the fourth synod; and partly the necessary remonstrances to its teachers, partly the representations, condemned by us, of some of its former members and members of other congregations against it, and most of all the rule we have adopted, have required great discretion and patience. But now that all attempts to come to terms with its teachers have failed, the shortcomings of others towards it have been recognized and disposed of, and its private differences, by which we do not wish to profit, have, without our interference, reached their inevitable result, the Congregation of the Lord declares herewith that this sect established in Conestoga with its two monasteries is nothing but a faction of the Baptists, from whom it has tried to steal its baptism and calling, and, after behaving in this wise and gradually, under pretexts of all kinds, alienating from the Baptists most of their upright spirits, has finally arrived at some semblance of a constitution, which, however, in reality has been invented by the Devil only in order that the approaching kingdom of Jesus Christ might be hindered in advance, the separatists excited most sorely against everything that smacks of a social order, religious people brought, through the horrible errors, into mistrust and fear towards future stirrings of grace, and finally so many souls that really desired to escape bewitched into a false teaching and society, so that if the Gospel came, nobody might be there to hunger after it. We have no instructions to offer its people, because we do not know how they have arrived at their present condition, whether God's anger has cast them off or only because His everlasting wisdom intended some good thing for them therewith, into which matter we are too aware of our own weakness to inquire, and are going to test it particularly in the case of every person who suffers in their fellowship, especially the captive conventual virgins of Kedar. May the Lamb tread this Satan under His feet shortly!

It is always painful to resuscitate the decayed remains of a religious dispute in which people no longer feel a vital interest. In this instance, it is sufficient to observe that the disharmony of temperament, antecedents, and opinion that existed between Beissel and Zinzendorf precluded their coöperation in any undertaking. Beissel found fault with the ardor with which the Moravians sought converts. It seemed to him an immoderate passion, a revolting lust for souls. This, however, was not a fundamental point of difference; it had its origin in the clash between two vastly dissimilar views of redemption. To this conflict the widely canvassed question of marriage, like the matter of zeal for souls, is secondary and subordinate. The two men contended with each other because there was an impassable chasm between their respective views of God, man, and the steps by which the two were to be brought into close relations with each other. Zinzendorf looked for a melting of the heart, quickly succeeded by an abiding assurance of safety under the guardianship of a loving God. To Beissel this seemed facile and superficial. For him sanctification was an agony of gradual death to self. As there had been two falls, so there had to be two redemptions. The kind of salvation the Moravians preached was, from his point of view, merely outward and legal. The deeper salvation could be gained only by complete abnegation, and a monastery was the only place where one could hope to persevere in a strict and lifelong plan of self-denial. Zinzendorf's conception of religion, implanted in the resourceful soul of John Wesley, gave solace and certainty to underprivileged thousands. It is still a vigorous force today, despite its inherent leaning towards sentimentality and cant. Beissel's spiritual descendants, in the year 1940, number fewer than five hundred, and among them some of his dearest principles and observances have fallen into desuetude. Has time vindicated Zinzendorf and rendered Beissel his just deserts, or is the victory really with Beissel?

VI

WISDOM'S HOUSEHOLD

A NARRATIVE of Conrad Beissel's life, however sparkling in some passages and fantastic or curious in others, soon becomes a bald catalogue of the Vorsteher's feuds, notwithstanding the author's unflagging efforts to inject a modicum of charm into his account. In the end, both biographer and reader are obliged to accept the ineluctable fact that there is not much else to recount. Intellectually, Beissel was largely an echo. Spiritually, he bears the impress of Pietism and presents nothing startlingly distinctive. His temperament is the only interesting and original thing about him, and it is the temperament of an unbending, untiring fanatic. It derives its power from the concentration that is possible only for a circumscribed mentality. If we could watch experience blunting his jagged edges and infusing a pastoral compassion, if not a warmth of fellow-feeling, into his frozen soul, this repulsive monotony would be mitigated in some degree. At times a superficial graciousness and affability masked the obsession that dominated his life, but when we undo the wrappings we find nothing but a blade of cold flint, which pierced not only those who matched their strength with his, but also the friends who embraced him. Strife was his sustenance. The ecstasy of combat was his animating principle. He lived for the tension of struggle. His successes were personal triumphs, and his failures humiliated him deeply because in every dispute or wrangle it was his self-love that was most at stake.

A person so fashioned by nature and circumstance necessarily imparted some traits of his character to the institution he founded. The complex society at Ephrata reflects the virtues and the foibles of its author. Its most ruinous weakness was an absence of coördination, a lack of centrality. Beissel was its head, but instead of endeavoring to resolve its discords, he pitted one part against another, ineptly applying the cynical maxim that bids a monarch control his subjects by preventing them from uniting in opposition to him. It is surprising that he retained the position of arbiter despite his flagrant partiality and want of moderation. This demonstrates the depth and strength of his personal influence but does not acquit him of the charge of prostituting his influence to mean purposes. In the founder of a religious community, who has the boldness to urge upon his followers the most excruciating sacrifices, anything less noble than the steadfast pursuit of a sublime objective is censurable. Measured by this standard, Beissel is found to have yielded deplorably to a temptation that attacks all those who undertake to guide others in matters of the soul. He encouraged his penitents to rely upon him and so became their divinity as well as their pastor. Engrossed in the stress of his own emotions, he could not be expected to cultivate the judicious balance that characterizes the wise and just ruler. He was impatient of the details of government because his own soul was chaotic. Ephrata was so intimately identified with Beissel that it partook of all his qualities, and, since Beissel was perpetually unsettled, Ephrata was always a prey to restlessness and disorder.

These lamentable truths must be stated emphatically, but there is a factor that counterbalances them. Beissel ruled, not over stocks and stones, but over souls. In a community recruited in no slight measure from people who had been exposed to Pietism of one hue or another, there were temperaments as froward and capricious as his own. Moreover, the settlement was not destitute of innocent, sincere devotion. The iniquity of a leader does not preclude virtue in his followers, particularly when the iniquity is the normally well-meant blundering of a self-conscious rustic who knows little about the tortuous operations of his own soul, rather than the deliberate and diabolical evildoing of a fiend. Undoubtedly many people at Ephrata were actuated solely or chiefly by a desire for perfection. They loved God, and, if Beissel sometimes minimized the difference between God and himself, those who erred under his guidance

erred in good faith. The life at Ephrata was marred by wilfulness and self-regard, but it was a rigorous life, and an urge
towards holiness was, on the whole, the most frequent motive
of those who subjected themselves to its privations. Partly in
slavish obedience to Beissel and partly in response to the mo-
tions of their own natures, the solitary and the householders
created a life of prayer and labor that commands interest quite
independently of Beissel's share in it. That life is the subject of
the present chapter.

Ephrata was known popularly as Dunkerstown, and to the
erudite as Parthenopolis. It was "an irregular *enclosed* village,
lying in a triangle formed by the turnpike, the upper, or old
Reading road, and the Cocalico creek." Rude fortifications,
probably built when the settlement was threatened during the
French and Indian War, were still to be seen in, or not long
before, 1770.

At the top of the hierarchy of dignitaries and functionaries
stands Beissel. He had chosen, at the start, to be a hermit, and,
in form if not in substance, he remained a hermit all his life.
The *Chronicon*, with no hint of disapprobation, confesses that,
in regulating the practice of the religious, he ventured to depart
fundamentally from the plan devised by the Fathers of the
desert. In the Eastern Church, which has kept many of the
features of primitive monachism, a monk spends many years in
the conventual life before daring to embrace the life of solitude,
which is replete with spiritual dangers for those who enter
upon it prematurely. Only at an advanced age, when he has
undergone the purgation of long and intimate converse with his
fellows and has eradicated the last vestige of selfishness from
his character, is he fortified against the insidious perils of the
hermitage, where his desires are no longer curbed by the necessities of a social life. Beissel began at the wrong end. To be
sure, he was never completely alone, but from the first he had
envisaged the eremitic life as the state that would suit him best.
Despite his immersion in the affairs of the community, he made
fitful efforts to shake off the trammels of responsibility and

enjoy a protracted honeymoon with his celestial bride. As a tyro he rushed precipitately into a mode of life for which only the seasoned adept is fitted, and, whenever he had an opportunity to learn the salutary truths that society alone can teach, he shied away from it. He coveted a position of isolated and insulated grandeur and at no time shared the peculiar trials of either portion of his community. He brought the solitary under the yoke of a common life, but he refused to bow to it himself. He attempted to direct where he had never condescended to obey, and his presumption was disastrous to himself and, in no negligible degree, to the religious. The decay of one Pietistic society after another indicates that Pietism was too much a personal affair to thrive in monasteries. Beissel himself is a conspicuous illustration of this truth.

The Vorsteher governed two distinct groups of Seventh Day Dunkers. The seculars retained the cohabitation of marriage, in the literal sense of the word, while the religious lived in solitude until the foundation of an order for each sex. There was an inevitable rivalry between the monks and the nuns, and the latter were more directly subject to Beissel than the former, but together they constituted a separate division of the settlement, and their interests diverged from those of the ordinary families. Apart from their common doctrinal beliefs—a very loose tie—the only link between the seculars and the religious was their devotion to Beissel.

The life led by the householders and their dependants will now be considered. Over them, in the main, Beissel enjoyed a uncontested mastery. The refractory conduct of a few members of the congregation merely accentuates the tractability of the rest. The Vorsteher demanded continence, obedience, and a generosity in almsgiving that, for all practical purposes, was voluntary poverty. The property of every family was at his disposal, and, in his heyday, the merest hint on his part that he desired a gift was sufficient to obtain it for him. His control of these submissive people was unbounded. He pried into their most private concerns. At the apogee of his power, he required them to scrutinize their souls every Friday night and give him a report in writing. The reports, called *lectiones,* were read publicly at the service on Saturday.

Even the simplest people at Ephrata were articulate, not to say loquacious, in religious matters, and eventually there must have been a prodigious number of *lectiones.* In 1752 a selection appeared under the title *Theosophische Lectionen.* These documents seem at first sight frank and naïve, and unquestionably they are so within limits; yet they were written for the Vorsteher's eye and therefore represent, frequently, not so much what the writer felt as what he knew Beissel expected him to feel, and, in addition, it is very likely that the *lectiones* were retouched before publication. Many of the expressions employed by the authors are conventional and stereotyped, and the sentiments are often commonplace. Scintillating originality is not normally a conspicuous feature of such writings. With all their defects, the *lectiones* disclose the outlines of the spirituality that held sway in the Ephrata community, and in examining them one must not fall into the error of discounting the substance because the form is hackneyed. The quaint piety of these serious people is often least false when it is most imitative.

In the published *lectiones* there are reverberations of many religious movements. It is not always possible to determine the antecedents of a given belief or mode of thought, and a scrupulous analysis is outside the scope of the present work. Dictatorial in questions of action, Beissel was not dogmatic in the proper sense of the word. His doctrines were not meticulously stated, and, for him, even the Scriptures—at least, so far as their language is concerned—had no finality. This vagueness and laxity of intellect permitted the entry of many strange persons, with many strange notions, into the fold. It is impossible to convey the gist of the *lectiones* in a few concise sentences. Besides being diffuse, they contain a luxuriant variety of inchoate apprehensions of divine things. The following digest is merely a review of the most interesting portions.

There is relatively little mention of the theosophy that oc-

cupies so predominant a place in Beissel's own view of reality.
There is a sharp sense of the irreconcilable opposition between
the world and the Kingdom, between flesh and spirit. The spiritual life is a present desolation with the comfort of a future
felicity. It is depicted under various images: a sowing with the
prospect of harvest, a painful journey to a land of beauty and
abundance, a widowhood that rejoices in the pledge of ultimate union with the heavenly Spouse, a fleeting barrenness that
God will some day fructify beyond human imagination, a
winter with the certainty of a spring to ensue. On the whole,
the language used in the expression of these feelings and convictions is sober and restrained. There are fewer absurdities
than a knowledge of the *Chronicon* leads us to expect. Along
with this soundness, there is an unmistakable strain of quietism.
The active virtues of the Christian life receive scant emphasis.
There is no sign of an urge to deliver this world from its thrall-
dom to evil. Union with God is vouchsafed only to those who
have annihilated all that characterizes them as human beings.
The end to which the seeker directs his efforts is the extinction
of his impure desires. Human life, except as its corruption is
softened by a striving towards holiness, is flagitious and de-
praved. The soul must study to render itself void, even to the
point of losing consciousness of itself. "If the first-created man
had not begun to think of himself he would not have deserted
the Creator." "The most necessary, best, and most certain
means of attaining to the true riches is to renounce oneself
and suffer the loss of all visible and created things." "God lives
without wants, because He possesses nothing." The last statement is striking, and the correct interpretation is presumably
that God is free of the greed that anchors so many men to the
world of carnal interests. He who lives emptied of needs belongs to God and will inherit the wealth of heaven. He par-
takes of the divine nature and, viewing things as they really
are, is reformed in God's likeness. Sometimes we find this truth
couched in words that recall the daring quasi-heresies of Eck-
hart and Tauler. Thus a writer affirms that "the soul is an ex-

halation (*Aushauch*) of the Eternal Father's divine power."
Spiritual poverty is the ground of all virtues. One must labor
to return to the "deep silence," the "great All of God," in
which one originated. Logically such a state would lead to the
complete banishment of sin. Probably many people at Ephrata
believed in the perfectibility of the soul in this life. One writer
asseverates that he "does not sin, for he who sins has not arrived at godliness, nor has he come to know the fullness of Him
who filleth all things." The God who is the object of these
strivings "is an incomprehensible Being; therefore He cannot
be found in comprehensible things." Beatitude is the abandonment of thought and every other conscious operation of the
human mechanism.

Probably the quietism of Ephrata stems both from a certain
interpretation (in the opinion of some experts, a misinterpretation) of an obscure portion of Böhme's theology and from the
Roman Catholic quietists—principally Madame de Guyon—
whose works were read diligently by many Pietists. Böhme's
conception of God as the *Ungrund* and a *Nichts* readily suggested the quietistic approach as most consonant with the nature of such an object of worship. In view of Sauer's taunt
that Beissel was indebted to the Böhmist Gichtel for some of
his doctrines, it is likely that Beissel learned "perverse quietism"
from the Gichtelians, perhaps directly in some unrecorded
contact or in his friendship with Haller, perhaps indirectly
through an acquaintance with Gichtelian writings. Whether or
not this is true, the force of Roman Catholic quietism was almost certainly felt among the Ephrathites. Tersteegen, one of
Madame de Guyon's most enthusiastic admirers and the director
of a religious community that closely resembled Beissel's, had
correspondents in Pennsylvania. In Beissel's youth, Poiret edited
Madame de Guyon's writings and worked steadily for the dif-
fusion of her teaching, with the chief articles of which Beissel
and some of his adherents must have been familiar.

Some of the *lectiones* are explicitly addressed to Beissel. In
one he is called "my dear Vorsteher," and its author declares

that he is entirely at peace because he has accepted "holy obedience." In another *lectio* Conrad is saluted as "Father." Finally, there is one *lectio* from overseas. It serves to remind us of the kinship between the *lectiones* and the other Pietistic collections of the period. One of the most notable is the *Geistliche Fama*, an astounding mélange of sense and nonsense. These literary ragbags illustrate the composite character of Pietistic associations. If the *Theosophische Lectionen* were our only source of information, we should be inclined to conclude that Ephrata was more nearly homogeneous than most other settlements of the kind. From other quarters we learn that it had its full allowance of freaks and dissenters.

A life of withdrawal from mundane concerns required some visible token of its character. The members of the community were known to each other by "church-names." A more conspicuous mark was the uniform or habit frequently represented in seals or drawings made at Ephrata. In the early days Beissel and the religious used the Quakers as models for their clothing. Later a habit was designed, and its inventors naïvely discovered, when their work was done, that they had unconsciously copied the apparel of the Capuchins. This raiment will be described presently. The seculars imitated the religious and for a time wore similar attire, except that their habits were not white, like those of the monks and nuns, but gray. Israel Acrelius, a Swedish Lutheran minister, who spent a day at Ephrata in 1753, remarks that the seculars wear their distinctive dress at church services and adds, "However, they have clothes of various colors and of the usual fashion." The habit of the seculars was therefore a kind of vestment or Sabbath uniform. During the week they were attired like ordinary folk. Eventually the householders discarded their habit.

When the Brotherhood of Zion was at the height of its splendor and sanctity, the religious life seemed to the householders so blessed a calling that they resolved to follow it themselves. A church, called Peniel, had recently been erected, and the seculars added a monastery to it. This building housed the

short-lived third order which, while it lasted, performed a useful service by supporting and ministering to needy widows.
The women were deeply in earnest and determined to remove
forever the danger of a relapse into the married state. They
had long since deserted their husbands' beds, but they were
still obliged to recognize their authority. A complete dissolution of the marriage tie was the only thing that would satisfy
them. Accordingly the husbands and the wives were solemnly
divorced. The legality of the act was very dubious, since it
consisted, apparently, in nothing more than the exchange of
letters of divorcement prepared by a Zionitic brother. In the
end, it was the women who once more took the initiative and,
reclaiming their husbands, brought the fatuous venture to a
close. Their children, for whom they had some residue of affection, did not share their elders' taste for the restraints of
religion and were growing up without oversight. The departure of the Eckerles disrupted the life of the community, and
in the confusion and the readjustment that followed it the
letters of divorcement were committed to the flames and the
householders resumed their former lives. Their monastery subsequently fell into the hands of the nuns and was named Sharon.
The other conventual buildings have perished, but Sharon remains standing to this day.

   During the earliest years of Beissel's public ministry the congregation had no church. The services were held in such farm-
houses as were open to the Vorsteher and his flock. In selecting
places for worship, the pastor showed no partiality towards the
prosperous, and frequently gave mild scandal to the more
sanctimonious members of his congregation by choosing some
rude and humble cabin, inhabited by people who were not
conspicuous for their piety. The services were potent for good
or evil, according to the disposition of the worshipper, and the
love feasts, which normally ended at midnight, at times were
prolonged until daybreak.

   Beissel retired to Ephrata in 1732, but the congregation had
to wait until 1735 for a meetinghouse, and even then it did not

enjoy exclusive possession of the building, but was obliged to share it with eight of the solitary. To this structure a second meetinghouse was soon added, only to be pulled down four years later. A third church, on Zion Hill, supplanted it, but the congregation did not occupy it long enough to grow accustomed to it. In the autumn of 1741 Peniel, a fourth edifice, was completed. Here the congregation worshipped until 1746.

In 1753 Acrelius was present at a service held in the old monastery on Zion Hill, which, as we shall presently relate, the monks surrendered to the secular congregation after Prior Onesimus' departure from Ephrata. The church had a capacity of about one hundred. At that time there was only one general service a month. Both sections of the community took part in it, the celibate brethren sitting in a sort of choir, which occupied one-third of the floor, while the nuns were hidden from sight in a gallery. The congregation proper was seated in the remaining two-thirds of the floor space, and Beissel had a seat between the monks and the seculars. Time had not greatly impaired the diverting pulpit manner he affected at the commencement of his public ministry. A sketch of his antics, drawn from the lifelike description of the *Chronicon,* has already been given. He no longer cavorted—if he had ever done so— like the Inspirationists, but the fiction of an immediate inspiration gave the service an impromptu and haphazard tone. It opened with a fifteen-minute hymn, for which the Vorsteher, after sundry contortions and grimaces, gave the pitch. After the hymn Jaebez read a chapter of the Old Testament. Beissel then began his homily, a jumbled discourse rattled off at dizzy speed. While delivering his sermon, the Vorsteher gave free rein to his distracting, and sometimes coarse, mannerisms. His hearers did not all respond in the same way. Some shed tears or gave other evidences of emotion. Others napped in stolid indifference. When Beissel had at last arrived at the end of this preachment, a psalm was sung, and then the meeting was thrown open for testimony. A pathetic old man made a valiant attempt to express himself, but was overcome by his emotions.

It was Beissel's custom to make a few critical observations on each testimonial.

Outsiders were not excluded from this service. It was probably designed as much to convert them as to edify those who were already members of the congregation. Apart from the singing, which had been elaborately developed among the religious under Beissel's direction, the details of the service were improvised. In trivial matters as in important ones Beissel was addicted to a slovenly reliance upon the chance inspiration of the moment, and he was often betrayed. To all except those who trusted him implicitly and revered him as God's emissary, he was a grotesque, pitiable figure. When he officiated at the Lord's Supper or a baptism, perhaps he had a more imposing manner, but Onesimus outshone him in sacerdotal dignity, and Beissel always had a poor presence. If it were necessary to describe his character and career in a single sentence, one might say with accuracy and justice that he was an insignificant man who made a lifelong effort to feel impressive. A surprisingly large number of gullible people accepted him as a half-divine illuminate, but, beneath his blustering bumptiousness, he was unconsciously skeptical of his own pretensions. Conrad the hard-headed peasant suspected that Conrad the messiah was a humbug. Conrad the messiah thrust these misgivings into a dark corner of his mind, and when they emerged they wore so convincing a disguise that practically everybody was deceived. Thus the shy, if they do not grow in diffidence, find peace only in the most blatant self-assertion.

To many of the younger Seventh Day Dunkers the solemn follies of their parents were absurd and the discipline under which minors were expected to live was galling. Courting and other worldly diversions were much more to their liking. The plain garb of the community seemed to them a badge of subjection. Their elders were betrayed into helping them to rid themselves of these onerous restrictions. At Ephrata the difference between the Law and the Gospel was a cardinal dogma. The one meant servitude; the other, freedom. The parents misapplied this teaching and granted their children a risky latitude in the matter of their daily deportment, with the rather disturbing result that the latter became extremely saucy and so annoyed their preceptors that nobody could be persuaded to labor with them. Beissel took the negligent parents to task. May 15, 1749 was kept as a fast day. Beissel improved the occasion to bring to an end many objectionable practices. The gaudy attire in which the young people had strutted was hurled into the flames.

In the school maintained by the Brethren and among the youngsters who had lately arrived from Germany there was a counterweight to this frivolity. They were amenable to guidance and, in emulation of their teachers, engaged in the exercises with which the reader is now familiar. By the end of the year their enthusiasm for religion was so keen that nothing short of a church of their own would satisfy them. For the action they took, Anabaptism and Dunkerism afforded many precedents. They became their own ministers and so were adopted into their own fellowship—an event signalized by a love feast and the Lord's Supper. Their seniors were delighted, and, as soon as an adult was designated to act as counselor to the young zealots, the householders were glad to entrust their refractory sons to him. Beissel showed unwonted common sense in his direction of this movement. The giddy young people who had shocked the settlement with their trumpery had been permitted to follow their own inclinations with regard to wedlock, so long as they did not compel their parents to become parties to their carnality. The godly portion of the youth deserved a similar reward, and Beissel did not withhold it. Curbed only by the moderating influence of their supervisor, they were almost completely independent. A special church for their use was planned, and materials for its construction were gathered, but the building remained unfinished. No policy was ever given a fair trial at Ephrata, and changes often occurred with a suddenness that knocked the wind out of its less mercurial citizens. The good boys soon confided to Beissel that they had scruples about their baptism—a state of mind that is not surprising, for Beissel's uneasiness about his own self-administered baptism had tormented him grievously, and, since the crisis of his early years in Pennsylvania was probably well known to the lads who consulted him, they were following his example in this as in everything else. The Vorsteher baptized half a dozen of the boys a little more than two weeks after their attempt to baptize themselves, and a few days later six were added to the number—in all, slightly more than half the total membership of the juvenile church. Decisive action frequently impelled some members of the community to dissent and schism. Certain brethren objected vehemently to the baptism, contending that it was invalid because the boys were too young. Undeterred by these sticklers for a literal application of Anabaptist teaching, Beissel admitted the baptized boys to communion. Two of them were chosen for the questionable honor of washing the feet of all the men in the community. Ultimately it became clear that Beissel's care had been lavished upon his young disciples in vain. The impulse to which the lads had yielded for a time with passionate ardor was exhausted at the end of a year and a half. The little society dissolved, and Beissel, who had seen such things happen before, was not unduly disappointed.

Scripturality was the criterion by which Beissel and his coreligionists, like the Anabaptists, were governed in their belief concerning the sacraments and their use of these ordinances. Their practice was based upon an interpretation of the sacred text that purported to be literal and free of the mischievous admixture of human reasoning. They were not altogether blind to the sacramental constitution of life in general, for, in the course of much experience of religion, they observed that the material was often the vehicle and instrument of the spiritual; but they never conceived of the sacraments as conferring indelible character or as communicating grace by virtue of the sacramental act itself. To put it differently, they rejected the Catholic view of the sacraments and adhered closely to the simple theology of the Anabaptists, who regarded the sacramental sign as worthless except when it was the token and evidence of a sound spiritual condition and disposition. In their struggles to be good, the Ephrathites were sustained first by a conviction of their true conversion, an indispensable preliminary to valid baptism, and, after that, rather by preaching and prayer than by sacramental ministrations.

There was no link between Beissel and the Holy Spirit; their intercourse was direct and uninterrupted. The Vorsteher, ordained by no physical imposition of hands, was theoretically the equal of St. Paul and owed no man anything. He might, and did, empower some of his adherents to exercise a portion of his authority. Like his eminent model, he ordained such persons in the apostolic manner, by placing his hands on their heads. At one time Elimelech actually ministered to the secular congregation at Ephrata, but ordinarily Beissel's representatives were permitted to exercise their ministry only in places that Beissel himself could not visit regularly.

It is not likely that the views of matrimony entertained at Ephrata were ever reduced to uniformity. The bond might be dissolved in order to free the parties for entry into a higher state of life. Opinion regarding the physical aspect of marriage probably fluctuated, and practice fluctuated more violently than opinion. The ideal was complete abstinence from sexual contact, but there is clear proof that this ideal was imperfectly realized.

In their theory of baptism and in the baptismal customs they adopted, the Seventh Day Dunkers followed, in the main, their Anabaptist forebears and the Schwarzenau conventicle of which they were, in origin, a branch. Baptism, according to their view of it, did not regenerate, but it was nevertheless a momentous transaction, for it committed the baptized person, before God and the congregation, to a lifelong perseverance in the calling of a Christian. So weighty an event needed to be invested with a glamor that would etch it deep into the memory of every participant. Sometimes it was the rigor of the ceremony, rather than its glamor, that produced this effect, and occasionally there must have been an element of broad comedy in the spectacle when a soaked sister or brother emerged streaming and embarrassed from the water or struggled convulsively during immersion; yet in the days when monks, nuns, and seculars assisted at baptisms performed in the open air, each group clothed in its peculiar habit, the sight was imposing. Maturity and conversion qualified the candidate for the sacrament. Both defied attempts to measure them precisely, and often laxity or an error of judgment opened the way to the unfit.

The following passage from Acrelius' book indicates how the candidates were baptized and, as a discussion between specialists, serves to show that in this as in other matters the Ephrathites, at least in some points, were singular and opinionated:

The time was further passed away by conversation between Müller and myself. I requested him to inform me as to their mode of baptizing, which he also did. "We seldom receive any others," said he, "than such as have been already baptized, and who thus have some knowledge of Christianity; but if they have been brought up in our Society, we first instruct them. When they come to the water, the Minister there puts to them the necessary questions, which are to be answered. Then the person falls down upon his knees in the water, places both his opened hands before his mouth, with the ends of his fingers turned towards his nose, so as to keep his nostrils closed, and the same with his mouth. The Minister then lays his right hand crosswise over the other's hands and presses them closely together, holding his left hand behind his neck, and thus plunges the person under the water. When the person who is to be baptized makes resistance during the performance of the rite, force and strength are employed for its completion. Without dipping them under the water, there can be no baptism. Is it not so?"

I answered, "I have nothing against your amount of water, but cannot understand why you will not allow of less water. When our Saviour, in St. John iii, speaks about what belongs to a true baptism, He says, *water and the Holy Ghost;* but not that it should be a whole river, more or less." "Nay," said he, "that cannot be sufficient, for the person must be submerged.

When Christ sent out His Apostles, He commanded them to baptize, which word cannot receive its significance in a small cup of water."

I referred to the English Baptists; how the Minister takes the person who is to be baptized, with one hand back in his collar, and the other in his waistband from behind, and so hurls him backwards, that his head is dipped into the water, and his feet turned up into the air, which must thus require the strength of two men in the Minister. On the other hand, the German Anabaptists, who are called Mennonists, conduct the person to the water, and there with their hands pour the water three times over his head. You of Ephrata, again, have your peculiar manner, which was never heard of nor seen before your time. You all profess to be Baptists, appeal to the first institution, and despise others. Which class of you all has now found the right way? He answered, "I believe we have." I said, "I will believe the same, but not before it is proved."

Behind the second entry in the Ephrata Register, which records the death, in 1728, of Peter Beller's daughter, there is a curious and moving story. Beissel was summoned from his nocturnal intercessions to baptize this young woman, who was near her end. He wished to administer the sacrament in the only way that was indubitably valid according to the Dunker theology, namely, in running water. This her parents properly forbade, and a tub was substituted for a stream. The girl's dying request was that Beissel conduct a service at her house the next Saturday. The service was held, but she attended it as a corpse. Her parents were so touched at her faith that they submitted to baptism.

The *Chronicon* contains an apology for rebaptism, which was so common at Ephrata that most of Beissel's followers were baptized four times or even more frequently. Twenty-four members of the Brotherhood of Zion, for example, were rebaptized after the evil Prior's departure. Nobody was compelled to submit to a second baptism, but, as no explicit prohibition of the practice was found in the New Testament and it was believed that Christian baptism had been administered in the days of the Apostles to many who had been previously baptized by St. John Baptist, the brethren who favored this method of marking decisive changes in their lives were confident that they had the support of Holy Writ. In this, the present writer holds, they were mistaken, but they undoubtedly had the support of some Anabaptist groups and were therefore neither so daring nor so original as they liked to imagine.

From 1738 until after Beissel's death there are instances of the baptism of the living for the benefit of the dead. Persons who desired a warrant for rendering this service to the departed could quote I Corinthians 15:29: "Otherwise, what do people mean by having themselves baptized on behalf of their dead?" It should be remarked, in passing, that there are indications of intercession for the dead. The register of deaths contains the names of some persons who did not belong to the congregation, and the most satisfactory explanation of the presence of these names is that relatives or others requested their inclusion in order that the departed might benefit by the prayers of the congregation.

There was no distinct sacrament of confirmation. The gifts of the Holy Spirit were bestowed through revivals and other spiritual exercises rather than in any sacramental act.

In some of the buildings erected at Ephrata provision was made for the *agape* or love feast. The purpose of this meal was to promote charity. The Ephrathites borrowed it from the original Dunker group. In 1738 Sauer attended a love feast at which almost one hundred and fifty guests were present. It did not end until midnight. A love feast given in honor of some important event was perhaps a lavish affair, but in 1753 the meal tempted nobody to gluttony. Acrelius describes it in the following words:

Sometimes the brethren and sisters come together, when they invite each other to their *love-feasts*, which, however, are celebrated in a very sparing style. If either party wish to hold a love-feast, it must be first notified to Father Friedsam, who grants permission thereto. If any of the brethren out in the country wish to hold this, he lets Father Friedsam know that his house can hold all the brethren and all the sisters, who are invited at the same time through Father Friedsam. If he informs them that his house can hold only a portion of them, then he has permission both to invite and to select his guests. If any love-feast is made within the convent, the brothers invite any sisters, or the sisters invite any brothers, at their pleasure. Sometimes the invitations are so secret that the others know nothing about it until the meal is prepared.

When Acrelius inspected the church of the Zionitic Brotherhood, he saw an altar. He inquired about its use and soon found himself involved in an intricate discussion.

We sat ourselves down to rest on a seat in the church, and I asked him whether the Lord's Supper was celebrated at the altar? He answered, "Yes, that is done by Father Friedsam, when one after another goes forward and receives the Sacrament in Bread and Wine; but this must be done on some evening, and with feet-washing afterwards." "That," answered I, "may be as proper as for the Lutherans in some places to use burning lights, although in the middle of the day. But," I asked, "cannot the Lord's Supper be celebrated at any time in the day, although it is not the evening?" Müller answered, "A supper cannot be held at mid-day; its time is in the evening." I replied, "That which regards time cannot be anything more than an external ceremony. We know that the disciples of Christ, almost immediately after His resurrection, most carefully considered almost every circumstance in the institution of the first Supper, such as to receive the Supper in a sitting posture, to sit reclining against each other, to celebrate the Supper in a house of entertainment, up one flight of stairs, and various other things. But after they understood that the service of the New Testament is not inseparably connected with any church usages, but that these are only to be regarded according to circumstances of convenience and propriety, then one external matter after another was omitted; and it is enough for us Christians to regard the Sacrament as it is in itself." Müller answered, "It is our duty as Christians to regard *the primitive state of the Church*, and not to make changes therein at our own caprice." I said, "*The spirit of the primitive Church* is sufficient for us; everything else that is external is less necessary, as also difficult to ascertain, and we now live in other times. How many Societies give themselves out as still retaining the usages of the primitive Church, which churches are, however, very different from each other?" He answered, "We can prove ourselves to have both the *spirit* and the *state of the primitive Church*. We keep our vows of chastity, we have all things in common among us, we observe the washing of feet, and other things." I said, "Each of these things were enough to talk about for half a day; but let us abide by the ceremonies of the Lord's Supper. If you will make any of those necessary which were in the first institution, why not all?" He answered, "It is enough to retain those which contain in them something that is symbolical, and which exhibits the value of the Lord's Supper." I said, "Take them all together, and the act thus becomes more symbolical. There is none of those just mentioned in which I cannot show something especially notable; yet I regard them all as indifferent. If, now, you will regard them as absolutely necessary, then show wherefore this and not the others?" Thereupon I perceived that the man was somewhat changed, and he answered, "The brethren live in the simplicity of their faith, and do not place a high value upon disputations. You must consider that we have lived here more than twenty years, and we must have learned something from our immediate intercourse with God during that time." "Well," said I, "if that is so, it is more than I know." From that hour I determined not to go any further into controversy than he himself occasioned and took pleasure in, so that I might not make myself a disagreeable guest.

In appending the maundy, or foot-washing, to the Lord's Supper, the Ephrathites again agreed with the First Day Dunkers. Like the *agape*, this practice is, of course, ultimately derived from the New Testament. Nevertheless, among the Seventh Day People it did not rest upon an independent study of Scripture, but had been adopted from the Germantown congregation.

Beissel, as a spiritual guide, received the confessions of many of his followers. The *lectiones* contain little, if anything, that is of a strictly personal and confidential nature. The Vorsteher did not feel an absolute obligation to observe the seal of the confessional. On one occasion he divulged a serious sin that had been confessed to him. The sacrament of penance, in the Catholic sense, was repudiated by all persons of Beissel's school.

Although the *Chronicon* records no instance of its use, the apostolic custom of anointing the sick with oil was probably practised at Ephrata. The Seventh Day Dunkers of our time affirm their belief in it in their official articles of faith.

The householders labored under manifold hindrances, of which parenthood and the ownership of property were perhaps the most distracting. Externally, nothing except the toil of the fields and shops impeded the religious in their pursuit of Wisdom, and even this necessary work need not have marred their recollection. In many respects the mode of life chosen by the monks and nuns resembled the Benedictine scheme, which mingled prayer and outward activity in such proportions that the latter reinforced the former. For the existence of a double community, each sex discharging the duties proper to its capacities and habits, there was sufficient justification in the long history of the monastic life.

Sound in many of its features, the attempt failed, and its failure can be explained without great difficulty. A mighty temptation to extravagance was implicit in the obscure theology of Jacob Böhme, and nobody at Ephrata had the discernment to perceive and guard against this peril. A sober, uniform, unruffled round of prayer and other employments that do not give rise to violent emotions is, of all types of life, the one most consonant with a monastic vocation. An atmosphere of emulation may well be fatal to it, and, if the religious resents his human limitations and refuses to take them into account, he suffers grievously. Böhme taught that Adam, in his original state, had not performed the grosser physical functions. Many aspired to a recovery of this supernatural life, and, as a means to that end, abstained from the flesh of animals and poisoned themselves by checking the natural action of their bowels. They conceived that a spiritual diet would be absorbed completely by the body, rendering the elimination of ordure unnecessary. They received nothing for their pains but severe constipation and the general lethargy that accompanies this condition. Another example of pious folly is the night watch, a vigil kept at first from midnight until four o'clock in the morning. There was no time for sleep between the end of the watch and the beginning of the day's work.

It would be incorrect to suppose that all the nonsense in the community emanated from the Vorsteher. He sometimes frowned upon the aberrations of unbridled zeal, but he never imposed a rule that would have preserved the religious from the extremes of asceticism and from the revulsion and recoil that are the punishment of unwise self-denial. Almost twenty years after he began to organize the monks, Beissel had still not given them a rule, or, if he had made a tentative effort in that direction, had abandoned it because of the resistance he encountered. Lacking both dogmatic formularies and precepts to govern their conduct, the brethren had no clear apprehension of their reasons for being together. Indeed, their motives were as diverse as their temperaments. The anarchy of their life made a profound impression on a keen observer. If we were not aware that, at the time under consideration, Ephrata was more than two decades old and the cenobitic life was already a venerable institution, we should infer from Acrelius' description that the solitary had been gathered in from their hermitages only a few months before.

Their rules, whether of the church, the household, or other usages, are as yet only oral, and are frequently changed, as seems to be demanded by edification. It is said that the brotherhood lives in the freedom of its conscience, and therefore without laws; and it is thought that some of the brethren do not yet know what the others believe. At first they regarded it as a sin to kill any animal, and still more so to eat flesh. Now they say that this is left to each one's freedom to eat it or not; but what liberty is there in eating what is not found in their storehouse? At first, also, it was regarded as a sin to use horses for working, and they themselves dragged home their own wood, and for this purpose put on themselves a suitable harness. Now they labor with horses and oxen, which, however, they treat very kindly. This, with other things, causes me to think that their work is still in its beginning, and stands, as it were, in a state of ferment as to whether anything shall come of it hereafter or not; also, that the freedom so much talked of is nothing but an encouragement to others to unite with them. I am sure that no one is regarded as a genuine brother in that house, unless he sleeps upon a hard bench in his usual clothes, however they may prate about their freedom.

Some importance must be attached to the relation between the settlement and the society that environed it. Each of the great religious orders of the Christian world was planned to meet an insistent contemporary need and is indebted for its initial growth to the success with which it met that need. Save for a few industries of limited value, Ephrata had nothing in its constitution that was nicely adapted to the necessities of the time. It could not draw upon large funds of public sympathy. Its contacts with the great world were accidental. It was one of the first of a long series of ideal communities that sprang up on the tolerant soil of North America. Both separately and collectively these communities have played a negligible part in the civilization of the continent.

The sisters lived under a rule, but among the brethren, after the disastrous collapse of the Eckerles' ill-advised scheme, rules that constrained the conscience were almost totally absent. Rules of a less authoritative sort existed in profusion. Bound with the published *lectiones* is a set of the latter type. Beissel reprinted his *Mystische Und sehr geheyme Sprueche* in the new collection, with a few unimportant verbal changes. The rules urge upon the religious the sedulous cultivation of such virtues as humility, detachment, and recollection. They show considerable knowledge of what the monastic life requires of those who follow it. The counsel they give is very sound, and it is a pity that they were so often disregarded. The religious is advised not to judge hastily, since people's motives are not always to be judged by their actions; not to be too certain of his sanctity, not to assume a false humility; not to inflict his spiritual sorrows upon others; to be courageous in sadness and to fear when things go well; when these emotions balance each other, to maintain that balance; to do only what contributes to his neighbor's salvation and to judge neither his neighbor nor himself. All this argues a deeper insight into the mysteries of the spiritual life than is evident in the actual practice of the religious. The regulations intended for guidance in prayer indicate that quietism was the prevailing type of spirituality. One quotation will suffice as an illustration:

When you pray, be free of images, and empty yourself of all created things. And when you pray, pray for nothing that you can reach with your thoughts; otherwise you pray to the creature and not to the Creator. If you want to pray properly, penetrate with your will beyond the world and time, and you will reach the divine magic in which everything at which our prayer aims is found. If you have reached God's will in your prayer, you are heard.

Sanctity and wisdom are the same thing, and the guerdon for which the devotee strives is an esoteric illumination. The following passage is a lucid and simple statement of this view: "If you want to find the way to wisdom occupy yourself simply with such things as you do not understand; and do not talk about the things you do not understand; and when you understand it, always regard the thing as being loftier than your comprehension of it."

The most admirable religious rule ever devised by ingenious piety would never fulfill the expectations of its contriver unless those who purposed to practise it obligated themselves to observe it until released by death or dispensed by a competent authority. The sacrifice of private rights takes the form of a vow or set of vows, voluntarily made, after due reflection and probation, at a ceremony known as profession. This public solemnity places the religious in a certain recognized state of life, which has its proper duties. The three traditional vows of Christian monachism bind those who take them to the practice of poverty, chastity, and obedience. The manner in which the vows are to be kept is prescribed by rule, but, whatever observances it may enjoin, the underlying obligation is the same in all religious orders. It preserves the religious from his own caprice. Without vows, he might be swept out of his monastery by any fleeting impulse. Even if he remained, he would frequently be the victim of his own self-regard, and imperceptibly, without the restraint of vows and the rules that are their commentaries, he would mold his own manners and habits and, so far as he possessed the capacity to do so, other people's, with such subtle self-seeking that ultimately they would pander to his appetites rather than mortify them. Those who are most at home in the involutions of this delicate and perilous mode of life are most conscious of this perpetual menace.

Vows were made and received at Ephrata. Dr. William M. Fahnestock, depicting the past of the community in a sketch written about 1835 for the bustling America of that day, may be pardoned for toning down certain beliefs and customs that, if delineated with strict truthfulness, would have excited the mirth or contempt of his fellow citizens; yet, when he trifles with truth so shamelessly as to deny that vows were ever taken, he invites reproof. In 1735 four sisters promised to lead a common life. The form of this promise is uncertain. Vows were first pronounced by the monks in the year 1738, and the sisters soon corporately followed their example. Whatever may have been true of the sisters, the brethren, before that time, were not under obligation to persevere in the religious state. The professions were recorded in writing, and both orders had their hair cropped close. Many people in the settlement viewed these proceedings with lively disfavor, regarding them as a revival of Popish abominations. At a later period a considerable number of former Roman Catholics had become members of the congregation. Even if they did not join the sect early enough to contribute to the formulation of the rules that governed the orders, it can scarcely be doubted that most of the people who lived at Ephrata in 1738 or at any other time were conversant with Roman Catholic customs. Nevertheless, the precise nature of the vows can hardly have been understood by all those who took them, and at least a few of these individualists must have taken them with secret reservations. The form of the vow has not been preserved, but probably the professed person bound himself only to lifelong chastity. Poverty, in the sense of an abolition of individual rights to property, was not introduced until 1740. After a long trial in its most rigorous form, the rule was relaxed, and thereafter, while the ownership of the buildings and equipment remained in the hands of the community, the individual's title to personal belongings was recognized. When the monastery was occupied, in 1738, obedience became necessary, but it is not certain that this duty was mentioned in the profession. There was no lucid explication of the force and extent of the vows and, in the absence of a rule to implement them, they were abandoned to the vagaries of private interpretation. This is much less true of the sisters than of the brethren, but neither of the two houses presented a pattern of religious deportment.

Whatever the content of the vows may have been, they were sometimes broken flagrantly, publicly, and to the shame of the community. A number of sisters fled when Beissel placed a superior over them, but they soon returned and acknowledged her authority. Under Prior Onesimus the Brotherhood of Zion amassed a weight of property that was incompatible with holy poverty. Far more serious than either of these breaches of obligation were the marriages of those who had promised to lead a life of virginity. A certain Peter Gehr contracted a union publicly with Sister Rebecca. It was a spiritual marriage, and Gehr vaunted his self-control. His wife repented and was readmitted to the convent. He released her and entered the monastery. Here he remained only a short time. He took his leave, changed his mind, and, after a second sojourn with the brethren, forsook the communion of the Seventh Day Dunkers and remained alienated from them until he lay dying some twenty years later. Smitten with contrition, he called for some of the brethren, and made his peace with them and Beissel. He was buried at Ephrata in the habit of the brotherhood.

Beissel sometimes appeared to give a tacit approval to such a match. Peter Weitner, a member of the brotherhood, grew weary of the monastic life and became enamoured of one of the sisters. He had the effrontery to seek Beissel's consent to their marriage and was astonished when Beissel gave it. The Vorsteher was present at the wedding, and a monk officiated. Beissel's simulated simplicity had the designed effect. Weitner conceived scruples and could not consummate the marriage. In sore distress of conscience he applied to Beissel for a dissolution of the bond. His request was granted with alacrity, but, in this instance, Beissel almost overreached himself. The two parties exchanged written articles of divorce, which were valid among the Seventh Day Dunkers, but not in a court of law. After a time the virgin, who had incurred no slight obloquy, resolved to enjoy the benefits of her sin and invoked the aid of the law. At the sight of the documents, the judges were so outraged that they were disposed to proceed against the monk who had prepared them, but, on further consideration, they concluded that he had acted as a clerk and not as a magistrate and, fortunately for Beissel, did not prosecute him. They did, however, compel Weitner to live with his wife.

The love affairs of Anna Thomin, who was known as Sister Tabea in the convent, illustrate not only the turpitude of human nature, but also the fluid state of society in colonial Pennsylvania. It was possible, in the course of a single life, for a woman to be a nun, the fiancée of an indentured servant who was also a monk, and finally the respected wife of a wealthy business man. Sister Tabea became a nun at a rather tender age, and her native ability and ardent temperament rendered the life in time exceedingly distasteful to her. When the sisters had, on one occasion, a difference with Beissel, she was their spokeswoman, and so well did she carry out her instructions that the Vorsteher was estranged from the sisterhood. The brethren had purchased a personable young immigrant, and, finding him well-bred, had admitted him to their order. Sister Tabea became engaged to him, to the disgust of the brethren, who were concerned more about their monetary loss than about the failure of the youth's vocation. At the wedding Beissel prevailed upon her to return to the convent, and she did penance so vigorously that she received the name of Anastasia in recognition of her resurrection. Visits to other congregations were at last her undoing. She became a stranger to her fellow sisters and, after Beissel's death, married John Wüster, merchant, of Philadelphia.

In fidelity to the duties of the monastic state, the sisters outshone the brethren, and their greater loyalty is reflected in the numbers reported at various times. At no time were there more than eighty religious. In 1740 there were thirty-five brethren and thirty-four sisters. A few weeks after Prior Onesimus left the settlement in the autumn of 1745, the count of the brethren was thirty-four. Immediately after this, for a time, both communities sustained losses. In 1753 the brethren could muster only twenty-five, but the accessions to the sisterhood had more than counterbalanced the deaths and desertions, and the convent now housed thirty-five or thirty-six sisters. In 1770, two years after Beissel's death, there were fourteen brethren and twenty-eight sisters. Beginning with a slight advantage, the brotherhood dwindled in thirty years to half the size of the sisterhood. However, in 1785, there were seven men and nine women. The contrast between the ages of those whose names occur at the beginning of the burial register of the women's community and the ages of those whose deaths are recorded at its close is arresting. Those who died at the start were in their twenties or thirties, or even younger. At the end there were only a few superannuated veterans, and the last obituary is dated 1813.

The final disparity, striking as it is in view of the initial equality, requires no far-fetched explanation. Beissel's power over men fell far short of his power over women. The brotherhood was within his jurisdiction, and he enjoyed the right of surveillance over it, but he was well advised to concede it a generous degree of autonomy at the outset, for in a position of direct command he might have found himself brazenly challenged by an infuriated subject. With the sisterhood his relations were much closer. He did not venture to establish it until a member of the congregation made him the guardian of his daughter. In his ward and the Eicher sisters, who had long since acknowledged his spiritual authority, he had the nucleus of a community, with the prospect of being able to control its development. The adulation of devout women was a balm to Beissel's harassed spirit, and nothing could induce him to forgo the solace of familiar converse with the sisters. His liberty of entry and exit was open to suspicion, and it cannot be gainsaid that his friendship with the virgins exceeded the bounds of propriety. He presided at their love feasts and, as the only male present, had a very good time.

The inborn religiosity of women makes them a willing prey to charlatans as well as the submissive followers of men who have a legitimate claim to the possession of supernatural gifts. Beissel's severe life was a clear token of his sincerity, and it is easy to understand why women of delicate sensibilities preferred his gentle rule to the brutality of an uncouth husband. In a newly founded colony women are usually in great demand, but this was less true in Pennsylvania than in many other places, and Ephrata may have been to some extent an asylum for superfluous females.

Beissel's indiscretion was a bad example to those who could not distinguish between innocent familiarity and lecherous looseness. The brethren and the sisters mingled with little restraint. The men were frequently absent from the monastery on errands of business or piety, and, when the Vorsteher made a missionary tour, inmates of the convent were sometimes in his retinue. Few restrictions were placed upon the sisters' commerce with outsiders. Strangers who expected to find them starchy and distant or demure and bashful were a little shocked at the freedom of their approach and the readiness with which they clasped even a male guest's hand in the sorority grip. This manner of life had a toughening effect upon a strong and incorruptible nature, and bred hardy monks and nuns. It did not favor the weak, but rather compelled them to engage in an unabating struggle with instinct, and thrust into their hands the means of compassing their own ruin. This reprehensible laxity indicates that Beissel was less virile than he wished to appear; if his own concupiscence had been sharper, he would have employed a greater wariness in his association with females and no doubt would have urged a similar caution upon others. Because of his reckless contempt for the opinion of the world, the two monastic societies had a foul reputation in certain quarters, and a traveler could write, "Ihre vorgemeldte Closter-Schwestern aber bringen öfters lebendige Früchten in Gedult."

One would have expected few lapses of people who dressed with strict modesty; but it is a common adage of the monastic life that the habit does not make the monk, and many examples of disastrous infirmity prove that desire can penetrate innumerable folds of sackcloth. We are beholden to Acrelius for a lucid description of the habit worn in the Kloster.

The dress of the brethren is a long, close coat, the skirts of which overlap each other, and are fastened with hooks quite down to the feet, with narrow sleeves, and the collar fitted close around the neck; also a girdle around the middle of the coat. When they wish to be well dressed, a habit is also worn over the close coat, like a chasuble in front, which is thrown over the head; but back of the head is a cape or hood to draw over the head in bad weather, and below this is a round cape which hangs down over the back. In summer-time the clothes are of linen or cotton, and entirely white; in the winter-time they are of white woollen cloth. On work-days they have coarse coats usually fastened around them by a leathern girdle. But upon their Sunday-clothes the girdles are either of embroidered woollen stuff or linen. Members of the congregation living in the country dress like those in the cloisters when they come to their church. However, they have clothes of various colors and of the usual fashion. Some have inserted in front on their hoods a piece of pasteboard, which serves as a guard to the capoch when it is drawn over the head. The brethren of the convent wear no shirts, but have their woollen coats next to their body. In summer-time they go barefooted; if they wear shoes, they are either of the usual sort with strings, or they are of wool above and a leather sole below. Some wear straw hats when they are travelling over the country; but most of them use their cape or hood as a hat or cap.

The sisters' dress was also a long, close coat; but we noticed that they all had linen girdles. The hood which they always had over their heads was sewed on to the coat. Their coats are also of linen or cotton stuff in summer; in winter of wool, without any linen next to their body. They also go barefooted in summer.

This dress makes them look quite thin, which their scanty food aids, as shall be described hereafter. Hence they are very quick and rapid in their movements, are not troubled by their narrow doors or their steep and narrow stairs. It seemed strange that they could go so thinly clad in the autumn.

Acrelius viewed the claustral dress as a curiosity. To the fond sight of the monks and nuns the mystical raiment in which they ate, slept, and performed their labors and devotions was the garb of affliction in this life and an emblem of the glory they were to inherit in the next. In the deliberations that led to its adoption they were guided, more than they were willing to confess, by their knowledge of the religious life in the Roman Catholic Church. The *Chronicon* abandons itself to a long disquisition on the apparel of the two orders. To translate the whole of it would be an imposition upon the reader's good nature, but he will probably not object to a word or two about the names that were used for the various articles of dress. Both sexes wore the "long, close coat," called the *Thalar*. The women attached an ordinary hood to it. The scapular extended to the feet in front and to the waist behind. When the nuns donned the scapular over the *Thalar* and pulled their hoods down to their foreheads, there was little for the profane eye to see. The men, who would have been impeded by the scapular, found it more convenient to wear the *Ueberwurf*, the "habit . . . like a chasuble in front," which had two parts: a *Schurtz* in front and a *Schleyer* in the rear. Hanging from the *Schleyer* at the neck was a cowl, pointed at the top (*eine oben zugespitzte Mönchs-Kappe*), which could be used as a covering for the head. A *Mantel* was worn at divine service, and to this—rather superfluously, it seems—a second *Kappe* was affixed.

Only after the effects of laxity had become disquietingly evident did the brethren require applicants for admission to their order to undergo a period of testing. The habit was assumed at the conclusion of the novitiate, which was of a year's duration. An earlier adoption of this rule would probably have excluded John Regnier. There are two accounts of his experiences as a brother. The *Chronicon* charges him with being an extremist, who advocated the substitution of acorns for bread and emulated Elijah and the Rechabites in refusing to live in a house. The Vorsteher was suspicious of him and cautioned the brethren against his singularities. They paid no attention to his admonitions at first, but were finally persuaded to relegate the eccentric Frenchman to a hermitage. When he became wholly unbalanced, they expelled him. He traveled for a time with another fanatic, and later made his way, hatless and shoeless, to Georgia. He became a Moravian, returned to Europe, and married. He worked as a missionary in St. Thomas, went to Bethlehem, and, oppressed by the weight of Moravian discipline, forsook the Unitas Fratrum and returned to Ephrata. He entered the monastery, but his wife soon asserted her rights, and, suffering another nervous breakdown, he took his leave again.

Regnier relates these adventures somewhat differently. He was converted not long after his arrival in Pennsylvania and, in the course of a search for some method of obtaining holiness, joined the hermits at Ephrata in 1734. He was told that a strict life and bodily self-denial would enable him to accomplish his purpose. The Eckerles (their rise to power and subsequent expulsion will be narrated in due time) proposed that he enter with them upon the practice of an austere asceticism, and described their discipline in detail. Regnier eagerly assented and was for beginning without delay. The Eckerles, however, postponed the commencement of the projected exercises from day to day, in the hope that Regnier's enthusiasm would evaporate. Meanwhile he was not put under probation, but was given the rank of a brother, since he seemed to have attained the requisite degree of humility. He could, if he had wished, have been admitted to communion before baptism. At length, despairing of the promised aid, Regnier asked merely for assistance in the erection of a hermitage, where he might make the experiment himself. Notwithstanding the assurances they had given him that they would lend him a hand in building a cabin, the Eckerles were reluctant. Regnier, annoyed, asked them candidly whether they still believed in their own principles. They replied that ideally the principles were admirable, but it had been proved by experience that human nature was too frail to support them. After much discussion, Regnier's request was granted, and he began the struggle for sanctity alone. He applied himself so diligently to the task that he lost his wits. The brethren removed him from his hermitage, tore it down, and locked him up. For a time they tried to restore him to his senses with harsh treatment and then, finding brutality of no avail, gave him more freedom—with better results, for at last he recovered. On July 15, 1735, he took his departure.

Regnier's confessions are so frank that there is no reason to doubt the substantial truth of his story, which is helpful to the historian of Ephrata because it reveals the sentiments that prevailed at a critical time. The hermits had found their life unsatisfactory, and the excesses of such unstable recruits as Regnier probably helped to convince them that the time had come to exchange their private penances for the less spectacular but more salutary discipline of a common life.

What constituted the daily routine, when the rampant wilfulness and self-determination of earlier days had been brought under the yoke of obedience? The lack of an elaborate sacramental practice and regulated corporate prayer was most glaringly evident in the common round of the conventual life. Roman Catholic religious have their masses and their canonical hours of prayer. These devotions occupy a large part of the day, and the interval between one service and another can readily be filled with any of a number of exercises. At Ephrata celebrations of the Lord's Supper were infrequent, and love feasts were held, not according to rule, but whenever an individual or a group felt an urge to issue a batch of invitations. We have only very meager information about the devotional life of the brethren. The night watch appears to have been the only regular daily service. In 1745, not long after they found shelter in Kedar, the brethren made it their practice to assemble for a formal service in the morning and in the evening. It is impossible to determine whether they were renewing an old custom or adopting a new one. The single common meal of the day was served between six and seven in the evening. The remainder of the day was devoted to work and to such private prayer as the necessities of work permitted.

The menu of one of the suppers has been preserved. Besides bread, there were only three dishes: a mess consisting of barley boiled in milk and pieces of bread, pumpkin mush, and cheese curds. There was a strong sentiment against the use of meat, but the members of the community, except perhaps during the time when the ascetic impulse raged uncurbed, were not required to abstain from it. Upon taking their seats, the brethren were silent for a few minutes. One of their number then read from the Bible. A second period of silence followed. At length the brethren brought out their knives and wooden spoons, which they carried in bags in their pockets. When they had eaten their fill, they licked their utensils, dried them, and replaced them in the bags. Nobody uttered a syllable. The meal concluded with a second reading from Scripture.

We are more fully informed concerning the sisters' timetable. Like the rest of the community, they followed the Jews in beginning the day at sunset. There were twelve hours from sunset to sunrise and twelve more from sunrise to sunset, and they were numbered according to the Roman method. Supper was served at six. It was the only substantial meal. Breakfast and luncheon were permitted merely because of the weakness of the flesh, and the exceptionally devout omitted them entirely. From seven until nine in the evening the nuns wrote, read, or practised singing. At nine they went to bed and remained there until midnight, when a two-hour night office (*Mette*) began. It consisted of psalms, hymns, and prayers. At the conclusion of this service the sisters returned to their cubicles, only to get up at five. They meditated for an hour and then worked until nine. They rested from their tasks for an hour, perhaps eating a frugal breakfast, resumed their work at ten, meditated from eleven to twelve, and at midday had the final meal of the day.

This sketch is drawn from a curious work known as *Die Rose*, which has been preserved in two manuscripts. No mention of the afternoon has been made. This omission indicates that the exercises of the day were not so clearly prescribed as those of the night. Evidently the hours from sunrise to sunset were not well organized, and *Die Rose*, in discussing the question, outlines a reform, which provides for several periods of devotion in the course of the day. It would be interesting to know exactly how the time allotted to spiritual refreshment was to be employed. It was intended for choir services, not for private mental prayer, but there is no hint of the form these services were to take. It is not recorded that the project was executed.

Applicants for admission to the sisterhood were obliged to submit to a novitiate of a year and a day. It was the custom not to profess them until they attained the age of eighteen and a half, but a girl of uncommon piety and maturity might become a professed sister at eighteen. Apostates were restored on relatively easy terms. They were required to make two distinct requests for readmission, with an interval of three months between them. Having established the sincerity of their repentance, they were subjected to a year's penance, at the termination of which their names were removed from the black list and they were reinstated.

The sisters were divided into seven classes, and most of the actual discipline was in the hands of seasoned members of the community, who acted as petty officers. There was a great deal of gadding about, and this pernicious vice, which frequently destroys a religious vocation, is prohibited in *Die Rose*. The scanty allowance of sleep was not compulsory, and, if a sister desired to advance her perfection by denying herself a part or the whole of the time appointed for rest, she was permitted to do so. When weariness at last drove her to repose, she settled herself, fully dressed, on a narrow bench. Some were content with no support for their heads. Others allowed themselves the indulgence of a small block of wood or a pillow in which chaff took the place of sinful goose feathers.

It is commonly, though erroneously, supposed that all monks are sluggards and that the cloister affords unlimited opportunities for the indulgence of sloth. Ephrata can easily be acquitted of such a charge; it harbored few drones. Refractory members of the brotherhood, if they seemed disinclined to quit the community entirely, were persuaded to live in hermitages where they could coddle their grievances without unsettling their fellows. Assignments to tasks were announced on Saturday evening, and in view of the multiplicity of employments, only the fastidious failed to find congenial labor.

The complex economy of Ephrata, for which it was indebted to the genius of Prior Onesimus, was one of the marvels of Pennsylvania. It provided a wide range of occupations, and the highly trained specialist could follow his calling within a stone's throw of the unskilled laborer in the fields. In 1753 the religious owned one hundred and thirty acres. Under Prior Onesimus the holdings of the community had been much greater, but a large part of this land had reverted to its original possessors, the householders. Besides the ordinary crops, there were apples and grapes. The brethren not only tilled the fields, but also gathered wood for the fires and cut timber for the buildings. A few were fortunate enough to be able to devote themselves mainly or entirely to intellectual labors. The literary output of the settlement was phenomenal, although nothing of general interest was written by any of its members. For the less gifted there was an abundance of useful jobs. The brethren toiled in the kitchen, at the washtub, the loom, and the last; plied the needle; did odd chores; and worked at the mills. A slender creek supplied water power for a group of mills: a flaxseed oil press, a fulling mill, and a sawmill. In 1747 occurred a serious fire, in which the community lost the flour mill, the fulling mill, and the oil press. Six years later the first and the last of these had been replaced.

Next to Christopher Sauer's establishment in Germantown, the Ephrata Press was the oldest German printery in the colony. Many people who desired to have works printed applied to the monks. The products of the press were almost exclusively religious. For the Mennonites, in addition to the Martyr Book, a book of instruction and devotion, entitled *Die Ernsthaffte Christen-Pflicht, Darinnen Schöne Geistreiche Gebetter* (1745) was printed. With this is bound some Mennonite martyr literature, translated from the Dutch by Theophilus (Alexander Mack, Jr.). The Gospel of Nicodemus was published in 1748. Bunyan's familiar masterpiece appeared under the title *Eines Christen Reise Nach der seeligen Ewigkeit* (1754). The ghost-ridden third wife of the peccant farmer, whose story will be told in these pages, wrote her own account of the affair, which was printed with the Society's approval in 1761. A work directed against the slave trade was printed in 1763. This list, while not complete, exhibits the general character of the books published by the brethren.

The most laborious commission executed at the Ephrata Press was the printing of the Mennonite Book of Martyrs. It involved a serious financial risk for the printers, since the Mennonites were under no obligation to buy the 1,300 copies. The price was about one pound. The project occupied fifteen brethren intermittently for three years. The work was translated from the Dutch, set up, and printed on paper manufactured in the settlement; and all these tasks were performed by monks. The undertaking was so arduous that it tried the brethren almost beyond endurance.

A monastery exists principally for the systematic worship of God. Such immunities as the religious enjoy are designed to give them leisure for their unremitting labor of adoration, and the entire plan is at bottom a scheme of prayer. The refreshment of the body and the tasks of library, shop, and field are regulated in such a way as to subordinate them to the primary purpose of the foundation and to make them contribute to the fulfillment of that purpose. Ideally this is true of active orders as well as contemplative.

The shortcomings of the religious life as it was practised by the Vorsteher and his disciples may be ascribed, as we have observed, to Beissel's unfortunate temperament and his want of experience and instruction. His failure is redeemed in part by a luxuriant growth of sacred song, which at times, to be sure, threatened to lose its fragrance and become a rank and pestilent weed. The hymns and psalm tunes of Ephrata possessed a vitality that its other artistic works lacked. Nobody now reads Conrad's crabbed prose for pleasure or edification; his sermons bored a vast number of his contemporaries; but the music he wrote for the monks and the nuns of Ephrata is still occasionally sung today, and a competent scholar is at present engaged in an exhaustive study of it. In this melodious labor Beissel was assisted by both orders, and the prolific devotion with which it was pursued is an indubitable token of a transparent sincerity and a profound consecration. Frustrated in other directions, the genius of Ephrata burst into a frenzy of musical creation. The inspiration was so fertile and so sustained that, in admiration of it, one overlooks the blemishes of the Seventh Day Dunker conventual life. People who rendered thanks and praise to God so strenuously cannot, for all their silly aberrations, have been wholly unaware of the true nature of the life they professed. Music was the tongue in which they uttered their aspirations most easily. It was the idiom of angels, a mode of expression not fettered by the diversities and misunderstandings of language.

Beissel displayed a fondness and aptitude for music in his youth, and music, in his mature years, alleviated the pangs of his disappointment. It was a recreation, a discipline, and a medium of expression. He sought refuge in it when other things had failed him, and was amazed and overjoyed to find himself in his element. At the start, his acquaintance with the art was sketchy, and his attainments in musical theory were never great, but he knew how to employ other people's talents and did not fail to perceive that one of his followers, Ludwig Blum, a trained musician, could serve him to advantage. A choir was formed among the religious, and Blum conducted rehearsals—at first to everybody's satisfaction. In time, however, the sisters resented their subjection to him and entered into a plot with Beissel. Blum was very shabbily treated. The sisters retained him until they had learned all that he could teach and had communicated it to Beissel, and, when the teacher had placed all his knowledge in their hands, they discarded him brutally. A condign chastisement soon fell upon Beissel. The sisters found their new master exacting beyond their expectations. The sessions of the school were of four hours' duration, and, when Beissel was vexed, he spent as much as half the period in upbraiding his unhappy pupils. There was so much discontent among them that the school was suspended for a time.

Choir practice might quickly have become a mere diversion, if Beissel had not dilated interminably on its spiritual and dietetic requirements. As he conducted it, it provided many opportunities for the mortification of the spirit. Beissel was not satisfied with this and did not confine his discipline to the actual time spent in rehearsal. When he dismissed the exhausted choristers, he did not relinquish his control of their lives, but prescribed for them a regimen that was calculated to keep their voices "subtle and thin." In the preface to the *Turtel-Taube* (1747) he discusses the conclusions at which he has arrived after a careful inquiry into this intricate question. The flesh of animals and animal products, such as milk, cheese, butter, and eggs, hinder the cultivation of an angelic voice. Honey clears the eyes, but not the voice. Beans are too filling and stimulate impure passions. Wheat, buckwheat, potatoes, and turnips preserve the virginal purity of the voice and are therefore recommended foods. When he submitted his work to the brethren, Beissel deleted a remark about the harmful effect of sexual intercourse upon the voice, but they decided to retain the passage. "This was only fair," observes the *Chronicon*, "for who does not know that sexual intercourse not only stains the soul, but also enfeebles the body and makes the voice harsh and rough, so that one must have very blunt senses not to be able to tell a virgin from a matron by their voices?" It adds that the voice throws a great deal of light upon man's fall. Almost all voices are too low, and that is why people's voices drop when they sing in church. Religious who are true to their vows improve their voices. For this reason a youth with a bass voice may become a tenor in his old age.

The singing at Ephrata was the expression of a theology and a vocation. Beissel insisted that the voices of his choristers should not misrepresent their characters. Behind the celestial sounds there was a celestial life. The meretricious beauties of a service sung, as services so often are nowadays, by professionals whose musical attainments are far in advance of their morals, would have been an abomination to the Vorsteher.

Two descriptions of the Ephrata music indicate how impressive it was even to those who were not attuned to it. The first occurs in a letter written by the Rev. Jacob Duché, a priest of the Church of England, who visited Ephrata in 1771. He says:

The music had little or no air or melody; but consisted of simple, long notes, combined in the richest harmony. The counter, treble, tenor and bass were all sung by women, with sweet, shrill and small voices; but with a truth and exactness in the time and intonation that was admirable. It is impossible to describe to your Lordship my feelings upon this occasion. The performers sat with their heads reclined, their countenances solemn and dejected, their faces pale and emaciated from their manner of living, their cloathing exceeding white and quite picturesque, and their music such as thrilled to the very soul.—I almost began to think myself in the world of spirits, and that the objects before me were ethereal. In short, the impression this scene made upon my mind continued strong for many days, and I believe, will never be wholly obliterated.

What Dr. Fahnestock says about the past of the Ephrata settlement must be received with suspicion, but he may be accepted as a competent witness to his own emotions. The following quotation confirms and amplifies Dr. Duché's generous appreciation of the music sung at Ephrata.

Music was much cultivated; Beissel was a first rate musician and composer. In composing sacred music he took his style from the music of nature, and the whole comprising several large volumes are founded on the tones of the Aeolian harp— the singing is the Aeolian harp harmonized. It is very peculiar in its style and concords, and in its execution. The tones issuing from the choir imitate very soft instrumental music; conveying a softness and devotion almost superhuman to the auditor. Their music is set in four, six, and eight parts. All the parts save the bass are lead and sung exclusively by females, the men being confined to the bass, which is set in two parts, the high and low bass—the latter resembling the deep tones of the organ, and the first, in combination with one of the female parts, is an excellent imitation of the concert horn. The whole is sung on the *falsetto* voice, the singers scarcely opening their mouths, or moving their lips, which throws the voice up to the ceiling, which is not high, and the tones, which seem to be more than human, at least so far from common church singing appear to be entering from above, and hovering over the heads of the assembly. Their singing so charmed the Commissioners who were sent to visit the society by the English Government, after the French war, that they requested a copy to be sent to the Royal family in England; which was cheerfully complied with . . . This music is lost, entirely now, at Ephrata—not the music books, but the style of singing: they never attempt it any more. It is, however, still preserved and finely executed, though in a faint degree, at *Snowhill*, near the Antietam creek,

in Franklin county, of this State; where there is a branch of
the society, and which is now the principal settlement of the
Seventh Day Baptists. They greatly outnumber the people at
Ephrata . . . and are growing rapidly. Their singing, which
is weak in comparison with the old Ephrata choir, and may
be likened to the performance of an overture by a musical
box, with its execution by a full orchestra in the opera house,
is so peculiar and affecting that when once heard, can never
be forgotten. I heard it once at Ephrata, in my very young
days, when several of the old choir were still living, and the
Antietam choir had met with them. And some years since I
sojourned in the neighborhood of Snowhill during the summer
season, where I had a fine opportunity of hearing it frequently
and judging of its excellence. On each returning Friday evening, the commencement of the Sabbath, I regularly mounted
my horse and rode to that place, a distance of three miles, and
lingered about the grove in front of the building, during the
evening exercises, charmed to enchantment. It was in my gay
days, when the fashion and ambition of the world possessed
my whole breast, but there was such a sublimity and devotion
in their music, that I repaired with the greatest punctuality to
this place, to drink in those mellifluous tones, which transported my spirit for the time, to regions of unalloyed bliss—
tones which I never before nor since heard on earth . . . During the week I longed for the return of that evening, and on
the succeeding morning was again irresistibly led to take the
same ride . . . to attend morning service, at which time I always entered the room, as there was then preaching; but as
often as I entered I became ashamed of myself, for scarcely
had these strains of celestial melody touched my ear, than I
was bathed in tears—unable to suppress them, they continued
to cover my face during the service; nor in spite of my mortification could I keep away. They were not tears of penitence,
for my heart was not subdued to the Lord, but tears of ecstatic
rapture, giving a foretaste of the joys of heaven.

If these supernal notes could overcome a casual visitor and
a tepid member of the secular congregation, those to whom
they were the daily affirmation of a cherished faith were en-
thralled by them and conceived an extravagant reverence for
their author. Each of the orders prepared a sumptuous music

book for presentation to the Vorsteher as a testimonial of its affection. The one given by the brethren (a manuscript copy of the *Turtel-Taube*) was later presented to Benjamin Franklin by Peter Miller and is now in the Library of Congress. One can imagine the thoughts of these scribes as they toiled hour after hour over their work of piety and friendship. They had vivid memories of the tempestuous periods of instruction: the austere master, his fickle, unmortified pupils, the unsparing reproofs, the resentful sulking, the plots, counterplots, and bickering. They had paid heavily for their knowledge of the heavenly art, but, now that they had attained proficiency in it, they permitted gratitude to drown the remnants of less charitable emotions.

Despite the warm admiration any just observer is compelled to feel for the piety and industry of the Seventh Day Dunker religious, it must be recognized that their scheme of life had grave faults. (1) It was dualistic and made too sharp and arbitrary a distinction between matter and spirit, equating the former with evil and the latter with good. It blocked the way to a sacramental interpretation of the world. Its purpose was not to redeem the world, but to rescue people from it. It had no encouraging gospel to deliver to the world, and the world naturally ignored it. It urged upon those who accepted it a spiritual struggle that took no account of the insuperable limitations of the human soul and body, and when this struggle ended in defeat, it knew no way to recovery. The struggle itself was unreal, because the world was an illusion. Besides, a belief in the ultimate salvation of all men was widely accepted at Ephrata, and such a doctrine tended to stultify all attempts to withstand evil. (2) It failed to crystallize devotion into acceptable social patterns, without which an institution cannot survive the exhaustion of the impulse that gave rise to it. From this it follows that it could have no permanent hold even upon the faithful. (3) It did not succeed in striking a practicable balance between work and prayer, and the quietistic element was too prominent in its conception of the interior life. It made prayer a blank, hoping to find God in the void, and was disconcerted to discover that He was not there. Life inflicts a savage punishment on those who will not submit to its conditions.

VII

A CONTEST OF WILLS

THE tempestuous cacophony of Beissel's life, complex at first glance and bewildering in its diversity, becomes startlingly simple when one discerns the *motif* that recurs from beginning to end. Beissel perpetually asserts himself, almost always in covert ways, hiding from its victims and even from himself his yearning for domination over a following that could please him only by an imbecilic submissiveness. For a long time this claim to servile obedience is not questioned, or else, if anybody has the audacity to oppose it, the Vorsteher swiftly and with obdurate finality repudiates the offender. An unswerving maintenance of this brutal obstinacy preserves his supremacy from violation until he discovers, among his intimates, an adversary who in the pertinacious pursuit of his own will equals his master and, in many other respects, outstrips him. This rival was Israel Eckerle—later the redoubtable Prior Onesimus—one of the four sons of Michael Eckerle, a councilman of the city of Strassburg, who became a member of the Dunker conventicle in Schwarzenau. He died respected by his co-religionists, and his widow emigrated to Pennsylvania in 1725, taking her sons with her. During the voyage Israel was very ill. Frightened at the hazards of the journey and confronted with the prospect of a new beginning in an alien country, he solemnly resolved to alter his manner of life for the better upon his arrival in Pennsylvania, if God would grant him recovery. He was soon up and about, but a certain adolescent vigor made him reluctant to carry out his part of the bargain. The family remained in Germantown for two years, Israel serving a term of indenture in a pious household. Michael Wohlfahrt paid his respects to Frau Eckerle, and his ministrations, reinforced by Conrad Matthäi's spiritual solicitude for the widow and her sons, were so effective that the young man conceived an intense desire to see the Baptists of the backwoods. Presently the widow collected her possessions and her sons and set out for Beissel's part of the country, where, at first, the family frequented the meetings of the Mennonites. Finding, however, like so many Christians of our own day who try to accustom themselves to an unfamiliar style of worship, that they "did not like the service," they began to contemplate the advantages of joining the Vorsteher's congregation. In reply to their questions, their neighbors communicated to them the scurrilous gossip that filled the countryside. Subsequently the Eckerle brothers entered the service of Christopher Sauer, who was then still living in Conestoga. Sauer's memorable combat with Beissel had not as yet occurred. The Eckerles accompanied their employer to a Dunker service, and in 1728 Israel was baptized.

Four years later Beissel retired to Ephrata, where Emanuel Eckerle (Elimelech) already had a hermitage. During the next two years the remaining Eckerle brothers followed Beissel to Ephrata, Samuel (Jephune) a few months after Beissel's resignation, and Israel (Onesimus) and Gabriel (Jotham) in 1734.

In 1738 Zion Hill was adorned with a monastery, and Nehemiah and Jaebez were made the joint superiors of this new foundation, but their authority was not cordially accepted, and Jotham improved the opportunity to gain the allegiance of the brethren. When Beissel, tired of the anarchy that had prevailed, named Onesimus prior in 1740 and gathered the rest of the hermits into the monastery, there was a strong degree of resistance to the new superior. The brethren at that period numbered thirty-five. Onesimus soon displayed an energy and an administrative talent that Beissel lacked. He instituted a stern discipline, grounded upon the entire subordination of every inmate of the monastery to himself. At the outset Beissel did nothing to check him, and it was not until the Prior had become a formidable competitor that the Vorsteher began to understand into what perils the community was drifting. The monastery seethed with disaffection, but Beissel's apparent approval smothered every rebellious impulse. The Prior was a paragon of zeal and diligence, and it was difficult for his ene-

mies to find concrete grievances. Besides, he enlisted the help
of useful auxiliaries. However bitter the differences that existed
within the Eckerle family, they invariably yielded to a strong
esprit de corps when an outsider threatened any of the four
brothers. This solidarity in time nonplussed Beissel. Through
the Mother Superior, Onesimus won the support of the sisters.
The Mother did not hesitate to strengthen her own position
by playing off the Vorsteher and the Prior against each other.
Notwithstanding the deference with which he continued to
treat Beissel, Onesimus was swiftly gathering the control of
the religious into his own hands. The spirit of insurrection subsided. A movement to unseat the Prior failed by a narrow mar-
gin when Beissel employed his influence to maintain Onesimus
in power. Michael Wohlfahrt died, and the malcontents lost a
staunch leader. Nothing could halt the Prior's progress.

Having consolidated his position, the superior of the brotherhood set about executing a very grandiose plan for the development of Ephrata. He had resolved to convert his agglomeration
of odd fellows into a self-sustaining community. Under his direction, the brethren toiled incessantly. Serenity and recollection vanished before an increasing preoccupation with trade
and gain. Novices were compelled to surrender their possessions
to the brotherhood, and the apostate departed from the monastery penniless. The versatile Prior turned his capable hand to
every conceivable enterprise: commercial, educational, philan-
thropic, and religious. He bought a mill and, supplied with
wagons, carted lumber to Zion Hill for an addition to the monastery. He planned a vault for the dead, stone bridges, a boys'
school, and a life of ease for the aged. He schemed to gain
possession of the land surrounding the monastery, and in all
likelihood the establishment of a third celibate order for married persons who deserted their farms and children and
adopted a communal life is to be attributed to his resourceful
intellect, for although these people finally returned to their
fields, the brotherhood no doubt enjoyed the use of the
abandoned acres while the farmers were in retirement. The

cupidity of these holy men became scandalous. They did not shrink from taking impecunious immigrants into their service, under articles of indenture. Beissel, recalling his visit to the Labadists years before, shook his head lugubriously, but still did not interfere.

Onesimus was not only a brisk business man, but also a pompous ecclesiastic, delighting in the pontifical vestments with which he glorified his person and prolonging the services, in which he was the chief figure, until his auditors were ready to scream with weariness. Two of the brethren were designated to copy his sermons, and, when his energy failed and he felt too tired to exhort the meeting, one of his incoherent and interminable effusions was read as a surrogate for the prophetic voice itself. For nine months Onesimus displaced Beissel as pastor of the community. He occupied the Vorsteher's quarters, and seemed to have usurped his position, arrogating to himself the dignity and the prerogatives that belonged by right to Beissel as founder and patriarch.

The Prior had long since reduced all effective opposition, but a smoldering ill will continued to exist among some of the brethren, and the eclipsed Vorsteher excited a generous measure of pity among those who had known him in the heyday of his authority. The deadly combat between Beissel and his disciple was waged behind a front of charity, which was not altogether insincere. Nevertheless, the affection they cherished towards each other was not without an admixture of malice and ambition, and both of them knew that a rupture would occur eventually.

In order to ease the strain of their relations, the Prior with three brothers took his leave of the Vorsteher and spent the fall of 1744 in a visitation, in the course of which he and his companions had many adventures. After tarrying for a time at Amwell, they traveled to Barnegat, where some of John Rogers' followers had settled. These people were not far removed from the Seventh Day folk in doctrine, and the two communities had been in touch with each other for some time. Pressed to extend their peregrinations to Connecticut, where other members of Rogers' sect were to be found, the four brethren sailed to Black Point, seven miles from New London. Among the Rogerenes of Connecticut they were obliged to engage in the usual inconclusive discussions of abstruse theological mysteries. At New London they were the guests of Ebenezer Boles, a prosperous Rogerene. Their hosts paid the expenses of the return journey, provisioned them, and saw them off, perhaps with a certain relief, for the habit of the brotherhood had attracted much curious attention and excited some mistrust. On the way home the four wanderers would have been detained in New York by the authorities but for the good offices of a justice of the peace. At last they reached Ephrata and resumed their occupations.

Beissel and Onesimus had hoped that the latter's absence would work a miraculous change and break the deadlock that, viewed in its purely human aspects, appeared likely to end in irreparable mischief. The Prior, recognizing the impasse, concluded that a pacific adjustment was impossible, and made up his mind to oust Beissel without pity. The Vorsteher, under pressure, relinquished the residue of his authority, and the Prior, by way of emphasizing Beissel's degradation, capriciously forced him to move five times in six months. This vindictive attempt to exhaust Beissel's patience by means of trivial irritations would have issued in the Vorsteher's complete subjugation, if the Prior had not overshot his mark.

Beissel, on the verge of ruin, now made a desperate and astute effort to recover his preëminence. Ordinarily he met such a difficulty by indulging in a tantrum, but, despite the ineptitude he had shown thus far in his duel with Onesimus, he was driven in the extremity of his danger to use a cunning to which he rarely stooped. The Prior had taxed the endurance of the brethren to the limit. Many of them were touched with commiseration for Beissel in his disgrace. The deposed Vorsteher had merely to manipulate this sentiment in order to gain his end. He recaptured the loyalty of Jaebez and Jotham and after that needed only to wait passively until the revolt they fomented against the Prior had become potent enough to compass his antagonist's downfall.

For three weeks the community was in a turmoil. The repressed vexation and envy of years burst into a consuming blaze. The Prior moved feverishly about, hurling vituperative thunderbolts at the heads of those who were now bold enough to assert their attachment to Beissel. Consternation and panic seized him when it became plain that most of the brethren had been galled by his yoke and were avidly embracing this opportunity to rid themselves of the despot forever. He purloined forty pounds of the brethren's money and endeavored with its aid to induce the Mother to plead his cause with Beissel. The Mother's purchased advocacy had no effect upon Beissel, nor did he budge an inch when a brother tried to procure a reconciliation. He was at last conscious of the full extent of his peril. He was certain that the Prior had entertained designs upon his life. It would be a grave disservice to himself to let such a foe escape with a light penalty, and Beissel had resolved to mete out to him the harshest castigation in his power. A conclave was held, and Onesimus was banished to the fulling mill, where, according to the sentence imposed upon him, he was to console himself with the reflection that, when the brotherhood had been reconstituted in conformity with Beissel's wishes, he would be permitted to reënter, as a plain brother, the house over which he had formerly ruled, or, if this did not suit him, to live in solitude. Onesimus accepted this humiliation, but as he pondered its implications, it became clear to him that he could not brook the effacement of every token of his influence and the liquidation of his thriving enterprises. His brother Jephune and a certain Brother Timotheus supported him in his defeat, and with these two as his fellows he quitted the community on September 4, 1745, for the raw life of the frontier.

It was characteristic of the Eckerles that they learned only by the merciless bludgeonings of experience. Congenitally unable to contemplate the sad examples of others with profit, they persisted in their infatuated efforts to impose unacceptable plans and insupportable discipline upon the brethren. Jotham had remained behind. Unmindful of his brother's ruin, he behaved much as Onesimus had done and within a few months suffered the same ignominious dismissal. Like Onesimus, he haughtily declined to submit to the punishment inflicted by his outraged victims. Jephune made the long journey to Ephrata during the winter and led him off to the New River (Great Kanawha, W. Va.), where the Eckerles had established a rallying point for those who remained faithful to them in their disgrace.

No longer manacled by the inhibitions and sanctities of Ephrata, the Eckerles, while building up a dissident Seventh Day congregation, indulged their own preferences in their selection of a means of earning a living. Onesimus, like a discomfited general, wrote reams of apology and invective. Jephune became a quack physician, probably as well qualified to practise as most of his confrères in the dubious profession of frontier physic. There is no record of his performance; it may be conjectured that he sometimes, by chance, alleviated, but more frequently aggravated, the ailments of the pioneers. Jotham, smarting under the memory of his expulsion, forced a precarious satisfaction from the most lucrative calling in the economy of the border and, attired in the rough clothes of a trapper, trafficked in pelts. Timotheus and Ephraim had forsaken the brotherhood to cast in their lot with the Eckerles, and so grievous was the disruption consequent upon their defeat that for a time Beissel seemed permanently crippled. The merchants who had done business with the Prior were nettled at the collapse of the industries at Ephrata. The Eckerles commanded considerable sympathy among the Baptists of Germantown, and not a few of the brethren who had chafed under their rule on Zion Hill sided with them. Many of the solitary renounced the religious life, among them several of the sisters. These malcontents drifted towards Mahanaim, the village founded by the

Eckerles on the New River. Beissel did not stoop to parley with these restive souls, and in refraining from the application of pressure he showed good sense. Better ten adoring devotees than a hundred who claimed a voice in the management of communal affairs. If this stream of defections had not failed at last, Beissel's spiritual enterprise would have disintegrated irreparably. Sauer, glad of an opportunity to deliver a vigorous thrust, announced in his paper that all gifts made to Ephrata would be returned. Liquidation appeared imminent.

Beissel's resolute purgation of the brotherhood and the confessed inability of the renegades at Mahanaim to cope with the heterogeneous crowd that flocked to them combined to arrest the flow of Seventh Day people westward. In order to cleanse the religious of every trace of corruption, Beissel ordered a rebaptism. After a year and a half of servitude to the Prior, Beissel resumed his post of director and despot of the community. The brethren abandoned the Monastery on Zion Hill. The enormities of the Eckerles had polluted it, and some of the monks had an uneasy feeling that their former masters would still control them if they continued to inhabit it. Once more a building was erected as a monument to a change of sentiment. Ironically, the materials accumulated by the Eckerles for an addition to Zion were used for the new monastery, to which the brethren gave the name "Bethania." It remained standing until 1910 (or sometime during the next two years, since nobody remembers a definite date). The old monastery on Zion Hill was surrendered to the poor. The labor of building a new and undefiled home for themselves exhausted the energies of the brotherhood, but nothing could quench the spirit of mutiny, and the superiors who essayed to govern the contentious monks during the years immediately following the Eckerles' departure found little delight in their dignity. Jethro, installed as Jotham's successor, had to surrender his office, after four months, to Jaebez. Jaebez in less than half a year was so close to a nervous breakdown that he felt constrained to resign. With unmortified eagerness Jethro obtained a second term of office, which ended some three years later in his reduction to the status of an ordinary brother—so sore a blow to him that he wasted away and expired. The vacant post was given to Eleazar, a seasoned monk and therefore not likely to be a martinet.

While these things were happening in Ephrata, there were hectic times at Mahanaim. Timotheus and Ephraim abandoned Onesimus, neither, however, returning to Ephrata. Jotham fell a prey to homesickness, and both he and Jephune felt a measure of contrition when they recalled their obligations to Beissel. They would have capitulated but for Onesimus' bitter refusal to concede a single point. He coddled his resentment and shame, nursing a deep sense of injury and longing to be invited back to Ephrata on his own conditions. If he seriously expected to be reinstated in his forfeited dignity, he was to be disappointed, but the brethren, when the menace of his tyranny was removed and time had begun to obliterate the memory of their agony, were mollified and gradually lost their vehement detestation of the discredited oppressor. After an absence of five years, he ventured to present himself at Ephrata, accompanied by his brother Jotham. His instability during the next few months indicates either that he was undecided as to the most expedient course to follow or that he had come merely to reconnoitre the ground. He was amicably received and the usual conferences, professions, and tergiversations ensued. Beissel treated him with simulated candor, and the brethren were not hostile. Onesimus and Jotham, unprepared for this mild reception, were overcome and averred their willingness to embrace the religious life again and cast all their wealth into the common stock. Under the stress of excitement this declaration was sincere enough, but Onesimus was rash and volatile, and his designs were to be altered from day to day. The sanctimonious pity with which he had been greeted was a little too nauseating. The two brothers left soon to renew old friendships, and in order to disarm mistrust they took a member of Beissel's faction with them as an escort. Hoping to ingratiate himself with the Baptists of Germantown, Onesimus paid his respects to

Peter Becker and a certain Gantz, who was Beissel's implacable foe. When they had finished their round of calls, Onesimus and Jotham appeared once more at the settlement. It is recorded, to Onesimus' credit, that he returned the forty pounds he had embezzled. It is impossible to determine the precise nature of this generosity; perhaps it was merely a conciliatory gesture, perhaps it was an act of reparation. At any rate, the apostates did not linger at Ephrata. Two months after their first arrival, they were on the way back to Mahanaim. Beissel showed them a parting courtesy and detailed two of the brethren to render them such aid as they could.

His more practical brothers failed to effect an expeditious settlement of the business that had served Onesimus as an excuse for revisiting the scene of his former grandeur. Inept in commercial negotiations and bored with idleness, he traveled back to Ephrata to explore the situation once more and gauge his prospect of success in an attempt to overthrow Beissel. The Vorsteher was so sure of his own ground that he placed no restrictions upon Onesimus, but the brethren would admit him only as a simple religious. Soon the garrulous visionary offended the brotherhood by delivering soporific sermons of unendurable length. He was ordered to desist and, deeply wounded, withdrew to private quarters. Beissel assumed a posture of imperturbable charity and baited Onesimus with condescending friendliness. If the Eckerles had invaded Ephrata in force, they might have tipped the scales in their favor. Onesimus had committed a blunder in returning without the backing of his adherents. Beissel had altered the tone of life at Ephrata, and Onesimus' influence was dead. There was no solace for him in the company of the brethren, who exulted in his impotence. There were moments when he could no longer abide his rage and chagrin, and at such times he vanished from his hut and trudged from one farmhouse to another, recounting splenetically the injustices he had suffered. Finally he discarded the habit of the brotherhood and sought shelter with a farmer in the vicinity. He had a rendezvous at Ephrata with his brothers and, fearing that they would steal a march upon him or make terms with the brethren if he did not intercept them, he stationed himself on the road and waited for them all day. In the dead of night Jephune reached Ephrata and learned of his brother's departure. At length Onesimus joined his brothers on the highway, told his tale, and dissuaded them from resuming the religious life.

The Eckerles had doubtless come freighted with a rich load of furs. These they bartered for supplies and articles that could be used in the Indian trade, and, having accomplished one of the purposes of their journey, they turned again towards the West, just as winter was beginning. They traversed the mountains with difficulty and repaired to a place not far from Fort Duquesne. They concluded an agreement with the Delaware Indians. It is possible that Onesimus tried to find distraction in evangelistic work with the Indians. If so, even though his apostolic enterprise reflects unfavorably upon Beissel, he cannot have made great headway, for Dunkerism of the Ephrata brand was too distinctly Pietistic to be marketed easily among the redskins. Whether or not a missionary urge animated him, Onesimus was engrossed, largely to the exclusion of other concerns, in his deadly hatred for Beissel and the machinations it inspired.

At the outbreak of the French and Indian War, the Delawares were obliged to admit that they could not be responsible for the Eckerles' security. Conducted by the Indians to a remote spot in the mountains, on the Cheat River, the brothers enjoyed a rude luxury in their new asylum. They were not wholly isolated, and Onesimus continued his correspondence with the Seventh Day Baptists in the East. He dispatched a vilifying letter to Ephrata. Five hours were consumed in the public reading of this communication. Jephune, probably on one of his business trips, had the effrontery to ask leave, at a service, to read a second letter. There were fifty sheets of it, but the congregation consented to listen. However, the opening sentences revealed the character of the missive, and Jephune was commanded to stop. He found a less inimical audience in Germantown.

During these years the shattered Prior subsisted on hope, and his hope was not entirely illusory. Disgruntled brothers renounced the regimented life of Ephrata, and two of them, Heinrich Sangmeister and Anthony Höllenthal, after an unsuccessful experiment in the anchorite's mode of life on the Shenandoah River in Virginia, threw in their lot with the Eckerles. Sangmeister, surpassing Jephune in brazen discourtesy, suggested that the Ephrata Press print one of Onesimus' diatribes, but the printer, properly loth to assist in the dissemination of a polemic that maligned Beissel, rejected the proposal tartly. Apart from the slender comfort and promise that such defections gave, the Eckerles had little encouragement. To be sure, they enjoyed a primitive abundance in their retreat, but there were ominous indications that their situation was becoming very dangerous. A party of Indians despoiled them of their clothing and rugs. The Delawares sent them a message informing them of the peril they ran in deferring their retirement to a more protected area. The settlers in Virginia suspected them of espionage. Onesimus was once imprisoned because he had laid himself open to the accusation of being implicated in the Indian raids. These incursions, by an embarrassing coincidence, commonly occurred within a short time of the trips the Eckerles made to Virginia, ostensibly for purposes of business. Far too often, when the trio had visited the settlements, an Indian foray followed hard upon their departure. Such regularity seemed scarcely fortuitous, and the colonists conjectured that these recurrent events were related. They pressed for the eviction of the Eckerles. Samuel Eckerle appealed to the governor in vain. The governor directed a military escort to accompany him to the trading post and remove the brothers and their belongings to a less exposed district. A small band of Mohawks, led by a Frenchman, surprised the little cluster of log cabins a few hours before the detachment reached its destination.

Onesimus, with mad tranquillity, remained seated at his writing table until the enemy captured him and tied his hands behind his back.

Onesimus and Jotham were dragged to Fort Duquesne and sold to the French. Their masters conducted them over the frozen lakes to Canada. At Montreal they were quartered in the Jesuit College. At long last they found themselves in a society that accepted monks and nuns as sane human beings and gave them the confidence they merited. Their captivity was not wholly a trial, for their sympathetic surroundings consoled them. In Quebec they almost starved, but the pious French Canadians, venerating their religious profession and ignoring their heresy, allowed them to solicit alms in the streets. Discovering that they could not be exchanged at once, the two brothers joined a batch of prisoners bound for France. The voyage was fatal to both of them. The long weeks in the fetid hold of the ship were unspeakable. Before they landed they contracted the malady that brought their restless lives to an end. They perished prematurely, in a foreign country, with many varieties of the religious life about them. Before his death, Onesimus entered a Roman Catholic order. It would have been better for a considerable number of persons, not excluding himself, if the Indians had captured him twenty-five years earlier.

Thus the lamentable story reaches its conclusion, and a few observations will now close this chapter. With the Prior we are not primarily concerned, and we cannot spare the time for an analysis of his career with a view to determining the motives of his bizarre antics; yet, since he serves as a foil to Beissel, we cannot dismiss him without trying, briefly, to do him justice. It must be allowed that he possessed uncommon parts. Perverse and grotesque as much of his conduct was, he had a genuine vocation to the life of virginity, which he might have realized in the broad impersonality of a great religious order. An ancient tradition, solemn offices, gorgeous high masses, and the expert guidance of competent superiors would have curbed and redeemed his excess of vitality, his genius for administration, and his talent for drama, as well as the other endowments that went so awry in the addled air of the Kloster. The true meaning of his character cannot be seen until he is contrasted with Beissel.

Judged by the ordinary standards of mankind, the Vorsteher stands far below his mightiest disciple. Onesimus overshadowed and outsmarted him, but he never wrested from him the prestige that belonged to Beissel alone. Even in the deepest adversity, the founder remained, notwithstanding appearances to the contrary, the spiritual head of the community. He possessed a unique authority, which nobody could inherit and nobody could successfully dispute. Usually, in religious societies, the founder and the organizer are not contemporaries. The founder erects the superstructure, which is often, from an economic point of view, exceedingly flimsy, though spiritually superb. He is succeeded by the practical genius who solves the problems of dollars and cents and bread and butter. At Ephrata, the two leaders flourished at the same time. Their conjunction wrecked the community. Beissel could never have made Ephrata pay, and it had to pay or perish. He financed the enterprise high-handedly by demanding donations of the housefathers. Such a system could not have endured indefinitely. Onesimus' efforts were directed towards an objective that in itself was legitimate and laudable. He tried to make the monastic community self-sustaining. His advent was premature. The force of Beissel's influence would have brought the foundation unscathed through the first generation of its life, despite his lax and almost unethical habits with regard to money. If, when Beissel died, Onesimus, instead of Peter Miller, had become the master of Ephrata, the Brotherhood of Zion and the Order of Virgins might still exist today.

VIII

"TO HIS LONG HOME"

The period of the Eckerles' ascendancy had terminated in their migration to the West, but they had left an indelible mark upon the settlement and upon Beissel. For a time the community was demoralized and unsettled. There were many who execrated Onesimus and all that he had accomplished; yet it would seem that, even when he was far away, the brethren still felt his oppressive power, which lingered, according to their notion, like a noxious gas. Everything that might preserve the memory of the fallen Prior and his iniquitous rule was abandoned, destroyed, or sold, and the last vestiges of his authority were banished by a sort of fumigation of the brethren's persons. In ridding themselves of his domineering presence they restored their former tranquillity, which had consisted almost wholly in the individual's exercise of an abundant measure of freedom, but the vexations of their common life did not vanish with their emancipation, and serious disadvantages attended it. Onesimus, for all his pompous gestures and ludicrous bombast, had a rare combination of talents. He alone had possessed sufficient penetration to become aware that the survival of Ephrata hung upon its success in producing goods for which the colony offered a market. His policy, soundly formulated, had been clumsily executed. His departure left the community with no policy at all.

Beissel now collected the shards of his broken authority and pieced them together. The tension of the years of conflict had altered him. For a year and a half he had been without status in the society. Worsted in many a combat with his former disciple, and ignominiously browbeaten, he found himself on the verge of old age. Defeat had cowed him, and he no longer had the aggressive energy of his prime. During the remainder of his life, an amiable but aimless timidity often manifested itself in circumstances that, at the peak of his vigor, would have provoked him to wrath and stimulated him to action. Yet his egotism survived, battered but not extinguished. He still had a keen sense of his own interest and was cunning enough to make some effort to safeguard his position. He did not fall a second time into the error of conferring too much authority on a subordinate. After his sore humiliation in the days of Onesimus' lordship, he entrusted the performance of sacerdotal ministrations to the superior of the brotherhood only when he had a good reason for doing so and was assured that the delegation of his functions did not threaten his security.

Occasionally he followed his inner leadings in defiance of all the warnings of reason. Philadelphia at that time harbored a charlatan named William Young, who duped him incredibly. Young was a rascal who had contrived to collect sizable sums of money for projects that existed only in his own fancy. He commanded an audacity that stunned his victim and left him so aghast at Young's brazen demands that he could not harden himself to reject them. The unctuous scoundrel employed this method with Beissel. About a year after Onesimus' deposition, Beissel received an amazing letter from Young. In this communication the wily rogue asked the community to lend him forty or fifty pounds, in order that, with this addition to the money he already possessed, he might establish his wife in a house and free himself to pursue his vocation at Ephrata. The petition was refused at first, but Beissel, snatching at an opportunity to gain a convert, drew upon his admirers' funds, and Young's bold request was granted. Beissel's correspondence with him brought about his baptism, which took place on February 28, 1747.

Young regarded himself as the local agent of the community. The recent convulsions at Ephrata had provided material for a great deal of malicious gossip, and it behooved the Sabbatarians to sink back into obscurity as quickly as possible. Young promptly opened a squabble with some sectarians in Germantown and obtained the approbation of the society for the diatribes he wrote. He prevailed upon half a dozen persons to

join Beissel's discredited band, and one of them, Henry Sangmeister, later wrote a damning account of his life in the community. Before many months had elapsed, Young required
thirty pounds, and appealed to his new brethren for succor.
Beissel yielded a second time and forfeited the confidence of
a number of his followers, who stopped contributing to the
common fund. The paper mill, however, made profits steadily,
and the Vorsteher enjoyed such veneration among those who
operated it that his inspiration was accepted and the money
was advanced. Young, instead of amortizing the debt on his
house, used the thirty pounds for the purchase of two penniless
immigrant shoemakers. Having spent the money for this purpose, he was still under the necessity of paying the sum that
was due on his house. The brethren were infuriated when he
had the impudence to apply to them a third time for relief,
but Beissel's enchantment remained unbroken.

Young was a slick sharper. His accomplishments outran his
integrity, and he soon mastered the cant jargon of the Kloster.
His assumption of authority became unbearable, for he took
the Beisselians to task when they visited Philadelphia without
informing him immediately of their presence. Early in the
summer of 1747 Beissel made a pilgrimage to the city with
twelve monks and nuns and conducted a love feast at Young's
house. The Vorsteher was in abject servitude to the hypocritical rogue, who improved the opportunity to furnish his
house at the expense of the community. Even in practical
matters Beissel submitted without protest to his judgment.
Throughout the journey, the demented leader taxed the
strength of his cadaverous subjects to the point of exhaustion,
and, if the devotion of the nuns had not triumphed over their
frailty, they would have been prostrated by the interminable
program of preachments, prayers, and professions of good will.
On the way home Beissel called on Conrad Matthäi, the only
remaining member of Kelpius' society. They were reconciled
after a long estrangement. The Vorsteher celebrated a love
feast among his English adherents at West Nantmill, where, by

dilating for hours upon the mysteries of human corruption and redemption, with the assistance of an interpreter, he wearied all those who had the hardihood to assist at the solemnity. The trip, which was much to Young's advantage, was not without benefit to the Seventh Day people. The appearance of the band of religious in Philadelphia excited a great deal of curiosity and reminded the public that the community was not extinct.

A year later Young was host again to a party from the settlement, and once more the community was forced to replenish his stock of household wares. His debts had reached the formidable total of two hundred pounds. His efforts to persuade the Brotherhood to assume his obligations were greeted with a clamor of indignation, but Beissel's inspirations could still on occasion move the community to folly, and the brethren borrowed the money from a business man in Philadelphia. Young gloated for the last time over the marvelous results of his knavery. The brethren were determined not to be importuned again by the insolvent trickster, and a deputation was dispatched to Philadelphia with instructions to disabuse him of any illusions he might entertain with regard to the possibility of further compliance with his outrageous requests. The brethren had a claim upon him for the debts they had incurred in his behalf. His retort to the assertion of this claim was the most remarkable piece of effrontery in his entire career. He sent them a bill for the damage he had suffered in his business by observing Saturday as the Sabbath. When it became evident that the brethren could no longer be mulcted, Young dissolved his connection with the society, but not until the community had released him from his obligations.

This is the most conspicuous, but not the only, instance of Beissel's gullibility, or, to use a word that some observers will prefer, perversity. The devices of the beggars and impostors with whom he had to deal must have been transparent to a man of Beissel's native canniness. It is probably true that he deliberately flouted common sense in allowing himself to be swindled by such people. His curious obstinacy caused serious discontent in the congregation.

About two years before the melancholy conclusion of Beissel's adventure with Young, Wisdom touched some of the English settlers in the neighborhood of French Creek and Brandywine and brought several families as well as half a dozen or more unmarried persons into the Seventh Day German Baptist community. Three of the latter group moved to Ephrata, but, finding the cramped life distasteful, did not remain. Beissel laid hands upon one of them, Israel Seymour, and appointed him to minister to his compatriots. He conducted services regularly under the vigilant scrutiny of the monks. After a short residence at Ephrata, Seymour made the response that so many before him had made to the outlandish manners of Sophia's suitors and the uncouth capriciousness of the Vorsteher. The brethren had learned how to alleviate the pangs of those who were in the grip of extreme nausea after excessive association with Beissel. They built Seymour a cabin in his own bailiwick, and he adopted the eremitic mode of life, with sensational results. The pious and the inquisitive thronged him, much as callers had flocked to Beissel's hermitage during his first years in Conestoga. A blooming damsel from the convent came to stay, pleading as her excuse an irresistible appetite for lessons in English. The cohabitation of these two votaries of Wisdom gave scandal to Seymour's congregation, and its members observed a diminution of his homiletical vigor, which they attributed to his loose life. At the end of a searching investigation, the Ephrathites informed him that two courses of action were open to him, and directed him to make a choice. He must marry his seductive housemate or seek safety at Ephrata. He answered by repudiating the girl, and she formally released him; but this renunciation, as the experienced surmised, was merely a prelude to their marriage, which was solemnized a few days later. It was a tempestuous match. Seymour's conscience smote him, and the brethren's generosity in providing a new house for the pair gave him no ease. Unwilling to blame himself, he ascribed his ruin to Beissel's invidious designs and charged the Vorsteher with putting temptation in his way. For a time he was beside himself with interior conflict, and when he recovered his wits he set out for South Carolina. He fought in an Indian war, underwent a second conversion, and redeemed his carnal weakness by becoming the pastor of a small congregation.

Conquests of this sort unfolded a vista of possibilities to Beissel, which he never explored because he lacked the resolution, imagination, and address to make a fruitful use of his gains. The inadequacy of his English hampered him. After almost thirty years in Pennsylvania, he did not venture to use it in a public utterance, but instead spoke German and availed himself of the services of an interpreter. If he experienced any impulse to enlarge his scanty attainments in the principal language of his second fatherland, it was checked by his indolence and pride more than by his want of capacity; and, above all, it was not the absence of qualified teachers that hindered him. Any of a number of persons might have been drafted as his tutor. From time to time neophytes of English blood and speech attempted to accommodate themselves to the round of life at Ephrata. In addition to Seymour and his companions there were Thomas Hardie, a man of unbalanced mind and, according to his own account, of illustrious antecedents, who spent six months with the brotherhood and afterwards, under its patronage, became a schoolmaster in the outlying districts of the inhabited land; an Irishwoman, who tarried at Ephrata for a short time; and others. The chaotic piety of the settlement rarely proved congenial to these strangers, and Beissel's stolid unwillingness to learn new habits or even to meet the demands of ordinary courtesy made it impossible for his community to assimilate them. One or more of them might have been made the means of extending his work to considerable numbers of settlers outside the relatively narrow and clannish circle of Germans. Beissel missed the opportunity, and his influence was restricted to a racial group that was soon to be outnumbered and in part absorbed, and even within these limits his doctrine commended itself to a pitiably tiny band.

Three matters remain to be considered as we follow Beissel through the dismal years of his dotage: the conversions that helped to offset the frequent desertions from the community; Beissel's commerce and combats with occult powers; and the excitement of the French and Indian War.

The Vorsteher's long arm spanned the ocean, and like other Pietistic exiles he remained in communication with his friends beyond the seas and was consoled by their replies to his verbose epistles. Among his correspondents was his brother, who was indebted to Beissel for his salvation. He lived in the Palatinate, at Gimsheim, where two townsmen, Kimmel and Lohman by name, were unexpectedly and vehemently assailed by the Spirit in the full enjoyment of their gaming and tippling. A revival occurred under their leadership, and the *Chronicon* intimates that it is to be traced to Beissel's diffuse exhortations, written in the abundance of his leisure and, often, in the depth of his disappointment, and posted with homesick emotion to their remote destination. Whether or not the movement, in its beginnings, is to be catalogued as one of the Vorsteher's achievements, it ultimately fell under his influence, and in this it was not untrue to itself, for early in its course it displayed tokens of its charismatic nature, and it is not rash to suppose that it was derived, like some of the most important ingredients of Beissel's own blend of faith, from the ecstatics of Cevennes, by circuitous channels. Those who yielded to the power of the movement withdrew from the established churches, the usual clandestine gatherings were held, the clergy inveighed against them, and at last the authorities took cognizance of the matter. An investigation took place, and many recanted. Eighteen remained unshaken by these proceedings, and the most prominent of them were fined. The Elector pardoned them but died too soon to enforce his order of restitution. The unfortunate sectarians fled to Herrnhaag and Gelnhausen and finally joined the stream of expatriates and took passage to Pennsylvania. The first contingent, which included several of Beissel's relatives, reached the colony in 1749. Two years later Kimmel and Lohman crossed the seas at the head of another party. Ultimately, if the language of the *Chronicon* is to be construed literally, all of Beissel's immediate kin made the long journey to Ephrata. Full of zeal, but destitute of resources, they were lodged, fed, and rescued from bondage by the devoted community. Not all of the newcomers, however, were beggars, and the hasty generosity of some, who offered to transfer their goods to the common store, had to be curbed. In numbers, the total gain to the settlement did not exceed a dozen or fifteen baptized persons, and the gain was not permanent. Kimmel pushed on to the stream known as the Bermudian (Warrington Township, York County, 15 miles from York and 102 miles from Philadelphia) and drew the married members of the Gimsheim group and others after him. The new settlement acquired a reputation for laxity, and Ephrathites of the more austere breed avoided it. When Kimmel's wife died, he accepted the monks' invitation to live as a widower in their monastery and persevered in this state until his death thirty years later.

Beisselianism, disseminated by evangelists of the skill of Lohman and Martin, followed the tide of migration south and west until the close of the colonial era, but it was so grotesquely at variance with the temper of the age, so unintegrated, and so mishandled by those who were charged with the publication of its teachings, that, before it was well launched upon its career, its advance was halted, and it scarcely crossed the limits of Pennsylvania. In the nineteenth century it was outstripped by its rival, the older form of Dunkerism, and even in Beissel's lifetime and at his very threshold, his sect encountered the most spirited competition. In the days of Beissel's arresting and alarming triumphs abroad, he suffered a severe loss at home. A schism occurred at Ephrata, and the dissident members formed a congregation of their own, to which Michael Frantz and, later, Michael Pffautz and others ministered, and which, at Beissel's death, roughly thirty-five years after the division, contained about fifty-three families and eighty-six baptized persons and was therefore slightly larger than the secular part of the settlement at Ephrata. This church cleansed itself of Beissel's polluting doctrines and was in communion with the Baptists of Germantown.

Henry Lohman was too brilliant to be endured in Beissel's vicinity, and the Vorsteher suggested that he settle at the Bermudian, hinting that their relations would improve if Lohman followed his advice. Lohman suspected that this apparently ingenuous candor was at bottom a stratagem of the Vorsteher's, but he soon received guidance that disposed him to fall in with Beissel's plan. The Vorsteher's wariness and the smart of his ancient hurts, to which he was not inclined to add fresh ones, prevented him from ordaining Lohman, but the latter prospered in the exercise of his ministry. The congregation at the Bermudian was organized in 1758 and Conrad's brother Peter was one of its charter members. However, the Baptists at the Bermudian had only a somewhat tenuous connection with Ephrata; some of them did not keep Saturday as the Sabbath, and Beissel's precepts and dictates were probably often disregarded.

George Adam Martin served this congregation until the end of Beissel's life, leaving it finally in Lohman's hands. Martin had been a First Day Dunker for almost three decades when, accompanied by John Horn, he met Beissel, was dazzled at the spectacle of his sanctity, found that his views coincided with the Vorsteher's, and became an advocate of Seventh Day principles. Martin recounted this experience in an autobiographical sketch, and both his reception and the manner in which he relates it are illuminating. The two visitors arrived unannounced. Martin, with the affected secretiveness of his kind, concealed his identity at first and disclosed it only when he could do so in the most dramatic fashion. Beissel washed their feet and Nägele dried them. The strangers then returned the

courtesy. Beissel fed them and conducted them about the settlement. At last they repaired to the church, where the sisters delighted their callers with a hymn. Martin and Horn acknowledged this attention by singing a hymn of their own, which
was slightly marred, or, at least, delayed, by the infirmity of
Martin's memory. He had forgotten the words and required
a little preliminary instruction from Horn. Beissel had requested Martin to make a few inspired observations, and the
latter obliged him, although he was not in a preaching mood.
The visitors were enchanted, and Martin and Beissel entered
into a nebulous pact, which, devoid of specific terms, was
nevertheless advantageous to the Vorsteher, in view of Martin's wide influence among the First Day Baptists. Beissel did
not stipulate that he was to sever his connection with the Germantonians, nor did he require him to accept a new baptism.
It was one of Beissel's rare exhibitions of tact. The one unfortunate consequence of Beissel's vague agreement with his new
friend was that the seculars at Ephrata were emboldened to
demand admission to the ministry.

The Vorsteher commissioned Martin to serve the congregation at the Bermudian, and in the absence of binding instructions Martin had a free hand. Beissel was pathetically eager for
a revival of his earlier splendor. A potent and extensive revival
at Antietam seemed a pledge of the realization of this hope,
and, indeed, with the decline of Ephrata, Snow Hill, on Antietam Creek, became the principal seat of the sect. Martin was
notably successful as a missionary, and, after several years of
service in the neighborhood of Antietam, he established himself
as pastor at Stony Creek, in Bedford County, where a congregation had been organized in 1763.

Beissel made three visits to Antietam and, despite his decay-
ing faculties, felt a lively return of his old zest in missionary
labors. So engrossed was he in the exploitation of a new territory that he could not remain at home. His overbearing impetuosity had mellowed into a self-effacing affability, but he could
never have outgrown his sly propensity for bending people to

his will by some covert device. At Antietam he gave way, in the beginning, to Martin, when a love feast was to be celebrated, and then, when he was pressed to officiate at a second love feast, consented only when he was given leave to conduct it in his own style and thus established a precedent and a norm, which the congregation observed thereafter. He also asserted his authority by ordaining Martin. One wonders what notions, if any, he had of the nature of ordination. Expediency guided him more frequently than any other consideration, and he was congenitally an opportunist rather than a person of conviction. The feeble gestures of his declining years were of little avail. Where Brother Martin taught, not all of Beissel's tenets were accepted. If Conrad's purpose in forming an alliance with Martin was to make delicate overtures to the Germantown Baptists, with a view to effecting a rapprochement, his designs miscarried completely.

Beissel may, at this time, have cherished hopes of gaining recruits from another quarter. A clergyman named Ludovic, animated by an impulse much like de Labadie's, brought a company of followers to Pennsylvania. Beissel assisted and exhorted him, but Ludovic was impatient of advice. The settlement he founded on Pequea Creek was soon dispersed by his death.

Unhappily, the size of a religious leader's following depends less upon his sanctity than upon the dexterity with which he trims his message to suit the tastes and capacities of his auditors. Either because he was sincere or because he was stupid, Beissel despised the rewards of such astuteness. Another factor is the leader's personal reputation, and if it contains a romantic element or a suggestion of turpitude, the effect is often remarkable. Both contributed to Beissel's bad name, but more decisive still was his alleged mastery over the invisible cohorts of the Evil One. We have seen him driving the spirits from the thickets at Ephrata and taming or circumventing the demons that inflamed his enemies with murderous ire. Long after his death his followers believed that he had possessed thaumaturgi-

cal gifts. There was nothing exceptional in this conviction. Not
a few Pietists had an avid, not to say morbid, interest in what
common parlance styles "the supernatural." They were steeped
in daemonism and spiritism. Beissel, in his struggle to recapture
the primitive glory and purity of Adam, was perhaps less disposed than many others to indulge in these superstitious speculations and to thrill and terrify himself with the inventions
of his own fancy.

For people who could exalt the Vorsteher to the level of
Christ, it was not difficult to ascribe to him the ability to
perform miracles. At least once Beissel had recourse to the other
world in order to rescue himself from an embarrassing situation in this. A constable had been instructed to serve a warrant
on Beissel and took the precaution to provide himself with a
companion before executing his commission. At their approach,
Beissel vanished into his cabin. One of them entered and examined every corner of the house, while the other guarded the
door. In some fashion, Beissel eluded them, and they started
home, nonplussed, only to see him, presently, emerge at the
doorway from which they had retired a few moments before.

In 1751 and 1752 there were plentiful harvests, and wheat
was so abundant that the farmers fed their pigs on it and still
had more than enough to make considerable quantities of
whiskey. During the same period the Brotherhood of Zion was
in one of its blackest moods, and its members were on bad terms
with the Vorsteher. Beissel entreated God to withdraw His
bounty, and the prayer was so well answered that three extremely arid summers followed. Beissel was puzzled and per-
turbed at his success. He applied to heaven for a mitigation of
the chastisement, but the only response he received was a little
rain. At length the brethren mended their quarrel with him,
Beissel was allowed to retract his somewhat vindictive petition,
and the drought came to an end.

In 1761 Ephrata witnessed the inglorious conclusion of a sensational train of supernatural manifestations. Beissel's virginal
radiance dazzled many women whose husbands possessed little

finesse in the art of love, and among these enchanted females was the wife of a virile settler. The husband's appetite for sexual congress was so keen that, when his wife denied him the pleasure to which he was accustomed, he formed an adulterous connection with a widow and at length endeavored to repair, in some measure, the wrong he had done by marrying his partner in the lascivious amour and moving with her to Virginia, while his first wife remained behind at Ephrata. His second wife presented him with three children and died, and the widower contracted a third marriage, wedding, this time, an adventuress, who boasted with impunity of noble origin, in a country where nobody had the interest or the knowledge to contest her claim. Both the man's former wives were dead but not appeased when the sequence of marvels we are about to relate began.

One night early in 1761 the second wife conversed with the third and disclosed to her the hiding place of a sum of money she had filched from her husband's funds. Subsequently she directed her successor to other caches about the house. Despite the ghost's amiable assurances, the afflicted woman was reduced to the most abject fright. Unseen hands plucked off her shoes and stockings, rent her dress, and tormented her with the most brutal horseplay. The spook surpassed herself one night by pulling a couch, with three persons on it, about the room. In the course of her antics she pronounced the name "Conestoga," and at last succeeded in making her victims understand that she wished them to return to the scene of her misdeeds. At this juncture, the spirit of the first wife gave a gentle assent to the second wife's behests, and the latter appointed a rendezvous in the large room above the church at Ephrata, designating the persons who were to assist at the ceremony that would bring all three wives into concord, and prescribing the order of service. Beissel was among those named. He was not at Ephrata when the party appeared, after being urged on, all the way, by the impatient spirit. He declined to obey the summons to return until divine guidance overruled his decision. At last the gathering took place, but the spirits did not keep

their tryst. To redeem the failure in part, the daughter of the
first wife and the daughter of the second were induced to act
as proxies for their absent mothers. The formula of reconciliation was recited, and the third wife was relieved of her predecessor's attentions. Beissel later committed to writing his
reflections on these weird occurrences. They contribute little
to the elucidation of what is at bottom probably hallucination
or fraud.

Equally puerile were the visions of Catharine Hummer, who
in a series of raptures gained an astounding knowledge of the
topography and customs of the other world. Her father, a
Dunker preacher, knew how to utilize his daughter's gifts. The
transports continued for almost three years. The curious came
in droves to see the ecstatic, and some of them heard angelic
voices raised in ravishing melody. Beissel, now a tired seventy-
five, urged the young woman to preserve her virginity and
hoped that her conversion would galvanize his effete foundation into fresh and triumphant vitality. Her marriage was his
last serious disappointment. With this consummation of her
real desires, the trances ceased.

The Vorsteher did not live to see the Revolution, but the
tribulations of the colony during the French and Indian War
stimulated him to a laudable exhibition of energy, which did
not escape the grateful observation of the government. Beissel
welcomed refugees, prayed for the troops, dispensed alms, and
toured the country, sometimes at the peril of his life, to comfort
the threatened colonists. The enemy advanced to a point within
thirteen miles of Ephrata, and even Beissel was alarmed. He
was about to order the evacuation of the settlement, when the
sisters set a splendid example of courage by informing the rest
of the community that they intended to remain. Beissel gained
confidence and, when the panic had subsided, dreaded the un-
friendliness of his enemies among the settlers more than the
cruelty of the Indians. Although the language of the *Chronicon*
leaves the reader in some doubt as to the sentiments that occasioned this apprehension, the colonists were probably incensed

at the conscientious unwillingness of the Anabaptist groups to serve in the militia. Short of shedding blood, Beissel and others of his persuasion were prepared to do almost anything for the relief of those who suffered because of the war. The government sent a company of infantry to insure the safety of Ephrata and recognized the services of the settlement by presenting it with "a pair of very large glass communion goblets."

Ten or twelve years before the Vorsteher's death, Peter Miller began a second term as superior of the brotherhood. Towards the close of Beissel's life, the management of the community must have fallen increasingly into his hands. The three constant temptations of man are wine, women, and song. Conrad had resisted women and was now beyond the reach of their solicitations. He had yielded, in his youth, to the spell of gay tunes, with their vain and sometimes, perhaps, ribald words, but he had long ago expelled all bawdy and frivolous doggerel from his mind and had discovered ample compensation for the loss of such things in his cultivation of sacred song. There is a strong likelihood that, in his last feeble years, he gave way before the allurements of drink. There were times when he certainly seemed inebriated: his speech was incoherent, his gait was unsteady, and he vomited. Many of his followers were scandalized and shunned him. Yet, when the testimony of his enemies has been given due consideration, there is no reason to conclude that he was an abandoned sot. If he took a drop to sustain his flagging strength, it may easily have proved too powerful a stimulant. Moreover, his habitual mode of preaching readily suggested, as did that of the Apostles at Pentecost, that his inspiration had been poured out of a bottle.

We must pause here briefly to discuss the testimony of Ezechiel Sangmeister. His memoirs were printed more than half a century after Beissel's death, and almost half a century after his own, when few, if any, of the Vorsteher's contemporaries were still living. Sangmeister seems to have had no intention of giving them to the public. He stowed them away securely in a wall, and only when somebody happened upon them were they published. If these astounding confessions had appeared during Peter Miller's lifetime, he would have defended Beissel with all the resources of his pen. Sangmeister puts no curb upon his spite. His vilifications of Beissel and others are incredible. He lived at Ephrata soon after the debâcle that drove out the Eckerles, and returned, after a long trial of the hermit's life, four years before Beissel's death. He depicts the Vorsteher as an unscrupulous hunter of souls, a petty plotter addicted to mean subterfuges, a drunkard, an incubus, and a lustful hypocrite. If we may believe Sangmeister, Beissel not only failed to preserve his own chastity, but also involved many of his spiritual daughters in his misconduct and contracted a venereal disease. The present biographer confesses his perplexity in face of a problem that can never be wholly solved, but, since there is no unimpeachable evidence that Beissel was untrue to his profession in any gross way, he prefers to dismiss Sangmeister's diverting gossip as a tissue of slanders. The witness himself was not above reproach; he engaged in a flirtation with a nun, and, even though she took the initiative, he should have disdained her advances. Moreover, he dwelt in an atmosphere of occult mischiefs and, to use a well-known phrase, "malicious animal magnetism." He had a greedy appetite for scandal and retailed with gusto every idle story he heard. He loathed Beissel so intensely that he remembered nothing good of him and magnified every faultfinding remark that was made in his hearing. His vindictiveness pursued Beissel even beyond the grave, and he was glad to learn that the Vorsteher had revisited his earthly haunts in a manner that demonstrated, beyond a doubt, that he had been condemned to the perdition he richly merited, in Sangmeister's opinion. For the information of those who care to read a few of Sangmeister's dirty tales in his own words, several quotations have been printed in the Appendix.

Until the day of his death, July 6, 1768, the Vorsteher puttered about at such chores as his physical condition still permitted. Shedding, one by one, the grudges that had exercised his tongue and pen, poisoned his prayers, and defaced his work, he made a clean breast of his shortcomings, omissions, and errors, and assumed responsibility for all the damage the community had suffered. If his passion for solitude was sincere, he was denied its gratification in the hour of death. The husbands and wives of Wisdom had gathered to hear his last profession of loyalty to the beliefs that had governed his life and would govern theirs a little longer. Miller blessed him, and the brethren saluted him with the kiss of peace. The agony of departure wiped out the last traces of hatred, and not until he was satisfied that no malice remained did Beissel stretch himself out on the hard bench for the closing ordeal. He bewailed his misuse of the long life he had spent upon earth and in the same breath expressed his amazed rapture at the sight of the beauties he was about to enjoy. The gaunt, silent faces watched him as he expired.

Conrad Beissel's memorial is a living community. His literary remains, except as they portray and illustrate the society in whose interest they were written, are insignificant. His sermons were delivered for its instruction and extension, and his purpose in pursuing the only art in which he excelled, music, was less to pamper his aesthetic tastes than to train his subjects, during their earthly lives, in the concord of the better life to which they aspired.

When the Vorsteher died, the monastic life at Ephrata was clearly destined to extinction. Mother Maria had been ousted some years before, and the religious had decreased almost to half the number Ephrata had boasted in its heyday. A friendly observer opines that it is not "likely that young people will join them to keep up a succession." This melancholy prospect did not improve. Peter Miller enjoyed a merited reputation as a savant, but he was neither energetic nor bold, and, if Ephrata looked to him to repair its shattered fortunes, it looked in vain. The two orders had dwindled, in 1814, to a membership of four. In that year the congregation was incorporated, and trustees took over the administration of the land and buildings. Catharina Kelp, the sister, and Johann Kelp, Jonathan Kelp, and Christian

Luther, the brothers, were confirmed in their rights for the residue of their lives.

To all appearances, the monastic life was now completely dead, but the years of gentle decline were prolonged and a handful of sisters preserved the feeble tradition. Ephrata was little more than an atmospheric ruin. I. D. Rupp injects a dash of sentiment into his description (*History of Lancaster County*, Lancaster, 1844, pp. 231–32):

What yet remains of Ephrata, is worthy a long journey to be seen; "its weather beaten walls; upon which the tooth of time has been gnawing for nearly one and a half century, are crumbling to pieces, rendering it more interesting from its antiquity. "Many traces of the olden time remain, but its life has departed.—There are, however, many delightful associations connected with the mouldering walls, and like some of the dilapidated castles, which are apparently falling to the ground, deserted and given to the rooks and owls, yet it contains many habitable and comfortable apartments." These are occupied by several single sisters, one of whom, sister Barbara, has been here fifty-five years; but under different Government; in former days the whole property and income belonged exclusively to the single brethren and sisters; but now by legislative enactment is invested in all the members, single and married. The sisters, since this enactment, in the convent, are *not* supported out of the common stock and their common labor, but each has house-room, which all the married members are entitled to, who require it, as well as firewood, flour and milk, from the society, who still possess some land and a mill, and their labor they apply to their own use, or dispose of it as they see proper."

There are difficulties in this account, but they need not detain us. Rupp seems to have used Fahnestock's article of 1835 in the preparation of his sketch. Fahnestock had written nine years before, "There are several single sisters remaining in the Convent, (one of whom has been there forty-six years, and another lives in a cottage, solitary life, sixty years,) but another government now exists." Rupp said nothing about the sister who had been in the convent for sixty years in 1835. She was probably dead. He gives us the name of the sister who had rounded out forty-six years in 1835 and fifty-five in 1844. Both accounts speak of "several single sisters," yet the name of only one occurs in the act of incorporation. One might speculate interminably and to no purpose concerning the conflict between the two historical sketches on the one hand and the act of incorporation on the other. Possibly all the single sisters except Catharina Kelp were pensioners and had no claim on the congregation. Other hypotheses might be advanced, but the matter is too trivial to warrant further discussion. These women led retired and mortified lives, and they may have kept up some semblance of the old conventual observances; but they were no longer nuns.

A few dying tremors of the upheaval that was Beissel are perceptible in our own generation. A Seventh Day German Baptist Church still exists. It claims five hundred members, but this is a generous estimate. At its most flourishing period the Ephrata community contained fewer than three hundred persons. There are now only three congregations. The small company at Ephrata numbers eleven. It contrives to dispense with the services of a minister. There are larger congregations at Snow Hill and at "The Cove" near New Enterprise, Bedford County, Pennsylvania. Until recently there was a fourth congregation in Somerset County. In the summer of 1940 Bishop John A. Pentz, the head of the denomination, died, and only two ministers now remain. The Rev. Benjamin F. Miller serves the church at Snow Hill, and the Rev. F. R. King officiates at "The Cove." The following confession of faith is accepted by the whole body:

ART. 1. We believe that all Scripture given by inspiration in the Old and the New Testaments is the Word of God, and is the only rule of Faith and Practice.

ART. 2. We believe that unto us there is but one God, the Father; and one Lord, Jesus Christ, who is the Mediator between God and mankind, and that the Holy Ghost is the Spirit of God.

ART. 3. We believe that the Ten Commandments which

were written on two tables of stone by the finger of God, continue to be the rule of righteousness for all mankind. We further believe that the active participation in war by military service in the army or navy is in violation of the sixth commandment and the teachings of Jesus Christ.

ART. 4. We believe that all persons ought to be baptized in water by trine immersion in a forward position after confession of their faith in Jesus Christ as the Son of God.

ART. 5. We believe that the Lord's Supper ought to be administered and received in all Christian Churches, accompanied with the washing of one another's feet previous to the breaking of the bread.

ART. 6. We believe in the anointing of the sick with oil in the name of the Lord.

ART. 7. We believe in the invocation of Infant Blessing.

ART. 8. We believe that all Christian Churches should have Elders and Deacons.

ART. 9. We believe the duties of the Deacons to be:

To provide for the Communion Service of the Church, and officiate thereat when necessary; to seek out and report to the Church all cases of destitution or suffering within bounds of the Church, especially such as arise from sickness; to provide necessary relief in behalf of the Church. They shall also be deemed co-workers in the ministry and counselors in spiritual matters. They shall continue in office for life or during good behavior.

ART. 10. We believe in observing the Seventh Day (Sabbath). He whom we worship was its first observer.

This creed contains no mention of the angelic life for which Beissel and his passionate associates yearned. The most vital and distinctive feature of Beissel's teaching has been quietly discarded. In their adoption of infant blessing, his followers have made a necessary concession to Protestant practice. This custom is, for all practical purposes, a substitute for infant baptism. For the rest, the formulary sets forth the conception of the Church to which the Anabaptists gave classic expression in their statements of belief.

A further trace of Beissel's work exists in one variety of American Rosicrucianism. Imperator Lewis, the pontiff of this group, regards himself as the heir of Kelpius and Beissel. In his account of the history of Rosicrucianism he says,

We are more concerned with its introduction into the New World. We find here, too, many books and records which give reliable and precise details of the coming to America of the first Rosicrucian colony from Europe, under Sir Francis Bacon's original plan, in the year 1694, and its establishment for many years first at Philadelphia, then at Ephrata, Pennsylvania, where many of the original buildings still stand.

IX

PHILOSOPHOLUS TEUTONICUS

━━━━━━━━━━━━━━━━━━━━━━━━━━━━━━━━━

IT is temptingly easy to sum up Beissel's life in one or more blistering epigrams and to stigmatize it as futile, mad, or preposterous; but no reputable biographer strikes off witticisms at the expense of the dead, and such misguided cleverness can be applied to Beissel only with the greatest impertinence. If at times the present writer has indicated Conrad's defects with a vigor that may be characterized as censorious or splenetic, he has acted in the service of truth and is eager to make amends for any overstatement into which the concentration of the moment may have betrayed him. Contemplated as a whole, the Vorsteher's character, in the plenitude of its frailty, rarely loosened its grip upon the verities to which he had vowed fealty in his youth. It is true that we do not discover in his obscure struggle the monumental grandeur of those Christian careers that have influenced entire cultures and left the impress of their holiness on long eras of human life, but he was not a false prophet, and the agonies he endured in the pursuit of his ideals are an indubitable token of the reality of his belief in them. He identified himself with the religion he professed, and in toiling to make a place for it he toiled to make a place for himself. What else could he have done? His timid preoccupation with himself and his habit of referring all events and problems to the tribunal of his own emotions were not deliberately cultivated; nature and circumstance formed him, to use his own language, in a matrix of tribulation, and, from the beginning of his life, it was impossible for him to face the world with the breezy assurance of the more fortunate. For one so lamed at the outset, he did well. Enough has been said, and he may now be left to the judgment of God, which will not wrong him.

Beissel's mind and thought are another matter. Without impeding the flow of the narrative unduly, we have improved the opportunity afforded by the first appearance of each new element in his complex theology to discuss its origin, but the digression, in every instance, has been kept within strict bounds. These passing references must now be systematized and amplified. The influences that contributed to the formation of the world in which he grew to the stature of an adult have been described at length. The reader, in following the story, has reconstructed for himself the type of life to which Beissel was introduced when he reached Pennsylvania. From his general surroundings he derived attitudes rather than ideas, and these attitudes have been dealt with elaborately. The ideas now engage our attention. The specific sources of the material that entered into the composition of Beissel's theology are Inspirationism, Seventh Day Sabbatarianism, Dunkerism, and Böhmism.

Inspirationism was a tonic to Beissel in the period of misery that followed his misfortunes in Heidelberg. The only valuable truth it had to impart was its affirmation of the Spirit's present power. This Beissel accepted and never discarded. He did well to cleave to it, because it swept away the bucolic shyness that might have been an impediment in his public life and enabled him to use both tongue and pen with facility if not with elegance. Yet it had its pitfalls, and it is to be regretted that Beissel was not endowed with the delicate discrimination that would have shielded him from the perils of too unreserved an abandonment to momentary impulses, which, in his simplicity, he traced to the Spirit. He became addicted to extemporization. Consecutive and constructive cerebration was a sign of too proud an attachment to one's own wits. It was better to be passive and limp in the Spirit's hands and listen for Its suggestions. It follows that nothing the Spirit uttered was ever the last word. Neither the reflections of saints nor the Scriptures themselves were invested with decisive authority. It is wise to live a day at a time and to exploit the present to its limits. The past dismays us and the future terrifies us, and it is best to live between them. Beissel, with the instincts of an ascetic, knew that this was the only way for him, but he made the mistake of trying to think day by day. This habit stunted his intellect. It is not strictly true to say that his writings present nothing more complex than the simple juxtaposition of ideas. He sometimes shows creditable skill in the manipulation of arguments. His profound saws—many of them appropriated, one suspects, without acknowledgment—are often neat and telling. Nevertheless, Inspirationism destroyed whatever capacity he may have had for sustained reasoning. Under its corrosive influence, his mind lost its power to see things as they are, and he forgot his debts to other minds. He probably never had a thought that was really of his own making; yet he passed off all his thefts as the fruit of his own brain and was guilty of no conscious imposture in doing so.

We need not restate the conclusions with which we ended our inquiry into Beissel's Seventh Day Sabbatarianism in Chapter IV. When he embraced this type of sabbatarianism, he already had a virtually complete theological system, so far as his heap of intellectual oddments is worthy of the name. He was steeped in Böhme's thought, and, while he may not have known all his master's writings at first hand, he was well acquainted with the substance of the passages in which Böhme magnifies the Sabbath. The despised and afflicted Jews had found solace in personifying the Sabbath and relaxing once a week in its company, as though it were a denizen of the eternal world sent into this to release them for one blessed day from an unbearable strain. Closely allied to this conception of the Sabbath and perhaps in a measure suggested by it is Böhme's doctrine, which came full-blown to Beissel and upon which he mused in the vacant hours of his early years in Conestoga until he invested it with a sublime loveliness and made it a type of all that his combative nature yearned for in vain. His master had discovered in the Sabbath the end of all strife and labor. It was the abode of Celestial Wisdom, the *Centrum* where the longings of the six weekdays and the six figures of toiling nature were fulfilled and their stormy lusts and strivings came to rest, the *Temperatur*, or poise, in which the tempestuous forces of the natural world found a certain equilibrium. Böhme regards the Sabbath as "the true image of God," fashioned by God eternally as a representation of His unutterable repose. "The seventh day, as the seventh property of eternal nature, is the transparent glassy sea before the throne of the Ancient of Days in Revelation 4:6 . . . The seventh day has been from eternity outside all time, for it is the formed Word of the divine understanding." This "true Paradise" is Christ, the Restorer of man, who through his unruly imagination has fallen a victim to confusion and multiplicity. Our present new humanity in Christ makes it possible for us to be "in the Sabbath" and to await "only the dissolution of the evil earthly life" and our entry into the life "where we shall keep the Sabbath not in this world but in the angelic world, in the world of light." The observance of the Sabbath was enjoined upon the Jews so that their day of rest might typify the "inner, holy, eternal Sabbath." With spectacular, but—to Beissel's critical eye—unconvincing agility, Böhme finally claims for the first day of the week all the splendors of the last. He contends that "the seventh day and the first belong together as one, for the six properties of eternal nature were all contained in the seventh as in a texture of the other six. The seventh property is a mystery or arrangement of all the others; and from the seventh day the first day took its origin and beginning." Beissel probably rejected this portion of the doctrine as a feeble device forced upon Böhme by his fidelity to Lutheranism. Separated from his guide by a century, he could apply Böhme's principles to practical questions more uncompromisingly than Böhme himself, and, in this instance, he had good reasons for pursuing an independent course. Nowhere in Scripture could he find an express abrogation of the Jewish law concerning the seventh day, and, therefore, he could not, with Böhme, follow the almost universal custom of Christendom; but he did adopt and hold fast to the main articles of Böhme's teaching, which, if it was sound at all, had a greater validity in eternity than in time.

Beissel's debt to Dunkerism requires little discussion. He may have learned from the Dunkers a certain hostility to formularies, but this he derived to some extent, as we have noted, from Inspirationism. The Schwarzenau sect taught him its view of the nature of the Church, its discipline, its conclusions from Scripture as to the Christian ordinances, its evangelistic technique, and its public worship. He was an eager and retentive pupil, but he was notably deficient in the supreme virtue of the disciple, a profound and abiding sentiment of gratitude to his teacher. Nothing sheds less luster upon Beissel than the perfidy he showed in his association with these people.

All other influences are reduced to relative insignificance by Böhmism, which was the regnant force in Beissel's life. It captivated him when he was occupied with a quest for finality, and he submitted to its fascination so willingly and irrevocably that, from the moment of his conversion to the end of his days, every new thought had to be trimmed to conform to the mystical doctrine in which he had discovered an infallible mentor to guide all his subsequent actions. In the remainder of this chapter an attempt will be made to trace the effect of these involved teachings on the Vorsteher's mind. Manifestly, his thought cannot be understood without a knowledge of the entire range of his literary activity. We have already devoted some space to a condensation of his earliest writings, and the preface to the *Turtel-Taube* has been quoted and discussed. A few comprehensive observations on his later work will now be made. A catalogue of Conrad's writings will be found in the Bibliography.

Conrad's fitful intellect prevented him from executing literary designs that called for the sustained application of his powers to a single subject. Though not given to the candor that lends charm to private correspondence, he was a sedulous letter writer, and, at times, when he fought clear of the tortuosities of his thought and for a moment dropped the pose he usually affected, he wrote simply, clearly, and with a certain rough vigor. His letters are rarely of inordinate length. Beissel expressed himself most happily in short pieces. A meditation, an exegetical essay, or a stilted prayer—he could dash off any of these at a single sitting—served his purpose, and he conceived a great fondness for this type of composition and acquired a high degree of skill in its use. At its worst, his prose is tedious and chaotic, and some passages are merely a grotesque jumble of metaphors. At its best, his style is earnest and impressive, but even when it is least artificial it still falls far short of the homely and unstudied charm it might have had if he had been interested in ordinary human things. In his hymns he remains confined within the pale of his limitations. Competent in the technique of versification, he was not endowed with the genius that makes measured syllables express what cannot be said in the less straitened vehicle of prose. He wrote, as all writers should, with a sense of being swept away by a current of revelation, but his first outpourings, unpruned and unpolished, were suffered to do duty as the final expression of his thought. He glided by degrees into a lifeless flatness, and a large portion of his work is unreadable.

The most highly prized of the Vorsteher's works was his *Wunderschrift*, which was printed in the *Deliciae Ephratenses, Pars I* (1773) and later (1789) published as a booklet without the notes that had accompanied it in the earlier edition. The tiny world that did him homage treasured it as a rare expression of truth, and, like some of his other literary performances, it was rendered into English, no doubt with a view to extending its influence. A cursory inspection of its contents will satisfy any unprejudiced reader that Beissel's intimates greatly overrated this mediocre production. Its diffuse prose and clogged thought must have rendered it an object of scorn to all but a few of the English-speaking colonists who had the enterprise to grapple with its obscurities. These defects might be forgiven, if the book were evidence of a startling insight into divine mysteries, but this it indisputably is not, and its arid pages present little save half-understood scraps of Böhme's rude but sublime view of man's pollution and redemption. Beissel represents these teachings as his own, and his claim may be admitted, since it is true that he appropriated them by practising them. Still, to live by a certain body of truths is not always to understand them, and, if the Vorsteher's apprehension of these ineffable secrets is measured by his ability to elucidate them, it must be confessed that the meaning of the Teutonic Philosopher's system as a whole escaped him. He was not a metaphysician.

Beissel begins with a reference to the experiences he underwent after his conversion, which occurred, as the reader will remember, in his middle twenties. With the boldness of untarnished innocence and a profound ignorance of life, he labored to extinguish his desire for women and was flabbergasted when a portion of his nature would not assent to this renunciation. It puzzled him that he should meet such vigorous opposition within himself, and he was troubled at the discovery that the struggle was suspended the moment he relaxed his efforts. Confronted with this difficulty, he adopted the expedient of transferring his problems to the universe and magnifying his private woes to cosmic proportions. He had been striving towards a *Temperatur*, a state of balance in which the virginal force in his nature and the "fiery male will," its enemy, would conclude their mortal combat. It was disclosed to him that his efforts had been misdirected, for peace between these two was impossible. After more than one false start, Beissel pulls himself together and strives heroically to come to grips with his subject; but he becomes entangled in one digression after another, and his mind darts from thought to thought with a disconcerting lack of connection.

Reduced to order and condensed, Conrad's history of man's commerce with Wisdom requires little space. The commencement of all our sorrows is to be found in Lucifer's insurrection. God, moved to fury, abandoned the female element in His nature and punished Lucifer by the exercise of His male sternness. He then spoke to His femaleness, saying, "Let us make man in our image." They created Adam, who was coupled with Wisdom and therefore possessed both male and female traits. He gazed too curiously at the copulation of the animals and became the victim of an urge to follow their example. The animals seduced Adam and were not altogether without blame for

the disaster that ensued. On the supposition that they were congenitally evil and had committed a sin in deflecting Adam from
his angelic course, those who are perplexed at the pain and death
appointed for them under the Old Dispensation may cease to
suspect God of an arbitrary ruthlessness in His treatment of
them. If Adam had not missed his opportunity, he could have
restored the balance that had existed before Lucifer's sin, finally
liberating himself from his body. Notwithstanding the first fall,
Adam was not wholly undone. God gave him the consort for
whom he yearned, and he had lost the integrity of his earlier
state; but, if Eve had withstood the serpent, it would still have
been possible for God to carry out His projected redemption
of the world, in which Adam was to be His agent and instrument. It is conceivable that Adam and Eve would have been
able to return to the "light-life" without dying. At the very
least, they would have had the power to spend a millennium in
immaculate purity and would have propagated their kind in
some spotless and miraculous manner. These possibilities were
not to be realized. Eve's resistance was as feeble as Adam's, and
man fell into a brutish sexuality, multiplying by a conjunction
that God contemplated with the most profound aversion. The
one had been divided into two, and now the two engendered
many. The Virgin Wisdom seemed permanently beaten, but a
few symbols remained to indicate that she hoped to recapture
the devotion of mankind. Thus, in the Old Testament, a virgin
was considered the only suitable bride for a high priest. Finally,
the Virgin Sophia impregnated the Virgin Mary. In Jesus Christ
there was a perfect balance of the male and the female. Adam's
side had been opened in order that his female portion might be
given a distinct existence. Christ's side was opened on the Cross
in order that the complementary elements might be reunited.
The end envisaged by Christ and all His disciples is the restoration of the entire creation to the *Temperatur* with which the
universe began. All things will return to unity.

Two remarks concerning this strange work may be made here.
The first is that the doctrine of a restoration embracing all

creatures has an unmistakably conspicuous place in it. Beissel indicates elsewhere that he holds this doctrine. The second observation is that John Hildebrand set forth the mystical theology of the community, in a writing entitled *Schriftmäsiges Zeugnis von dem himlischen und jungfräulichen Gebährungs-Werck*, with a lucidity that far surpassed Beissel's, if the work of which we have just given an abstract is to be viewed as Conrad's most successful effort at presenting these abstruse matters to his bewildered followers. It is to be regretted that Beissel esteemed this tract so highly, for in other places his exposition of the same mysteries is not obfuscated by his memories and feelings and he writes tidily and exactly, without the unintelligible torrent of words that too often disfigures his style and veils his thought.

Every riddle vanishes in this conception of the origins of our race. The desire of the sexes for each other is linked with Adam's catastrophic loss of his celestial properties. His lascivious imagination brought about all sexuality and division. Woman is the absence or want of man: man, the absence or want of woman. Each labors under a sense of incompleteness, for the perfect man is male and female. Human genitals are not a part of the image of God. The institution of circumcision proves that the secret members are an abomination to God. Carnal contact between the sexes is revolting to Him. In Christ the sundered maleness and femaleness returned to their primordial union and wholeness. The pursuit of Christ imposes upon us the necessity of forsaking the delectable objects of longing to which unregenerate man devotes himself. The abandonment of sex is only the most obvious of the renunciations such consecration requires. The world is illusory and has no real being. The spouse of Wisdom studies to eradicate every remnant of the *Ichts*, in order that he may be drawn back into the *Nichts*, into the divine *Ungrund*. The affinity between this doctrine and certain beliefs found in Indian and Islamic mysticism cannot escape the careful reader. When we are ingrafted into the new humanity, God is our Father, Christ our Brother, and the Holy Ghost our

Mother. Loyalty to Christ is equated with unflinching self-denial. Beissel's devotion to Christ was fidelity to a symbol of abnegation; there are few, if any, traces of the warm, sensuous affection that appears so prominently in the spirituality of the Catholic mystics. Beissel's theology ended in a rigorous quietism. According to the Law one might expect rewards for righteousness, but according to the Gospel man has no merits, and all God gives him is given graciously and freely, as to one who has earned nothing.

The Vorsteher, taking Christ as his model, assumed the functions of an intercessor, offering himself as a victim for other people's transgressions. This, as we have seen, brought him to the verge of blasphemy. He exhibits an impressive theological acumen in his nineteenth epistle, a paragraph of which is devoted to an exposition of the intimate association of good and evil. Like Böhme he maintains that there are three warring worlds: the temporal world, the abode of light, and the abode of darkness. They are perpetual rivals for mastery over man. Böhme's philosophy is the ultimate source of Beissel's belief in will as the most significant factor in the cosmic struggle and in the conflict fought out in man's soul. Beissel grasped at least some of the cardinal doctrines of Böhme's system and spoke the Böhmistic patois with the readiness of long familiarity. His literary remains bristle with such Böhmistic words and phrases as these: *sophianische Weiblichkeit, principium, massa, magia, magisch, essents, centrum, imagination, Freuden-Reich, Lebens-Kräfte, Fabel und Babel, matrix, temperatur, phantasien, limbus, Welt-Geist, element, inqualirend, syderische Linea, tinctur.*

It is highly improbable that Beissel acquired his knowledge of Böhmism wholly from a systematic study of the sage's writings. His mentality could toil with vigor upon any subject that gripped it, but his interest in speculative questions was confined to their devotional and eschatological implications. To plumb the boundless profundities of Böhme's baffling tractates was an exacting task, for which the wizard of Conestoga had the time and the materials, but not the appetite. Böhme's collected writings, in the monumental edition of 1682, circulated widely. Whether in this form or individually his works were on the shelves of many who were shaken by the religious storms of Beissel's generation. More than once in the course of Beissel's life a treatise of Böhme's must have reposed in his lap as he thumbed his way from one knotty passage to another and at last closed the volume with a sense of being out of his depth. Assurance soon took the place of bewilderment. A vital sympathy enabled pupil and preceptor to clasp hands over the century of time and the disparities of mind and soul that divided them. They had the same defects. Both wrote a graceless, uneven German; both dealt cavalierly with the canons of language and reasoning; both had the narrow, persistent ardor of the self-instructed. Outwardly they followed the same course from a humble station to one in which they enjoyed the attention of their social superiors and the adulation of those to whom they communicated their knowledge of the dazzling mysteries unveiled to them. Both were men of unwavering confidence, pursuing a difficult and elusive ideal with devout courage. Beissel's biographers a little too patently underline his uniqueness and would have the reader believe that nobody stood between God and the Vorsteher. The most remarkable thing about Böhme is this very independence of human lore, the absolute freshness with which he assailed the problems of philosophy and theology. Here and, it may be, elsewhere in the *Chronicon* the godly authors have made the disciple look as much like the master as they dared. In reality, save for these few adventitious points of agreement, the two lie far apart. Böhme is one of the immortals. If we grant Beissel a place not far from the head of the honorable company of Böhmists perhaps we give him more than his merits warrant. Beissel had the complications of the mediocre. Böhme's heavenly singleness of motive and steadfast tranquillity, which he coveted, were denied him. He was not of Böhme's stature.

The light broke upon Beissel at his conversion in Heidelberg. From the moment of his introduction to Böhmism he was taught to think of it as a body of divine and life-saving doctrines. For

him it was never a desiccated philosophy. Hence, while Conrad
might in odd moments bestow a glance upon Böhme's own
books, they did not provide his sustenance. It cost him less labor
to understand Böhme in the interpretations of Gichtel and
Arnold. His removal to the new world did not cut him off from
intercourse with those who shared his reverence for Böhme.
He fed on the living faith of his fellows. Therefore in time such
of Böhme's unutterable discoveries as he found within the range
of his intellect became detached from Böhme's name. They
were the common inheritance of all those who acknowledged
the superlative sanctity of the Teutonic Philosopher. Of course,
one is impelled to ask whether Beissel was guilty of premeditated
intellectual theft in adopting Böhme's teachings and passing
them off as his own. If there is any guilt, the international
dissemination of Böhmism palliates it. Böhmism was common
property, and people helped themselves to it freely. The most
deluded of Beissel's followers may have failed to recognize that
he had pirated many of his leading ideas from Böhme, but certainly the borrowing was obvious to all those who had even a
smattering of the mysteries.

Beissel's service to Böhmism was spiritual, not intellectual.
It had never occurred to the Teutonic Philosopher that the
worship of Wisdom demanded the repudiation of family life.
He married while he was still young and lived in peace and
fecundity with his wife for thirty years. Subsequent contenders
for Sophia's hand chafed at the hindrances of matrimony and,
assuming an exceedingly bold position, declared that at best it
retarded the redemption of the human race. Beissel had a goodly
number of predecessors. Their passionate, but ordinarily barren,
struggles foreshadowed Beissel's fruitful combat with the hosts
of darkness. Wisdom had offered its secrets to Adam's stricken
children through many seers. In the summing up at the end of
Beissel's biography Gichtel and Arnold are warmly commended
for their valiant zeal in the propagation of this type of Böhmism
and a tribute is paid to the gentle Kelpius, who, in establishing
a Böhmistic sect, accomplished almost as much as the Vorsteher.

Beissel is the most eminent of this saintly line. His foundation endured.

In its quaint way this is a marvelously exact statement of the truth. Beissel had a consuming admiration for the fraternity on the Ridge. At first he must have been appalled at the lamentable plight of this now feeble fellowship, which a few years before had seemed vital and lasting. Forced by its failure to look for a place of retirement in Conestoga, he took his leave of it with a deep insight into the deficiencies and blunders that had contributed to its decay.

It is not explicitly stated in the *Chronicon* that Beissel was addicted to the study of Arnold's works, but his appearance in the list of the Vorsteher's precursors compels us to devote a few lines to this most charming and sincere of Pietists. Gottfried Arnold (1666–1714) is known principally for his courageous and original studies in church history, from which he banished polemics to admit a semblance of scientific objectivity, and secondarily for his tasteful religious poetry and his indefatigable pastoral labors. Nauseated at the profanation of the Lord's Supper and other scandals that were inseparable from the ecclesiastical system of his time, he declined, in his youth, to assume the cure of souls and spent a number of years as a tutor, venturing out of the congenial privacy of this employment for a single year to occupy a professorship at Giessen. During this period he was a militant Pietist. He engaged in an eager correspondence with Gichtel and devoured the writings of the English Böhmists. Under these influences he conceived an enthusiasm for mysticism, although he lacked mystical experience and was hindered by an impetuous and aggressive temperament in his strivings towards contemplative detachment. Indeed he never assimilated Böhme's theology even when he was most proficient in the use of its curious locutions, and, in his mature life, he left it behind as a discipline that had no meaning for him. Arnold wielded a prolific pen, and before he outgrew the tortuous intricacies of Böhmism he had composed a number of works that bear the stamp of its influence. Chief among these is *Das Geheimniss der göttlichen Sophia* (1700). Not long after the publication of this work, his *Das eheliche und unverehelichte Leben der ersten Christen* appeared (1702). Its subject is marriage. Arnold's position does not diverge, in any important respect, from the teaching that determined Beissel's final opinions concerning this most delicate matter. It is possible that Beissel read the book and gave it his approbation. His sole adverse criticism would have been that it was not sufficiently austere. Save for this, he would have endorsed it.

A late manuscript copy of the first appendix to this work was in use among Beissel's people. From this scanty evidence Sachse rather precipitately drew the conclusion that Beissel had borrowed the main elements of his mystical theology from Arnold. His theory has little support. It is true that Beissel's followers read a great deal of mystical literature, and it may be granted that Arnold's writings were held in high honor. They contained a compendium of the Teutonic Philosophy—at least such parts of it as commanded the attention of the people who were likely to read Arnold's works—but there is no proof that Beissel learned his Böhmism from them. However, further argument in this strain would be wholly useless. The appendix was not written by Arnold at all. In the preface he imparts the helpful information that the author of the appendix is a learned person of academic renown.

Whatever the Vorsteher may have assimilated from the works of other Böhmistic commentators or from Böhmistic discourses or conversations, Johann Georg Gichtel (1638–1710) made the deepest impression upon him. Since Sangmeister mentions Gichtel's writings in a manner that implies an acquaintance with them among the servitors of Wisdom at Ephrata, we may be certain that Beissel knew them in his prime. Nothing forbids the conjecture that he was initiated into Gichtelianism at Heidelberg. Irrefragable proof of Beissel's dependence upon Gichtel cannot be offered in the present discussion, which, as patient inquiry has failed to uncover a single copy of any of Gichtel's works, must make shift with the information that can be extracted from a few biographical sketches.

Gichtel was a person of extraordinary intelligence. In his early days he learned several oriental languages with ease and took a lively interest in other branches of study. A clerical career seemed the choice both of nature and of grace for a stripling who cultivated brain and soul with equal success. The matter was still undecided when Gichtel's father died. The young man's guardians directed him to begin the study of the law, and Gichtel, already pliant under the Spirit's decrees, did not resist. His spiritual experiences were in a manner like Beissel's and he had some of the Vorsteher's most glaring faults. He did reasonably well in the practice of the law, but his mind was on better things than the bagatelles about which pettifogging lawyers dispute. His misadventures and follies are pitiable and amusing. None the less, the influence of his ardor and sincerity and his indubitable knowledge of Böhme's works, which he published in the first complete edition in 1682, brought him fame and elicited either the most unquestioning loyalty or the most virulent contempt. During his long residence in Amsterdam, he attracted a considerable number of disciples to the city and its environs. The spell of his introspective personality did not suffice to maintain unity among them. A measure of his authority passed into the hands of two men after his death. Johann Wilhelm Ueberfeld became head of Gichtel's followers in the Netherlands. Johann Otto Glüsing, captain of the Gichtelians in Hamburg and Altona, was the author of *Leben der Altväter in der Wüsten*, which was in the library at Ephrata. The sect adopted the name "Engelsbrüder" and lasted at least until 1789.

Conrad's *Theosophical Epistles* are the direct offspring of Gichtel's *Theosophical Epistles*. Gichtel appropriated the name from Böhme's *Theosophische Send-briefe*. The reader may object that Beissel could have been under Böhme's immediate influence. For reasons already given, this is unlikely. So far as it is possible to form an opinion from quotations, it was Gichtel's vehemence, not the meekness of Böhme, that echoed in Beissel's mind when his pen dashed phrenetically over the paper. Gichtel's *Eine kurze Eröffnung und Anweisung der dreyen Principien und Welten im Menschen* may have helped Beissel to an understanding of Böhme's three contending worlds.

The affinity was even more intimate, and in the convictions they cherished with regard to wedlock and the priesthood of Melchizedek there was an identity of thought between Gichtel and the Vorsteher. Gichtel loathed marriage; his flesh crawled at the mention of it. In Böhme's works there was much to sanction this extreme position, but Böhme, in the actual affairs of life, tolerated marriage. Beissel follows Gichtel. Both had sex appeal, which they endeavored to sublimate, but, while they succeeded well enough with their own appetites, those of their female admirers remained unsubjugated.

From Gichtel came the guidance that enabled Beissel to fit his afflictions and his ambitions into a coherent picture. In one of the publications of the Zionitic Brotherhood the truth concerning the priesthood of Melchizedek is unfolded in the following words:

This office may by no means be administered by a man, because the man's rule does not appertain to the Church, but is an official service that has its origin in the world of darkness. Rather does it require a person who has been prepared by very lofty tests of suffering; and because such a person, by the work he does, exposes himself to the devil's assaults, he must in a certain measure be quite other than he outwardly seems to be, so that the devil may not find him. He must not be obliged to procure nourishment and sustenance for his soul when he has begun to perform the duties of this priesthood, but must beforehand in his whole life have become God's to such a degree that he can spend his time in the tranquil Now of eternity in God's presence; yet he must, out of love for God and his neighbor, have descended to the common level of men in order to become a cause of their salvation. The highest necessity must have driven him to it, the work must be his heaviest load, so that, when the time of sifting comes, he may lay it before God's

feet, raise his hands in innocence, and say, "Lord! Thou know-
est that I have not run myself." Furthermore, he must have
met the demands of righteousness, in order that it may be his
friend, and, in case of need, his defender. In short, he must
have lost his soul and found it again, so that he may place it
before his brethren as an anathema.

This is a general portrait that requires only a few additional
strokes to make it reproduce the lineaments either of Beissel or
of Gichtel. Both bore pain cheerfully for the cowardly and
besought God for the frivolous, who neither dreaded the pangs
of hell nor craved the delights of heaven. Wherever a soul had
lost the power to pray for itself, these men braved the poundings
of Satan and the indignant bolts of the insulted Creator in an
effort to reconcile the defeated sinner with God. To Protestants
this seemed a pernicious and abominable type of madness. So it
was, if the man who practised it exalted himself far above
humanity and claimed to be the peer of Christ. So long as the
pleader retained an acute sense of his own creatureliness, his
sacrificial exercises were not repugnant to Scripture. Bold as
it may appear to say so, every Christian is a Christ, and many
Christians have found it a comfort to believe that God permits
them to suffer for the misdeeds of their fellows. Beissel did not
monopolize the honor, but regarded all consecrated virgins,
male or female, as members of this priesthood.

Upon this lofty note a study of the manifold influences that
shaped Beissel's theology may well be brought to an end. A
great deal has been left unsaid. Not a little of it would be tedious
to the reader. We shall content ourselves with registering our
conviction that the Vorsteher, in synthetizing the multifarious
elements we have catalogued and described, deprived them all
of their fertility. This singular conjunction of ideas died with
Beissel. Enthusiasm for Böhme had not perished completely
even after the turn of the century, for in 1811–12 Jacob Ruth
published Böhme's *Christosophia* at Ephrata, thus issuing the
first American edition of any of Böhme's works in German; but

this interest is not the work of the Vorsteher, who was neither the only nor the most accomplished Böhmist in Pennsylvania. His will, his courage, and his hardihood rank higher than his intellect.

APPENDIX

CONRAD BEISSEL AS HE APPEARS IN
SANGMEISTER'S *LEBEN UND WANDEL*

". . . der Jacob N. des Eichers Tochter eine Nonne geschwängert hatte, (doch ohne Wissen der Brüder, es wurde aber bald offenbar, denn sie bekam drey Kinder auf einmal,)" I 93.

" 'Nachdem ich (sagte sie) mit meinem Manne in Ephrata komen, und wir voneinander geschieden waren, so besuchte ich den Conrad sehr oft; indem ich mich nun eines Tages sehr weit und vertraut mit ihm eingelassen hatte, und mein ganzes Herz entdeckt; so legte ich mich auf den Abend meiner Gewohnheit nach, in meine Kammer schlafen: Indem ich nun wachend auf dem Rücken da lag, so sahe ich den Conrad in Gestalt wie einen Schatten, zu meinem Fenster herein kommen, fiel auf mich drein und vermischte sich mit mir, mehr empfindlicher und wohlthuender als mit meinem Mann jemalen. Nachdem er wiederum fort, so kam ich sehr in Noth darüber, nicht wissende was ich denken oder davon machen solte; indem ich nicht wusste ob so was durch die Magia geschehen könte, etc.

'Kaum war es Tag worden, so besuchte mich der Conrad Beissel, und frug sogleich wie es mir die Letzte Nacht ergangen? Ich erzelhte ihm dañ meine Versuchungen, und alles wie mirs gangen; er sagte dann: "Ey mein Lebtage, was wilt du dann anderst? Das ist ja gut! Dass dirs so gangen ist; das ist ja das einzige Mittel was dir und denen andern Schwestern den Mangel des Mannes ersetzen kann." ' " III 51-2.

"Um diese Zeit erzelhte mir die Schwester M. dass der Vorsteher sich nun fast immer um den andern Tag vollsauffen und brechen thäte, und so mächtig nach dem starken Getränke rieche, so dass die ältesten Schwestern einen Abscheu an ihm hätten: Auch sagte sie dabey, dass wann er ihr unters Gesicht käme und mit ihr zu reden anfienge, sie ihn fragen wolte, ob er mit gutem gewissen, vom weiblichen Geschlecht frey blieben sey? Sie wüsste wohl dass er ihr nicht antworten könne. Dann sie wusste nur zu wohl wie es mit ihrer Schwester und ihm gegangen war, andere zu geschweigen: Und wer weiss, wie mit ihr?" IV 11.

". . . sondern der Conrad Beissel selbsten, kam in wunder-

liche Zustände, dann durch den vielen Umgang mit denen
Weibsleuten, bekam er endlich einen offenen Schaden an
seinem heimlichen Gliede, welches oft im Gehen den Boden
besudelte . . ." IV 13.

BIBLIOGRAPHICAL NOTE

THE complete truth about Beissel has been preserved in the mind of God, and one would look in vain for it in any other place; the feeble faculties of a mere biographer cannot hope to recover it. Despite the slender prospect of success, I have plodded through the material, without shirking the boredom of many a somnolent afternoon passed in the society of some of the weakest minds of the eighteenth century, not to mention the defectives of subsequent generations. In the course of this research, I have assembled a crushing weight of information, most of which I shall banish from my mind, now that this book is about to be delivered to the printer. Simply to enumerate the works consulted would exceed the space allotted to this bibliography. Since I have had the good fortune to solve one or two obvious problems, I may fashion this material into a coherent article for the improvement of the expert. Here my task is much lighter. It will suffice to name the writings that contribute the greatest amount of information, and where a broad designation will serve for a fund of material I shall employ it in the hope that brevity will stimulate curiosity.

Among the Vorsteher's intimates none found the unbiased mean, and even those who gazed upon his works from afar were usually incapable of an impartial judgment. Except for a few inadvertent lapses, the *Chronicon* (done into English by J. M. Hark, Lancaster, 1889), an approved biography, unswervingly vindicates the Vorsteher. No reputable scholar would neglect to subject such testimony to a painstaking scrutiny. A more serious deviation from the truth is brought to light when we strive to determine the nature of *Das Leben und Wandel des in Gott ruhenten und seligen Br. Ezechiel Sangmeisters*. Shall we dismiss it as a tissue of calumnies, or shall we grant that from time to time Ezechiel imparts precious information? We are soon driven to the conclusion that the author's animosity has corrupted every line he composed. The cardinal sources must be employed with caution. Their glaring faults are corrected, in a measure, by other sources of smaller compass but greater soundness. These, of course, are often tinctured with the authors' sentiments. With ruthless penetration Sauer points out Beissel's shortcomings, but who would deny that he mingles truth with falsehood? We are deeply beholden to him for *Ein Abgenöthigter Bericht* and his reports to the devout in Europe, but it would be rash to remain blind to the aversion with which he regarded Beissel's ruses and poses. Acrelius in his *A History of New Sweden*—I quote from Reynolds' careful rendering, after consulting the Swedish to elucidate dubious matters—writes as an interested and curious inquirer and recounts his conversations and observations with disciplined exactitude. He was one of many guests and sightseers. Of those who found it diverting to record their impressions of Ephrata we may cite, by way of example, Jacob Duché (*Observations on a Variety of Subjects*, 3 ed. London, 1791, pp. 66–7) and an officer of the vanquished British army (?) (Edinburgh Magazine, May, 1785(?)). Regnier lingered to try his vocation and told his story in *Das Geheimnis der Zinzendorfischen Secte oder eine Lebens-Beschreibung Johann Franz Regnier*. Mittelberger must have devoured scores of filthy tales to write as he did concerning the misdeeds of the Closter-Schwestern. Gruber was well-disposed, and his concise remarks furnish a handful of facts. Morgan Edwards had a wide knowledge of Baptist communities. I have profited by every sentence he wrote about the Seventh Day German Baptists.

The *Geistliche Fama*, the *Büdingische Sammlung*, and Fresenius' *Bewährte Nachrichten* are replete with a diversity of matter, in part written by Seventh Day Baptists, in part the work of people who were so situated as to be able to observe one phase or another of their perplexing life. Some of Sauer's comments are embalmed in *Acta Historico-ecclesiastica* XV, pp. 210–6.

Primary sources have been rendered into English, quoted, edited, and elucidated in modern periodicals and collections of studies. In this labor the Historical Society of Pennsylvania, the Pennsylvania German Society, and the Lancaster County Historical Society have been laudably conspicuous. W. M. Fahnestock's article "An Historical Sketch of Ephrata" (*Hazard's Register of Pennsylvania* XV, 11 (March 14, 1835), pp. 161–7) is a misleading quasi-primary source. The same writer falls into the same errors in "Baptists, Seventh Day, German" (*He Pasa Ekklesia*, Philadelphia, 1844, pp. 98–111). C. Endress' "An Account of the Settlement of the Dunkers, at Ephrata" (*Hazard's Register of Pennsylvania* V, 21 (May 22, 1830), pp. 331–4) should be mentioned as one of the most pungent writings on Conrad and his adherents.

The reader may be reminded that I have dealt with the work of the Ephrata Press in Chapter VI. Before the settlement obtained a press of its own, Beissel and those who seconded him with their pens were dependent on Bradford, Franklin, and Sauer. Franklin printed the first Seventh Day German Baptist hymnal, *Göttliche Liebes und Lobes gethöne*, in 1730. Almost to the end of Beissel's life new hymnals appeared at intervals of a few years. The press could not keep pace with the poetasters; either for this reason or because written exemplars were preferred, manuscripts were extensively employed. Before we leave the subject of manuscripts, it will be convenient to mention Sachse's monograph, *A Unique Manuscript by Rev. Peter Miller (Brother Jabez)* (Lancaster, 1912); *Die Rose oder Der angenehmen Blumen Zu Saron geistliche Ehe-verlöbnüs (Schwester-Chronic)*, my best source for the description of the life led by the virgins; *Betrachtungs-würdige Anmerckungen von der Natur und Beschaffenheit des ehelichen und unverehlichten Lebens;* the Ephrata death registers; and some oddments in the library of the Historical Society of Pennsylvania. It may be said categorically that the writing done at Ephrata was bad, whatever the form selected for thoughts that were themselves deficient in vitality and, not seldom, worn with repetition. One would suppose that a ghost story would stimulate the narrator to an unwonted feat of tale spinning, but the haunted wife who appears in Chapter VIII, when she composed her *Abgeforderte Relation der Erscheinung eines entleibten Geists*, displayed as little control of her pen as she had of her nerves. The *Erster Theil Der Theosophischen Lectionen*, to single out a striking specimen from the Ephrata community, is uncommonly monotonous and would provoke an educated man of the present generation to violence. In research these tawdry hymns and drab confessions shake off the torpor of extinct devotion. One who ponders them long enough to detect the elusive hints that lurk in many a bizarre turn of language will arrive at a comprehension of the cravings that devoured the emaciated brothers and sisters.

These are the materials upon which scholars and journalists have worked. Little that they have written is of independent value. Sachse's volumes are widely known, and in reading them I first made Beissel's acquaintance. Sachse labored under the disabilities of the pioneer. His works contain faults, but most of them are light. Most historians will allow that Seidensticker's monograph *Ephrata, eine amerikanische Klostergeschichte* (Cincinnati, 1883) is unequaled.

The riddle of Beissel can most readily be solved by a determined delving into the writings in which he recorded his interior life and unfolded his views. He was on the brink of middle life when *Mystyrion Anomias* began a literary career that filled many hours of his life for the next four decades. A catalogue of the Vorsteher's works will put a term to this rambling discussion.

Mystyrion Anomias: The Mystery of Lawlesness, 1728, English version by Michael Wohlfahrt, 1729.

Mystische Und sehr geheyme Sprueche, 1730, English version (99 mystical proverbs) by Peter Miller. *Theosophische Sprueche* (*Theosophische Lectionen,* 351–95), 144–242 = *Mystische Und sehr geheyme Sprueche,* 1–99.

Die Ehe das Zuchthaus fleischlicher Menschen, 1730.

Urständliche und Erfahrungs-volle Hohe Zeugnüsse (*Deliciae Ephratenses, Pars II*), 1745: *Vorbericht* [3–8]; *Gemüts-Bewegungen* I–XXXVIII, 1–58; *Theosophische Episteln* I–LXXIII, 59–294.

Eine sehr deutliche beschreibung wie sich dieses hoche u. wichtige Werck dieser unserer Göttlichen Sing Arbeit erboren, 1746 MS. Preface revised and printed in *Turtel-Taube.*

Das Gesäng Der einsamen und verlassenen Turtel-Taube, 1747, English version of prefatory material in J. F. Sachse, *The Music of the Ephrata Cloister* (Lancaster, 1903), 52 ff.

Conrad Beissel's Letter Book, 1751(?)–1756(?) MS.

Theosophische Gedichte (*Theosophische Lectionen,* 1752, 396–431)?

441 hymns (*Paradisisches Wunder-Spiel,* 1766, 1–296).

Deliciae Ephratenses, Pars I, 1773: *Vorbericht* [3–8]; *Wunderschrift,* 1–48; *Reden* I–LXVII, 49–340.

Göttliche Wunderschrift, 1789 (*Del. Eph. I, Wunderschrift*): *Vorrede* [3–4]; text, 1–31; *A Dissertation on Mans Fall, Translated from the High-German Original* 1765 by Peter Miller; "an elaboration of Beissel's *Dissertation on Mans Fall*" (J. F. Sachse, *A Unique Manuscript,* 4), presented by Peter Miller to Franklin in 1771.

Geistliche Briefe eines Friedsamen Pilgers, Welche er von 1721. bis an seine 1768. darauf erfolgte Entbindung geschrieben, 1794.

"57 'Apophtegens (*sic*) taken from the Father's Writings'"
(J. F. Sachse, *A Unique Manuscript*, 34–44).
"Apology for Sacred Song" (J. F. Sachse, *The Music of the
Ephrata Cloister*, 24–6).

Beissel's reputation was so great that he was credited with
a small volume written by an unidentified numerologist after
1800. If the "*Mystische Abhandlung*" is to be assigned to Conrad, he dictated it from the tomb. I have examined the muti-
lated copy in the collection of the Historical Society of
Pennsylvania. The first printed page is numbered 5. The last
page is numbered 92 and ends in the middle of a word. The
latest date given in the preserved part of this work is 1809.
If Conrad had prescience of the Messina earthquake (1783)
and of the French Revolution or communicated his reflections
regarding such matters to his sectaries many years after his
death, we need not deny him credit for a writing in which,
if it is genuine, he must have taken pride. However, even the
manuscript title-page does not attribute the book to Beissel
with complete confidence. I need merely to quote it in order
to demonstrate that it is worthless: "*Mystische Abhandlung
über Die Schöpffung und von des Menschen Fall und Wieder-
brin[g]ung durch des Weibes Saamen. Conrad Beisel zuge-
schrieben. Ephrata. Druck der Brüderschaft. Im Jahr (ohnge-
fähr 1745).*" The person who wrote the title-page knew less
than nothing about the provenience of the book. The "*Mystische Abhandlung*" lacks Beissel's peculiarities. Even if it could
be shown to have been written during the Vorsteher's lifetime,
the date would not be conclusive.

It is all but certain that Beissel did write an opuscule called
*Mystische Abhandlung über die Schöpfung und von des
Menschen Fall und Wiederbringung durch des Weibes Samen.*
The date is 1745. I am inclined to regard the masterpiece in
question as the earliest edition of the *Göttliche Wunderschrift*,
in which case there are three editions.

INDEX

Acrelius, Israel, 115, 117 f., 122 f.,
 124 ff., 128 f., 136 f., 208
Adam, 64, 127, 176, 192 ff., 197
agape, 124, 126
Altona, 46, 200
Ames, William, 37
Amos, Brother, *see* Jan Mayle
Amsterdam, 45, 200
Amwell, 92, 94, 154
Anastasia, *see* Anna Thomin
Anhalt, 8
Antes, Heinrich, 101
Antichrist, the, 65
Antietam, 147 f., 174 f.
Apocalypse, the, 64
Arnold, Gottfried, 26, 197 ff.
Augsburg Confession, 16
Aushauch, 114

Bacon, Sir Francis, 185
Baptists, 20, 75, 77, 94, 105, 123, 208
Baptists, English, 31, 59, 92, 123
Baptists, Keithian, 39, 67 f.
Baptists, Rogerene, 62, 154 f.
Barbara, Sister, 182
Barnegat, 154
Baumann, Matthias, 47 f.
Baumannites, 48
Bebber, van, *see* Bebern, von
Bebern, Henry von, 34, 42
Bebern, Isaac von, 43, 47, 49
Becker, Peter, 38, 42 f., 55 ff., 75, 160
Bedford County, 174, 183
Beghards, 19
Beguines, 19
Beissel, Johann Conrad, birth, 2; education, 3, 21; itinerant journeyman, 21-22; Heidelberg and Pietism, 26-29; banished from city, 27; Berleburg and Inspirationism, 29-33; departure for America, 34; arrival in Germantown, 40; retires to Conestoga, 42; to Mill Creek, 43; returns to Conestoga, 47; first disciple, 50; becomes pastor of German Baptists, 54; baptized, 57;

beginning of community at Ephrata, 70-72; conflict with Germantown Baptists, 75-78; withdraws to Ephrata, 79-81, 84; death, 180
Beissel, Peter, 173
Belgic Confession, 16
Beller, Peter, 123
Berleburg, 29, 35
Bermudian, the, 172, 173, 174
Berne, 15
Bernhard of Saxe-Weimar, 10
Bethania, 158
Bethlehem, 104, 138
Black Point, 155
Blum, Ludwig, 145
Bohemia, 8, 101
Böhme, Jacob, 26, 41, 66, 114, 127,
 188-189, 190, 191, 195, 196-197,
 198, 199, 200-201
Bohemia Manor, 43, 46
Bohemian Brethren, 19
Boles, Ebenezer, 155
Bourignon, de, 46
Bradford, 59, 209
Brandenburg, 8
Brandywine, 169
Brethren of the Common Life, 19
Bromley, 26
Bucks County, 67
Büdingen, 29
Buttlar, Eva von, 25

Canada, 163
Carl, Doctor, 30
Carolina, 50
Casimir, 7
Casimir of Berleburg, 29
Cathari, 19
Catholic League, 8 ff.
centrum, 188, 195
Cevennes, 32, 171
Charter of 1701, 36
Cheat River, 161
Christian IV, 9
Chronicon Ephratense, 3 f., 43, 48,
 50, 66, 68, 75, 76, 78, 86, 96, 103,